IMAGES
of America

GADSBY'S TAVERN

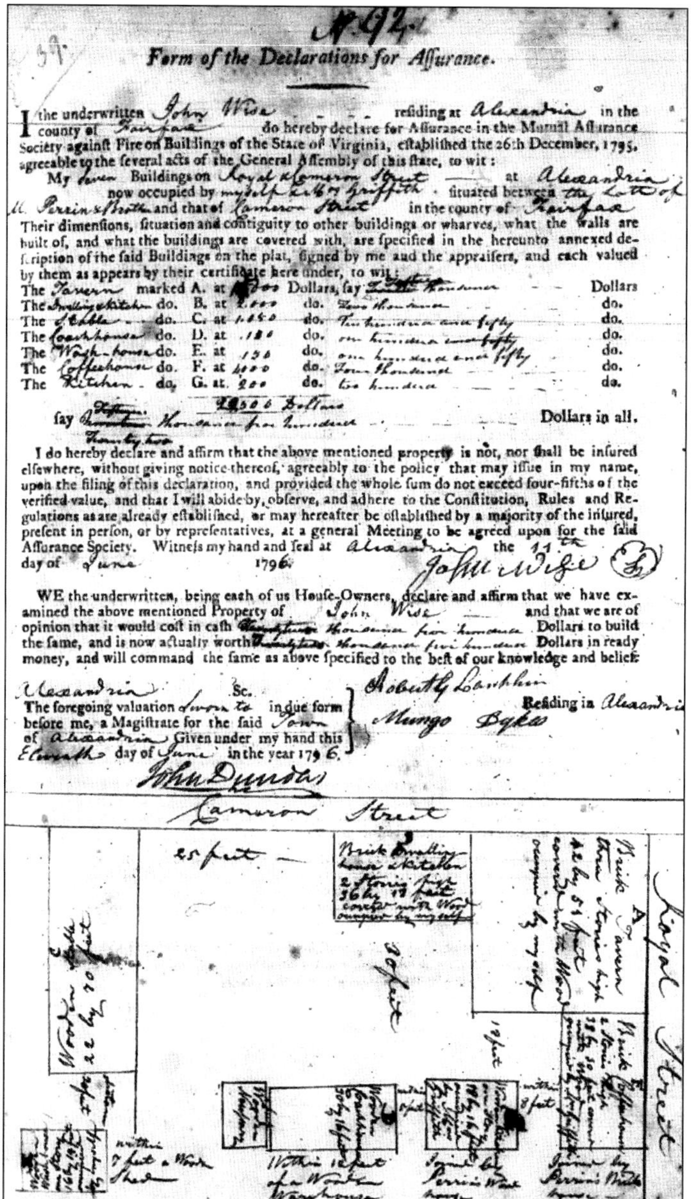

No. 92.

Form of the Declarations for Assurance.

I the underwritten John Wise residing at Alexandria in the county of Fairfax do hereby declare for Assurance in the Mutual Assurance Society against Fire on Buildings of the State of Virginia, established the 26th December, 1795, agreeable to the several acts of the General Assembly of this state, to wit:
My seven Buildings on Royal & Cameron Street at Alexandria now occupied by myself & Gilbert Griffith situated between the Lott of M. Perrin & Brother and that of Cameron Street in the county of Fairfax
Their dimensions, situation and contiguity to other buildings or wharves, what the walls are built of, and what the buildings are covered with, are specified in the hereunto annexed description of the said Buildings on the plat, signed by me and the appraisers, and each valued by them as appears by their certificate here under, to wit:

The Tavern	marked A. at	15000 Dollars, say	Fifteen thousand	Dollars
The Dwelling & Kitchen	do. B. at	2000	do. Two thousand	do.
The Stable	do. C. at	1050	do. [illegible] hundred and fifty	do.
The Coachhouse	do. D. at	150	do. one hundred and fifty	do.
The Wash-house	do. E. at	150	do. one hundred and fifty	do.
The Coffeehouse	do. F. at	4000	do. Four thousand	do.
The Kitchen	do. G. at	200	do. two hundred	do.

22500 Dollars

say Twenty two thousand five hundred Dollars in all.

I do hereby declare and affirm that the above mentioned property is not, nor shall be insured elsewhere, without giving notice thereof, agreeably to the policy that may issue in my name, upon the filing of this declaration, and provided the whole sum do not exceed four-fifths of the verified value, and that I will abide by, observe, and adhere to the Constitution, Rules and Regulations as are already established, or may hereafter be established by a majority of the insured, present in person, or by representatives, at a general Meeting to be agreed upon for the said Assurance Society. Witness my hand and seal at Alexandria the 11th day of June 1796.

John Wise (LS)

WE the underwritten, being each of us House-Owners, declare and affirm that we have examined the above mentioned Property of John Wise and that we are of opinion that it would cost in cash Twenty two thousand five hundred Dollars to build the same, and is now actually worth Twenty two thousand five hundred Dollars in ready money, and will command the same as above specified to the best of our knowledge and belief.

Alexandria Sc.
The foregoing valuation sworn to in due form before me, a Magistrate for the said Town of Alexandria Given under my hand this Eleventh day of June in the year 1796.

John Dundas

Robert Lanphier
Mungo Dykes
Residing in Alexandria

Tavern owner John Wise insured his property at the corner of Cameron and Royal Streets against fire damage through the Mutual Assurance Fire Company. The policy, dated June 11, 1796, protected a tavern, dwelling and kitchen, stable, coach house, wash house, coffeehouse, and kitchen that were valued at $22,500. This document details the location, dimensions, and construction materials of each building on the lot. (Library of Virginia.)

On the Cover: The facade of Gadsby's Tavern was being restored to its 18th-century appearance in 1936, in preparation for the return of its original 1792 front door. Sold in 1917, the door had been installed in the American Wing of the Metropolitan Museum of Art in 1924. (Library of Congress, Historic American Buildings Survey; photograph by John O. Brostrup.)

IMAGES
of America

GADSBY'S TAVERN

Gretchen M. Bulova

ARCADIA
PUBLISHING

ISBN 978-1-4671-2320-4

Published by Arcadia Publishing
Charleston, South Carolina

Printed in the United States of America

Library of Congress Control Number: 2014950627

For all general information, please contact Arcadia Publishing:
Telephone 843-853-2070
Fax 843-853-0044
E-mail sales@arcadiapublishing.com
For customer service and orders:
Toll-Free 1-888-313-2665

Visit us on the Internet at www.arcadiapublishing.com

To the members of American Legion Post 24 and the local groups and individuals whose remarkable dedication and passion preserved this important historic landmark.

Contents

Acknowledgments

While much has been written about the early history of Gadsby's Tavern, it has always been my dream to share its rich 20th-century story. This is a story about the preservation of a national landmark as seen through the eyes of the past and present volunteers and professional staff who share a love for Gadsby's Tavern. I want to first thank the museum staff, especially Frances Abbott Lyon, who had the foresight to painstakingly collect and organize the newspaper clippings, meeting minutes, museum research files, and images that document the modern history of Gadsby's Tavern. Then, three huzzahs to Lance Mallamo, director of the Office of Historic Alexandria, and the current staff of Gadsby's Tavern Museum (Liz Williams, Callie Stapp, Michele Longo, and Emily Soapes), for their support of this project and their patience while I spent hours digging through files and photographs in their offices. I owe special thanks to the many friends and colleagues who helped make this publication a reality. Suzanne McDougal kindly volunteered her publishing expertise and gently kept me focused and on track. She deserves special recognition for her countless hours scanning photographs and editing caption text. Ellen Donald spent many late nights editing caption text and kept my spirits up with her endless enthusiasm. Anna Frame expertly scanned and edited the museum's slides, negatives, historic photographs, and archival materials. Julia Downie from the Alexandria Library Special Collections staff is a hero for retrieving and scanning photographs from its extensive collection. Barbara Helsing searched the Little Theatre of Alexandria's archives for "just the right" photographs. Finally, my sincere appreciation goes to Richard Bierce, Warden and Harriet Foley, Linda Mills, Carl Nold, and Mark Reed for helping to identify members of American Legion Post 24 and museum volunteers. And, of course, my heartfelt thanks go out to my wonderful and supportive family.

Unless otherwise noted, images in this volume are from the photograph collection of Gadsby's Tavern Museum. The following abbreviations are used in photograph credits: the Alexandria Library, Special Collections Branch (ALSC); the Library of Congress (LOC); and the Historic American Buildings Survey at the LOC (HABS).

INTRODUCTION

I found elegant accommodations at Gadesby's hotel. It is observable that Gadesby keeps the best house of entertainment in the United States.

—John Davis, 1801

Since Alexandria's founding in 1749, a tavern has stood on the lot at the corner of Royal and Cameron Streets. The story of Gadsby's Tavern, however, begins in 1785. Gadsby's Tavern Museum consists of two buildings, a c. 1785 tavern and the 1792 City Tavern, both constructed by local tavern keeper and entrepreneur John Wise. The buildings take their name from John Gadsby, who operated the tavern from 1796 to 1808 and raised the level of tavern keeping in Alexandria to new heights. As the premier establishment in early Alexandria, the City Tavern was known by travelers far and wide for its fine accommodations, elegant parties, and useful amenities. Gadsby's Tavern embodies the history of taverns as the social and business centers of our emerging nation.

By 1790, Alexandria was an affluent and thriving seaport. When boundary stones for the District of Columbia were laid out in 1791, Alexandria became part of the new capital for the young nation. John Wise was just one of the many astute businessmen in Alexandria to see the potential for wealth inherent in Alexandria's new status in the nation.

In 1792, Wise undertook the construction of the larger of today's two Gadsby's Tavern buildings. The new tavern building was four stories tall and featured 14 sleeping rooms, coal-burning fireplaces, an enormous and elegant ballroom with a musician's gallery, multiple dining rooms, and its own ice well. Wise's City Tavern symbolized a new era in Alexandria's lodging industry. It must have been an impressive and towering sight on the streetscape. When Wise opened his new City Tavern on February 6, 1793, he promoted it by announcing that "he has laid in a large stock of good old Liquors."

In 1796, John Gadsby leased the new City Tavern from owner John Wise. At 30 years of age, Gadsby was a gifted businessman who had come from England in 1795 and managed a subscription tavern on the Alexandria waterfront. In establishing his new business as a premier destination, Gadsby furnished the best parlors and bedchambers with luxury items such as fashionable mahogany dining tables, feather beds, and coal grates. A room-by-room inventory taken in 1802 provides a glimpse into the appearance and furnishings of Gadsby's City Tavern.

Soon after Gadsby assumed the lease for the City Tavern, the establishment came to be known as Gadsby's Tavern. Gadsby himself referred to the business as the "City Tavern," a traditional name for fine taverns in cities and towns in America and a name that indicated to travelers that this establishment was the best in town. By March 1798, Gadsby decided to add "Hotel" to the name, which further elevated its status.

Gadsby used sophisticated marketing skills to elevate his establishment to the finest in the area, but it was his reputation for throwing a great party that sealed his success. Gadsby was known for entertaining George Washington, especially for his elegant celebration of Washington's Birthnight. This special Birthnight Ball was initiated in Alexandria by John Wise as early as 1787, and General and Mrs. Washington attended this important community event in person in both 1798 and 1799. Gadsby also entertained Pres. John Adams in 1800 and hosted a lavish inaugural banquet for Pres. Thomas Jefferson in 1801.

In 1802, John Gadsby took over the lease of the smaller tavern next door and operated it as a subscription coffeehouse. Until this time, the smaller tavern, while still owned by John Wise, had been leased to a series of other tavern keepers. While little information remains about Gadsby's coffeehouse business, it is known that Gadsby subscribed to at least 32 newspapers as amenities for his patrons.

Gadsby's City Tavern and Hotel, with its large ballroom and private dining rooms, was the site of many Alexandria social, political, and business endeavors. Local organizations such as the St. Andrew's Society, the Jockey Club, the Potomack Company, the Washington Society, and the Mutual Assurance Society held meetings at Gadsby's. The tavern also became a place for others, such as itinerant merchants, craftspeople, and entertainers, to conduct business and offer services. At Gadsby's, one could purchase a ticket to see a hot-air balloon, have one's teeth fixed, take dance lessons, select the latest and most fashionable jewelry items, or learn about upcoming house sales.

Of course, neither John Wise nor John Gadsby could have operated successful enterprises without a large labor force. This labor was mostly enslaved. In 1802, Gadsby owned 11 slaves who supported the operations of the City Tavern and Hotel. Gadsby was also purchasing, selling, and hiring slaves—especially those that possessed specialized skills that would ensure high-quality services and accommodations for his customers. Among Gadsby's many enslaved workers, hostler James Lewis was willing to risk running away to obtain his freedom. On August 30, 1808, Gadsby ran an advertisement in the *Virginia Journal and Alexandria Advertiser* for the return of his longtime stableman.

John Gadsby ran the City Tavern and Hotel until July 1808, when he moved his tavern operation to the Indian Queen Hotel in Baltimore, at the other end of his stagecoach line. Looking to further his enterprises, he moved back to the Federal City. In 1827, he opened the National Hotel, where he became famous for entertaining Washington society. In September 1836, at the age of 70, Gadsby retired from the hotel business. The *National Intelligencer* announced Gadsby's retirement by saying, "This gentleman so well known throughout the country as proprietor of the hotel which bears his name, having acquired a handsome independence by his exertions, has retired from the hotel business." John Gadsby died on May 15, 1844, and was buried in his family vault at Congressional Cemetery. As for John Wise, he continued to own a series of taverns, selling the City Tavern just prior to his death on October 31, 1815.

Known as the City Hotel, the buildings continued to be operated by a succession of tavern keepers throughout the 19th century as a hotel and then boardinghouse. The taverns were often visited as a tourist attraction for having been frequented by the Founding Fathers. By the turn of the 20th century, the buildings had fallen into disrepair and their future looked bleak. In 1917, the Metropolitan Museum of Art purchased architectural elements from the once-famous hostelry and sparked an interest in saving the tavern buildings. This publication is the story of the 20th-century preservation of historic Gadsby's Tavern and the individuals and organizations that worked tirelessly to save and restore the buildings.

One

Historic Gadsby's Tavern

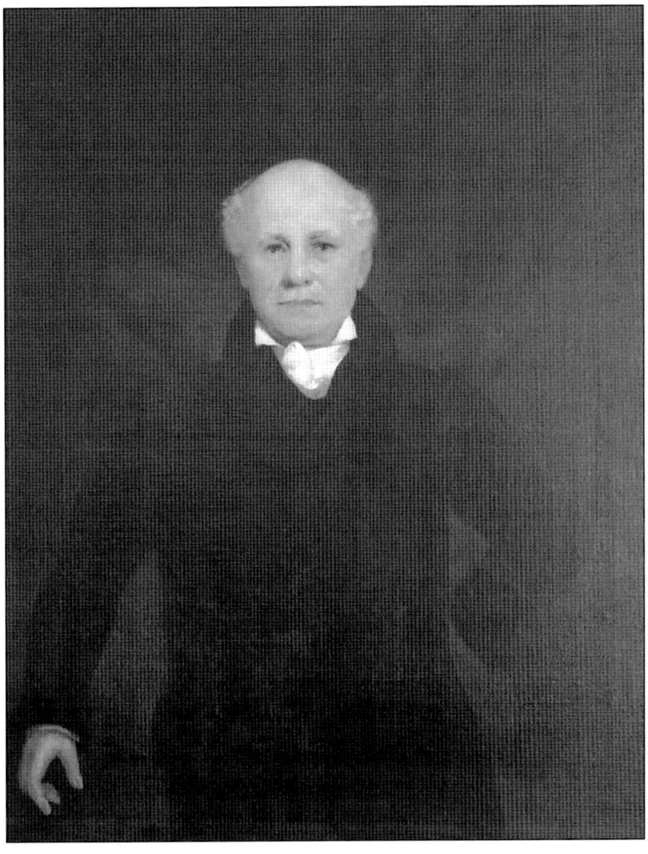

John Gadsby was the most notable tavern keeper to have operated the business at the corner of Cameron and Royal Streets in Alexandria. He was renowned for the excellence of his hospitality. Period travelers noted that Gadsby's had the reputation of being a superior establishment. His March 13, 1798, *Alexandria Gazette* advertisement stated that he supplied "every article for . . . comfort and convenience." Though he ran the tavern only from 1796 until 1808, his reputation and association with the buildings survived into modern times. This 1840 portrait is the only known likeness of John Gadsby. It and a portrait of Gadsby's third wife, Provey, were painted by his grandson John Gadsby Chapman. Both portraits were acquired at public auction in 1930 and donated to American Legion Post 24.

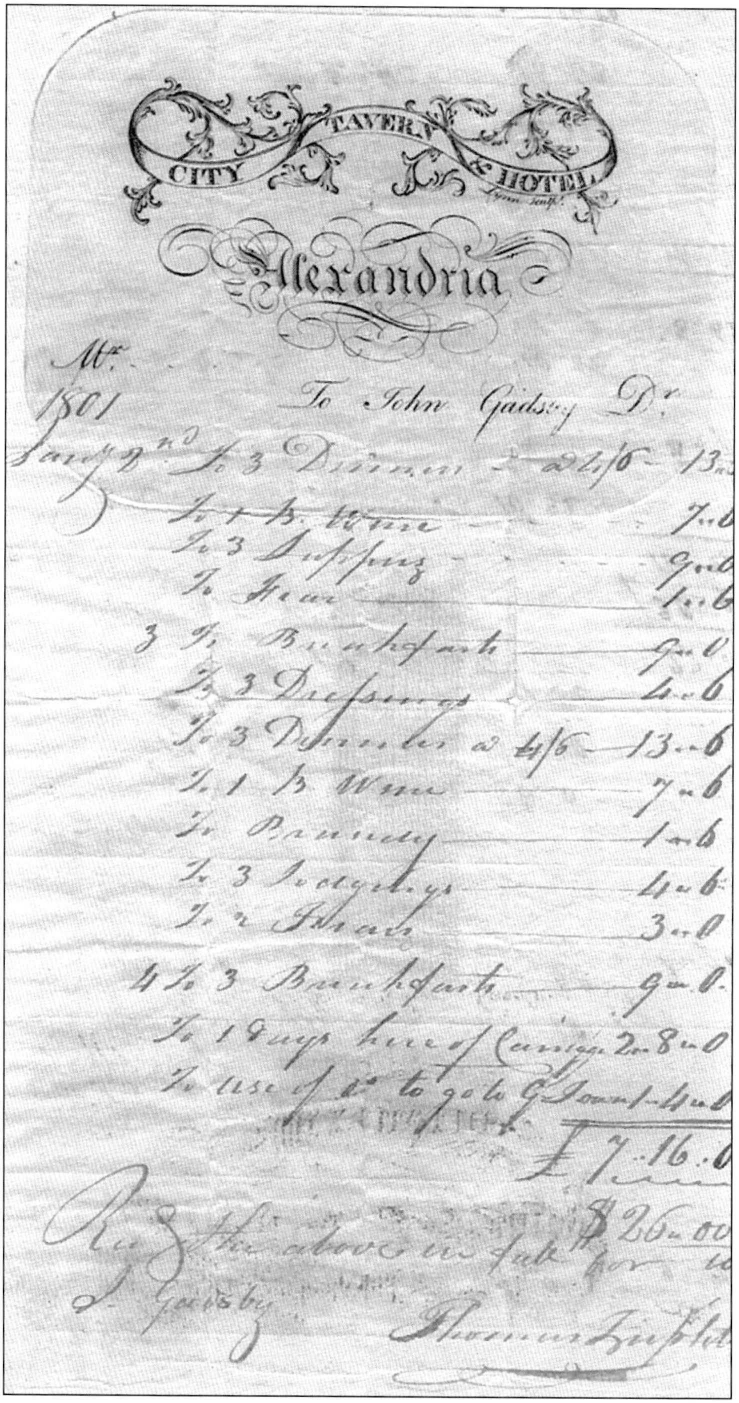

City Tavern & Hotel
Alexandria
Mr.
1801 To John Gadsby Dr.
Jany 2nd To 3 Dinners @ 4/6 — 13..
To 1 B. Wine — 7..6
To 3 Suppers — 9..0
To Fire — 1..6
3 To Breakfasts — 9..0
To 3 Dressings — 4..6
To 3 Dinner @ 4/6 — 13..6
To 1 B. Wine — 7..6
To Brandy — 1..6
To 3 Lodgings — 4..6
To 2 Fires — 3..0
4 To 3 Breakfasts — 9..0
To 1 Days hire of Carriage — 2..8..0
To use of do. to go to G Town — 4..0
£7..16..0
$26..00
Recd the above in full
J. Gadsby
Thomas [illegible]

This rare January 2, 1801, bill for John Gadsby's City Tavern and Hotel details food, beverages, carriage use, and lodging costs incurred by a Mr. Latimer. Documents like this bill, business ledgers, newspaper advertisements, and travelers' accounts detail the goods and services provided by the tavern and their prices. In general, travelers were satisfied with their tavern stay, though sometimes they found it costly.

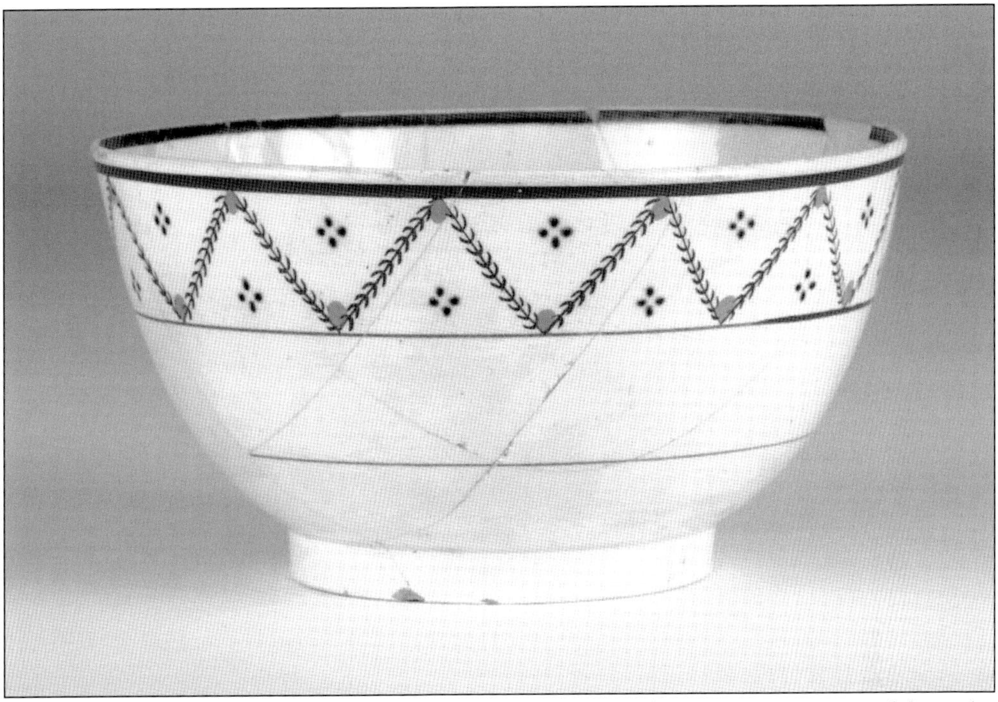

This punch bowl, along with fragments of similar bowls in other sizes, was excavated from the courtyard of Gadsby's Tavern. Dating to around 1796, this painted ceramic bowl was typical of the wares imported to Alexandria from England. (Collection of Alexandria Archaeology.)

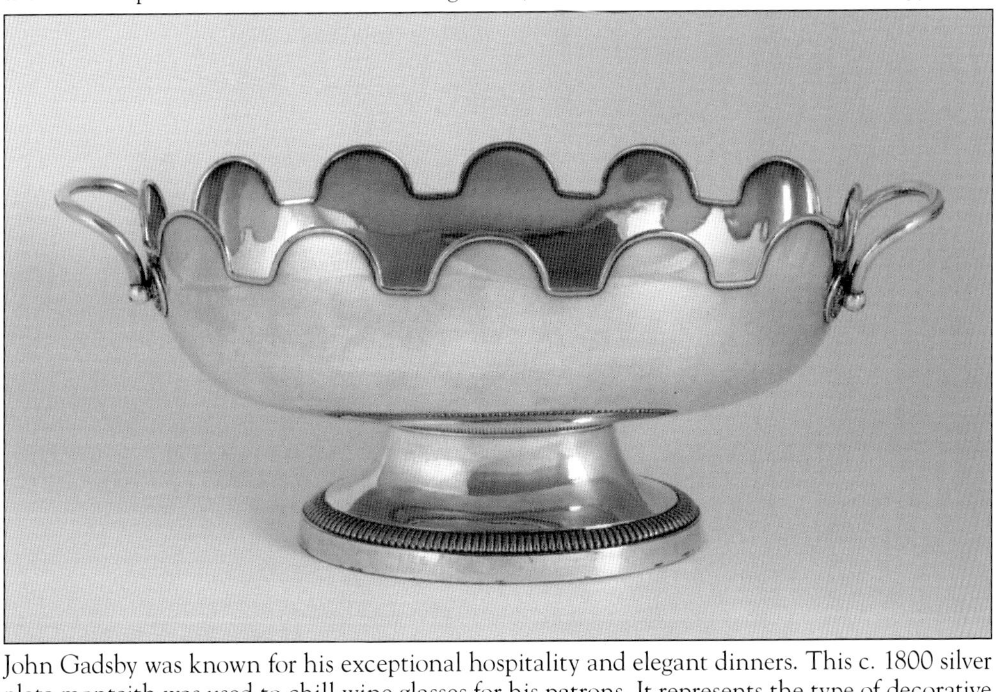

John Gadsby was known for his exceptional hospitality and elegant dinners. This c. 1800 silver plate monteith was used to chill wine glasses for his patrons. It represents the type of decorative yet practical item that helped Gadsby make a name for himself and his tavern. The base of this piece is stamped "Gadsby" to identify its owner.

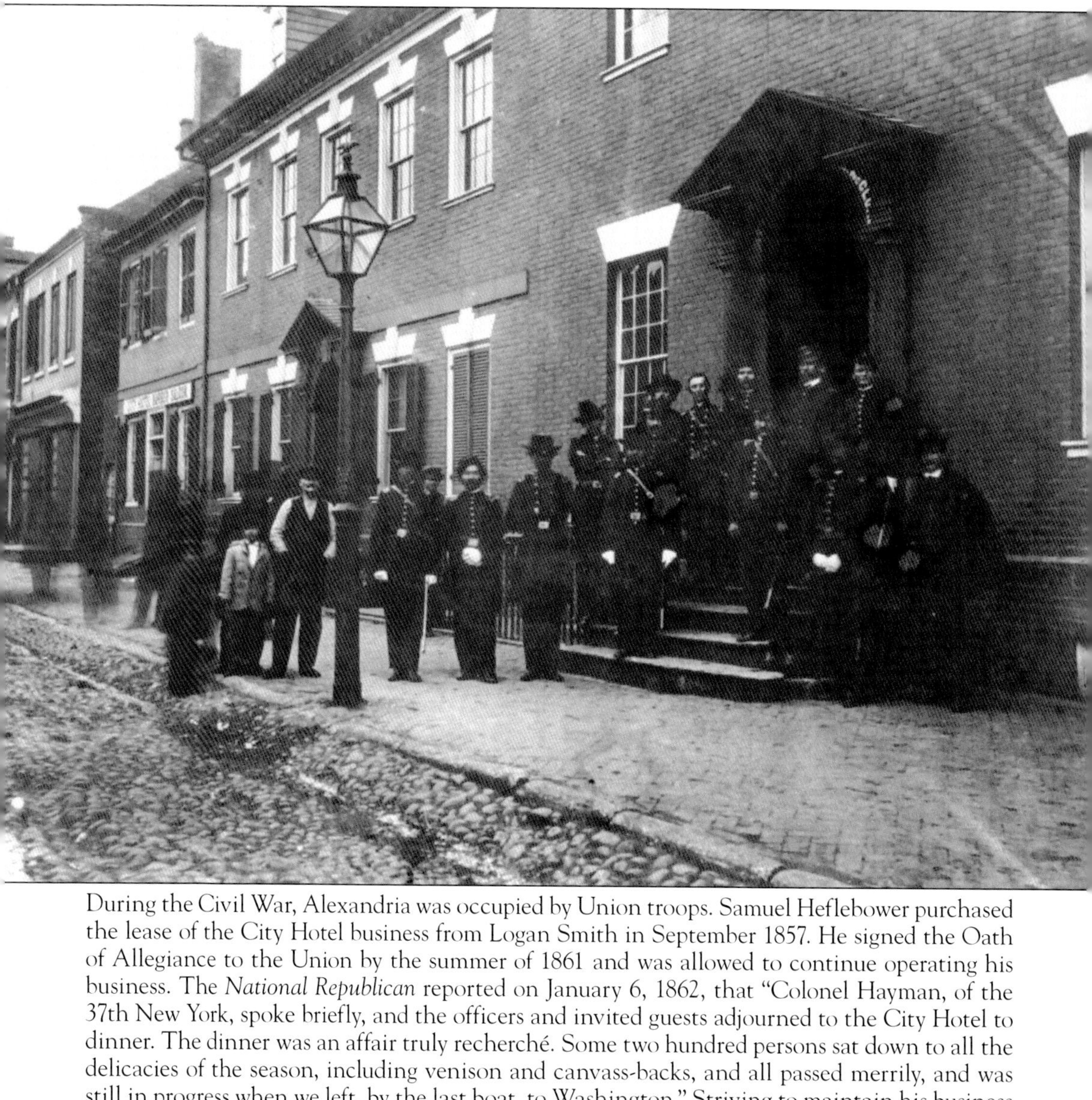

During the Civil War, Alexandria was occupied by Union troops. Samuel Heflebower purchased the lease of the City Hotel business from Logan Smith in September 1857. He signed the Oath of Allegiance to the Union by the summer of 1861 and was allowed to continue operating his business. The *National Republican* reported on January 6, 1862, that "Colonel Hayman, of the 37th New York, spoke briefly, and the officers and invited guests adjourned to the City Hotel to dinner. The dinner was an affair truly recherché. Some two hundred persons sat down to all the delicacies of the season, including venison and canvass-backs, and all passed merrily, and was still in progress when we left, by the last boat, to Washington." Striving to maintain his business and reputation, Heflebower advertised in the *Alexandria Gazette* that "This old and well-known house continues to offer to the resident sojourning and traveling public every comfort and convenience. Obliging and attentive assistants, a well-spread table, and pleasant sleeping rooms have long been among the essentials of this establishment." (Special Collections and University Archives, Colgate University Libraries.)

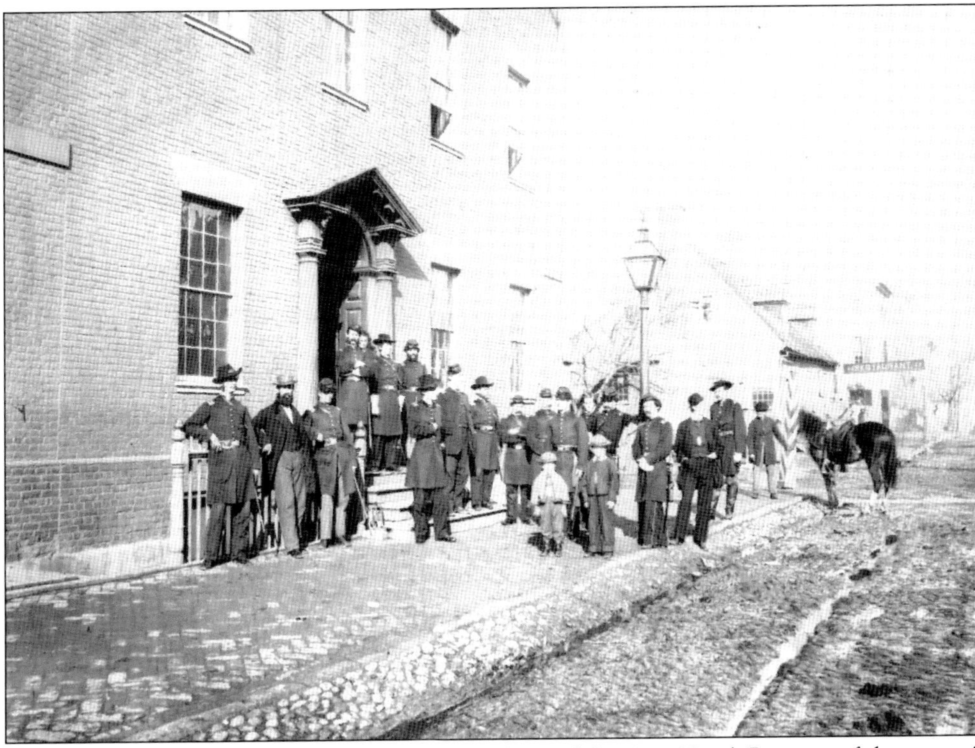

Officers of the First District Volunteers pose in front of the City Hotel. Because of the tavern's association with George Washington, the buildings were seen as a tourist attraction by soldiers. In July 1863, hotelier Robert McClure from Philadelphia purchased the remainder of Heflebower's lease, along with the furnishings and fixtures. He continued to manage the City Hotel until 1866. (LOC; photograph by Andrew J. Russell.)

Francis Pierpont, governor of the restored Government of Virginia, was headquartered at the City Hotel in August 1863. By then, the Ballroom had been divided into three suites. According to 1937 biographer Henry Ambler, Pierpont wrote his family on August 23 that his quarters consisted of a room "connected with a nice parlor, which according to tradition had been Washington's Ballroom. The orchestra where the musicians sat was still preserved."

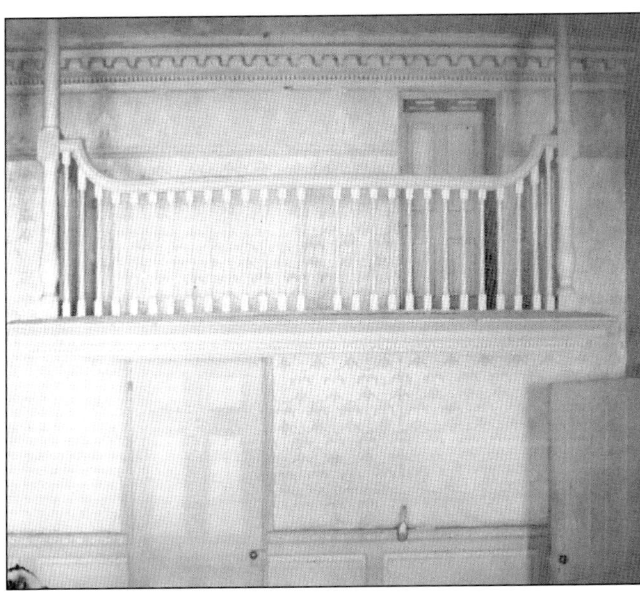

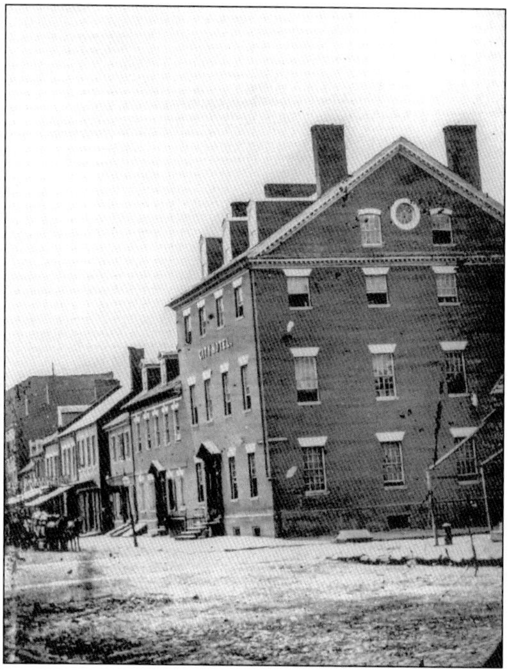

In 1749, Charles Mason purchased lot 45 at the first public auction for land in Alexandria. He was required to construct a brick building on the property by 1752. His 1752 tavern, known as Mason's Ordinary, is seen in its original appearance in this c. 1862 photograph. Mason's Ordinary is third from the right, next to the two taverns built by John Wise in 1785 and 1792.

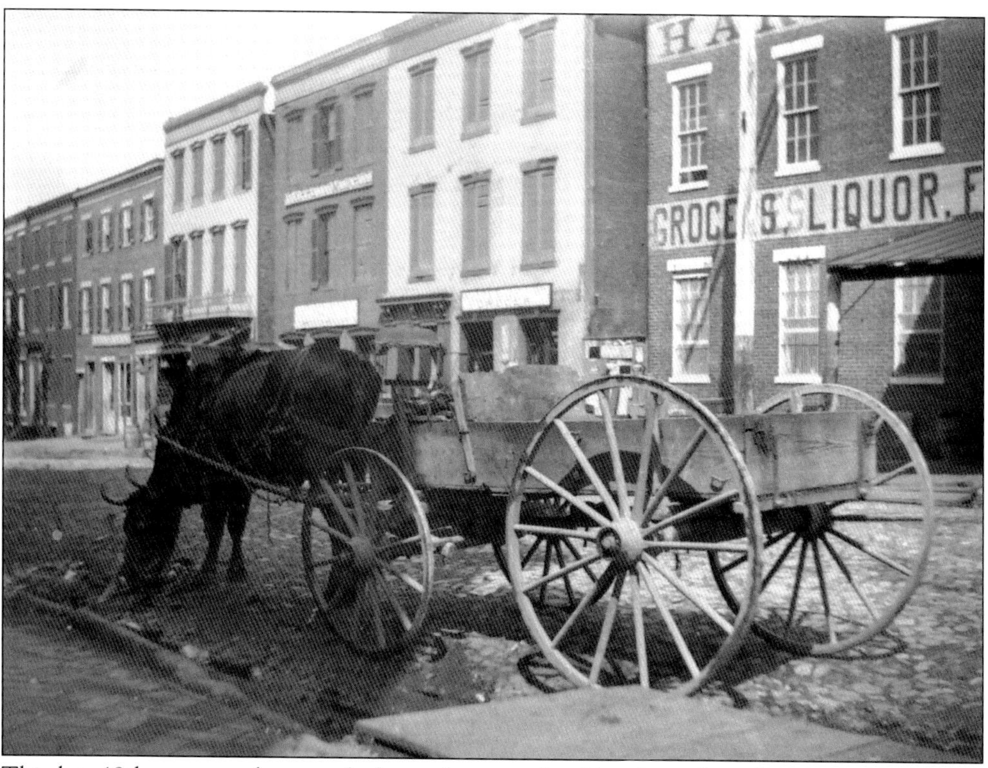

This late-19th-century photograph shows the street-level hatch to the subterranean ice well at Gadsby's Tavern. Built adjacent to the tavern in 1793 by John Wise, a tunnel linked the ice well directly to the tavern's basement. The brick-lined well, 17 feet in diameter, could hold up to 68 tons of ice, which was loaded through the street-level hatch and insulated with straw. (ALSC.)

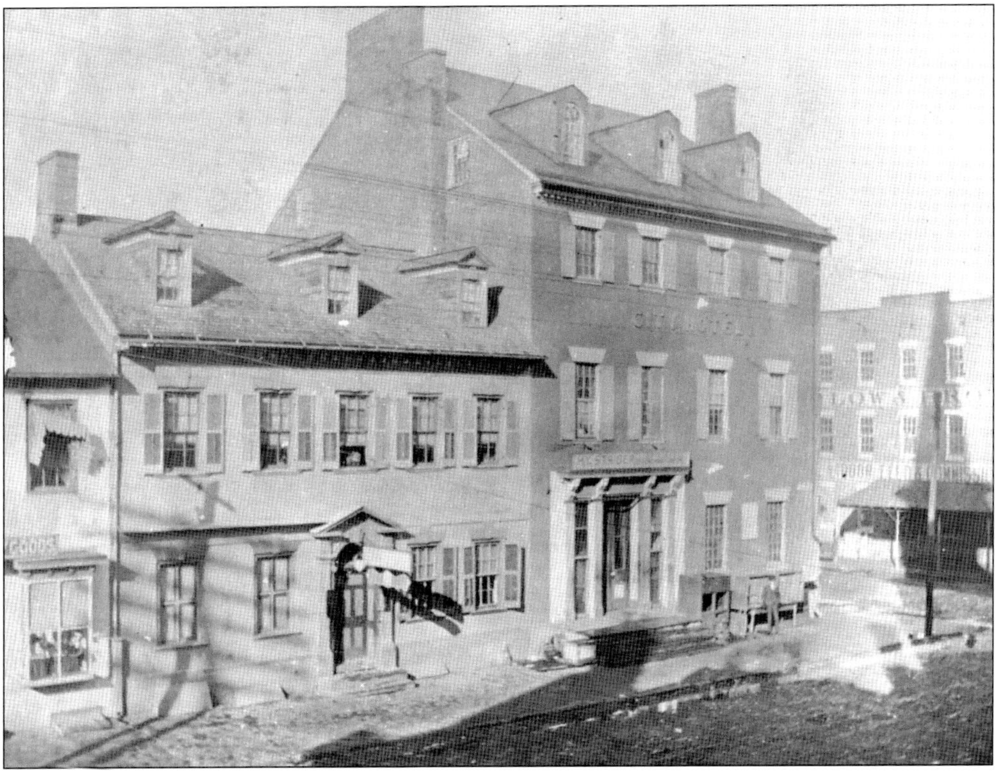

The Irwin family, who had purchased the taverns from John Wise in 1815, remodeled the City Hotel in 1878 in an effort to improve business after the economic depression caused by the occupation of Alexandria during the Civil War. The facade was modernized with an Italianate double door, the first-floor interior was remodeled, and a wing was added to provide additional hotel rooms. (ALSC.)

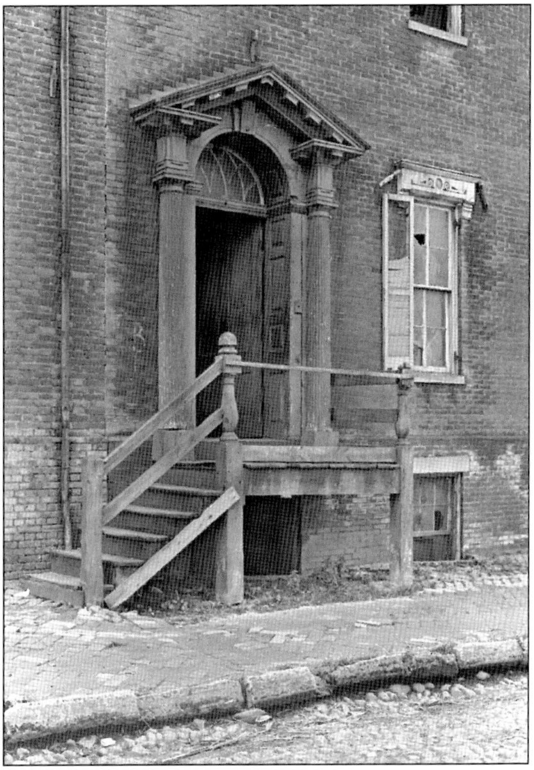

The front door to the City Hotel was moved around the corner to the Cameron Street entrance of the newly constructed hotel wing. This was the original doorway through which George Washington and other famous tavern guests had passed. The new wing is thought to have been constructed on top of the foundations of an earlier tavern, referred to by John Gadsby as "White Hall." (Historical Society of Washington, DC.)

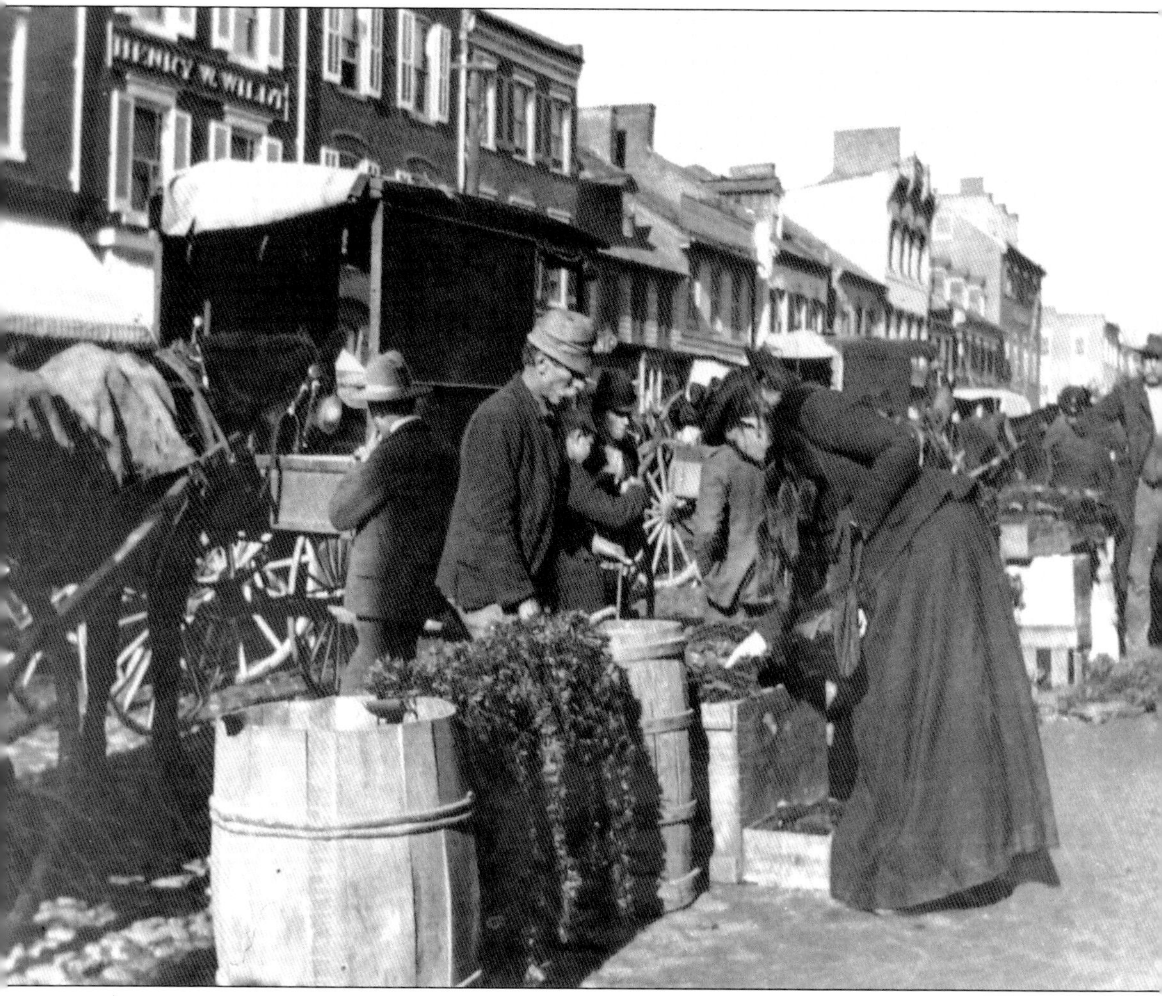

The two Gadsby's Tavern buildings can be seen on the far right in this c. 1895 photograph of the market on Royal Street. For more than 100 years, the City Hotel dominated the landscape of Alexandria. Between 1895 and 1897, the Potomac Literary and Social Society advertised its meetings "in the handsomely furnished parlors (Washington's ball room) in the City Hotel building," utilizing the gallery for musicians during events. (ALSC.)

The Gadsby's Tavern buildings were in a prime location, directly across from city hall. Proximity to the city courts, government offices, and market stalls that were a part of the complex brought additional business to the taverns. City hall, labeled "Town Hall and Market House" in Frank Leslie's *Illustrated Newspaper* of October 5, 1861, was destroyed by fire in 1871. (ALSC.)

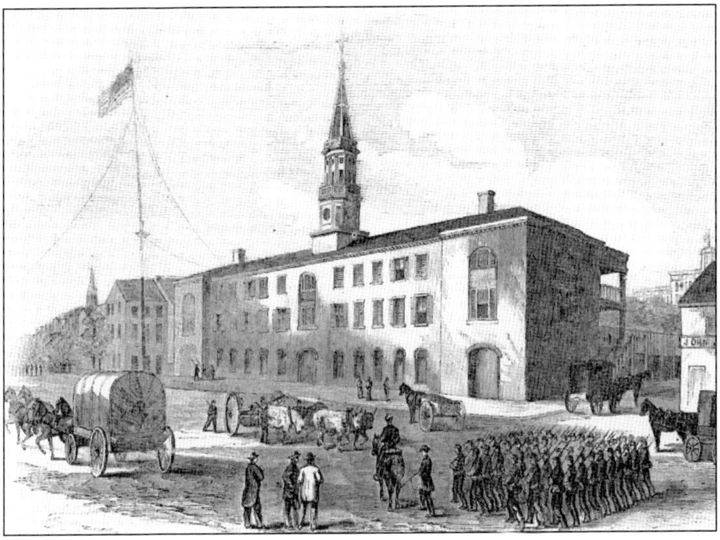

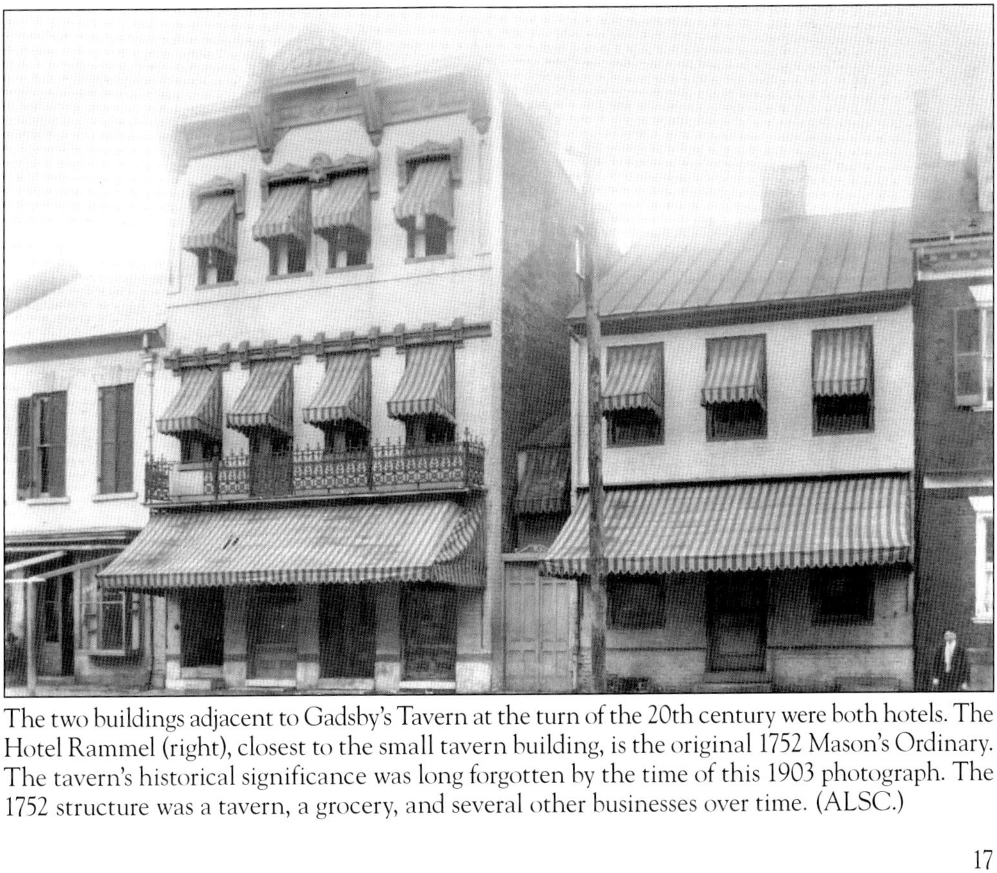

The two buildings adjacent to Gadsby's Tavern at the turn of the 20th century were both hotels. The Hotel Rammel (right), closest to the small tavern building, is the original 1752 Mason's Ordinary. The tavern's historical significance was long forgotten by the time of this 1903 photograph. The 1752 structure was a tavern, a grocery, and several other businesses over time. (ALSC.)

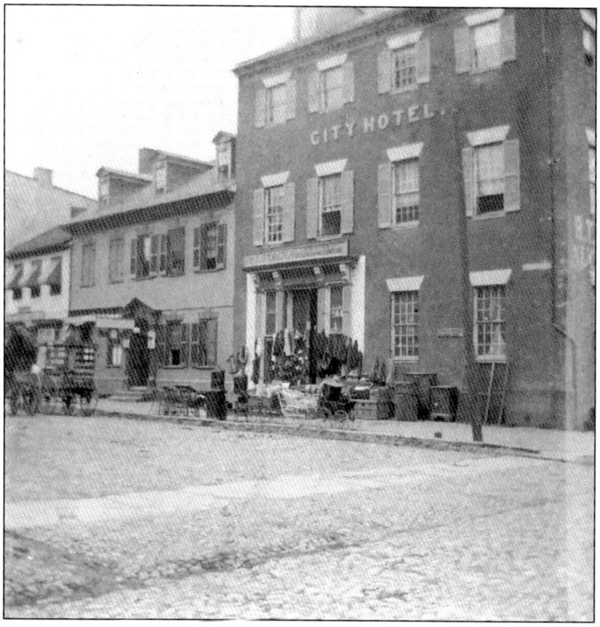

By the early 20th century, the two tavern buildings were serving as a boardinghouse, and first-floor spaces were leased to shoe, clothing, and furniture dealers. This c. 1915 photograph shows the business of Hugh L. Strider, a secondhand merchant who sold goods out of the front of the City Hotel. His brother J.H. Strider operated a printing office in the basement. (Collection of Craig Keith.)

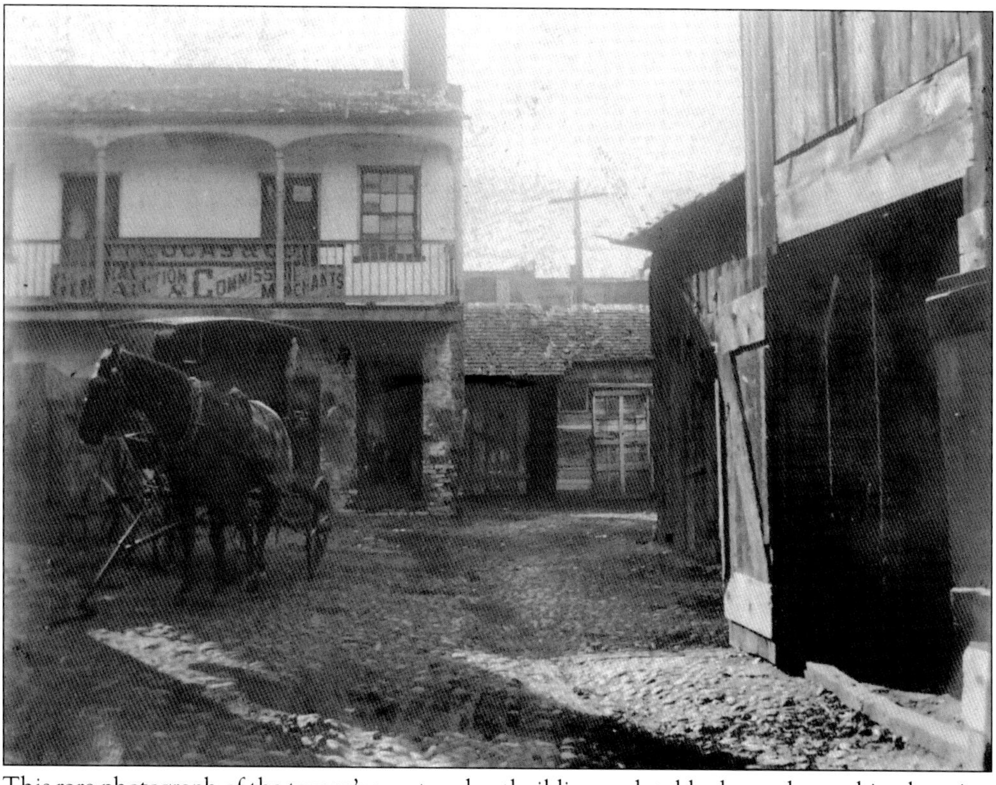

This rare photograph of the tavern's courtyard outbuilding and stable shows the working location of R.T. Lucas and Company's auction business, which advertised on the Cameron Street side of the City Hotel structure. Robert Lucas was active in the community, serving as sheriff, city councilman, and city sergeant. After suffering a stroke, he gave up his business in August 1892, offering his remaining stock for sale. (ALSC.)

Seen here around 1924, a clothing store operates out of one side of the smaller tavern. Note that there is a separate store entrance as well as a shop window. By this point, the former Hotel Rammel (the original 1752 tavern) had merged with the hotel next door to become the Belvoir Hotel. Mason's Ordinary was now covered with a new, more modern facade. (ALSC.)

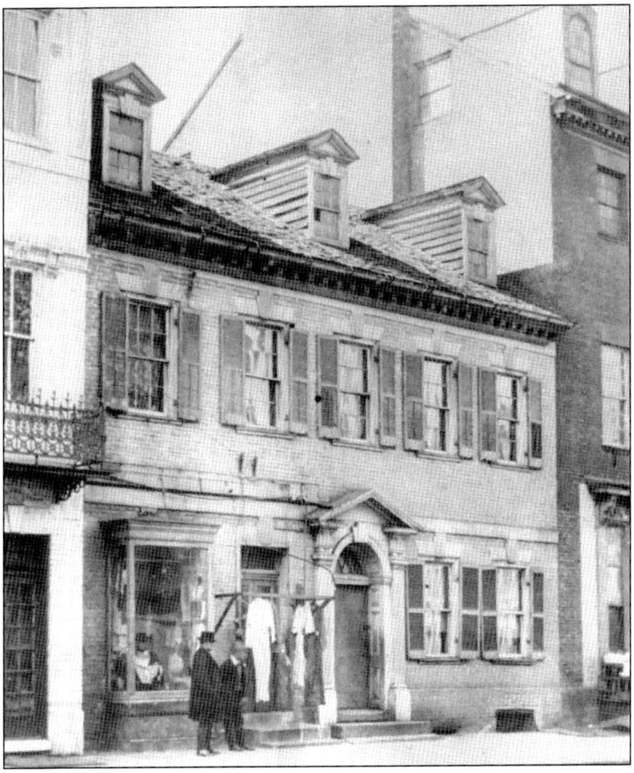

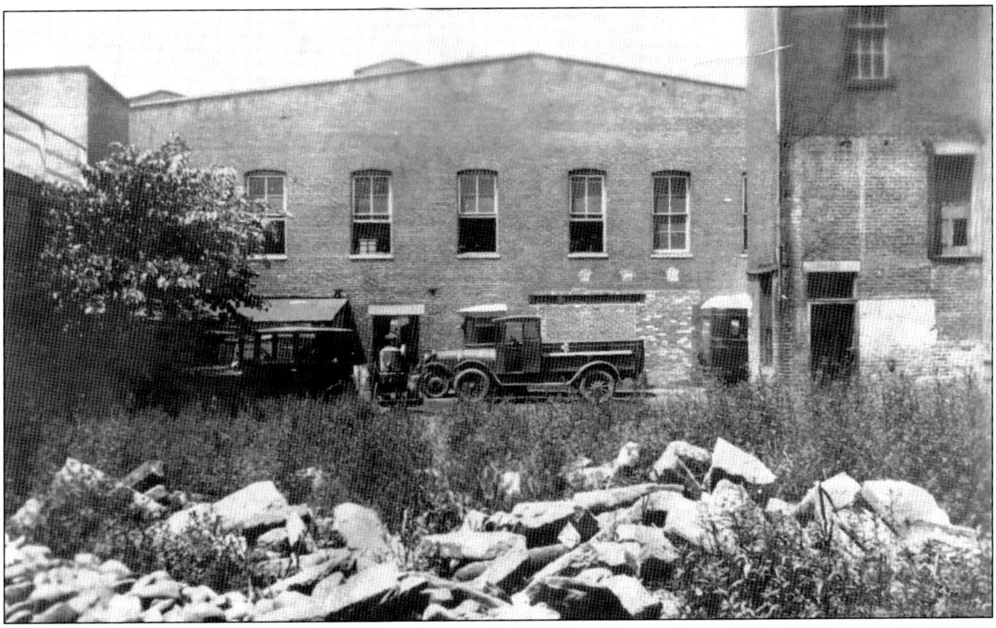

A July 27, 1907, *Alexandria Gazette* article noted, "Old Buildings Demolished. The rear buildings of the old City Hotel, at the southwest corner of Royal and Cameron streets, are being torn down, having been declared unsafe. The buildings are a part of the original hotel and were in use as a kitchen . . . during Washington's time." The remains of the 1907 courtyard demolition are seen here around 1929. (ALSC.)

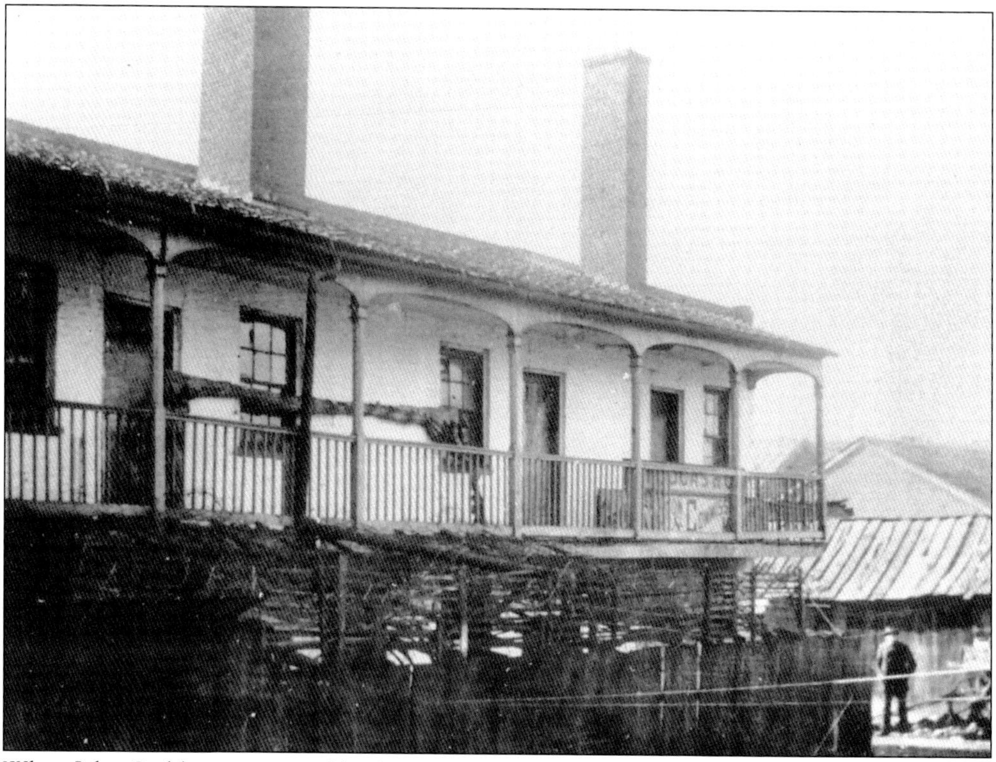

When John Gadsby renegotiated his lease with tavern owner John Wise on July 8, 1802, for a full 15-year term, he was required to make several improvements to the business. These included painting the interior of both taverns, constructing a brick stable at the rear of the property, building a brick house on the south side of the lot, and adding a brick wall along the remainder of the south property line. The 1802 brick house is about 100 years old in these two photographs. To comply with the terms of the lease and construct the new structures, earlier outbuildings, such as the kitchen, coach house, and necessary were torn down. As part of this lease, Gadsby incorporated the smaller tavern into his successful business, as a subscription coffeehouse. (Both, ALSC.)

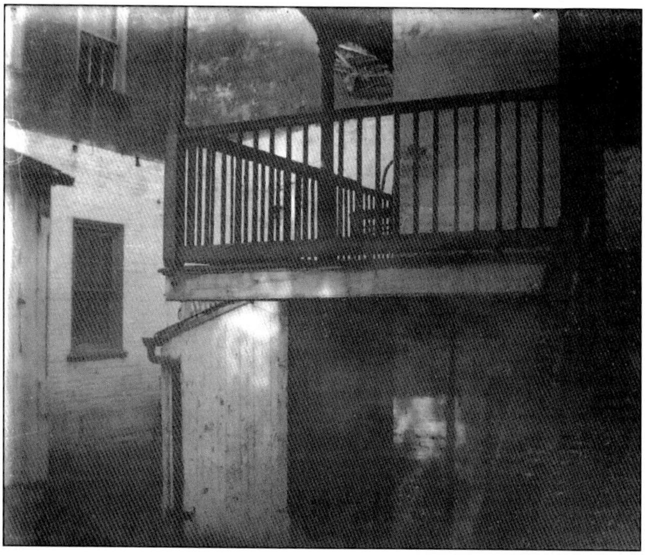

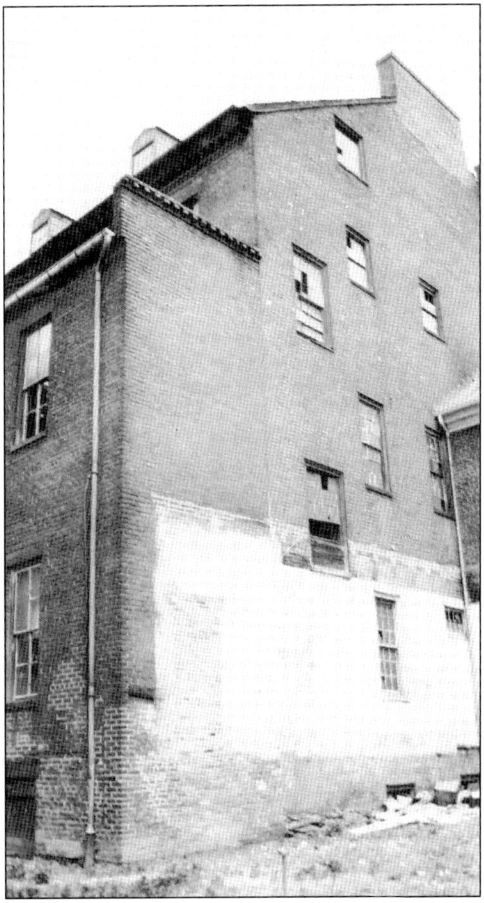

These courtyard views of the City Hotel and smaller tavern building are from a c. 1929 scrapbook. The white paint on both buildings and the mark above the paint where a porch roof was attached to the bricks are the only surviving evidence of a covered structure that connected the back and side doors of the two taverns. This addition may have been constructed as part of the 1878 modernization of the buildings. While a few businesses and boarders still occupied the site, broken windows speak to the building's overall neglect. In the photograph below, the spire of city hall across the street looms over the smaller building. The emptiness of the courtyard is a far cry from the once-bustling area that had been the working heart of the taverns. (Both, ALSC.)

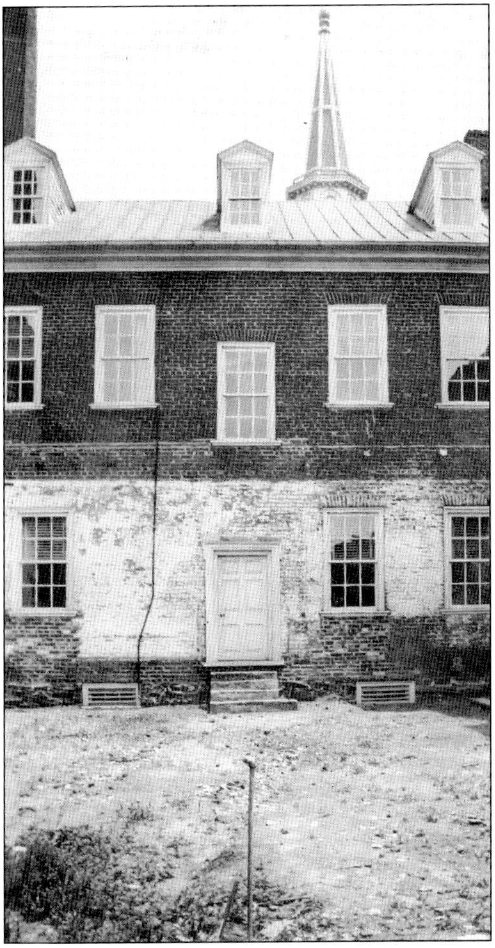

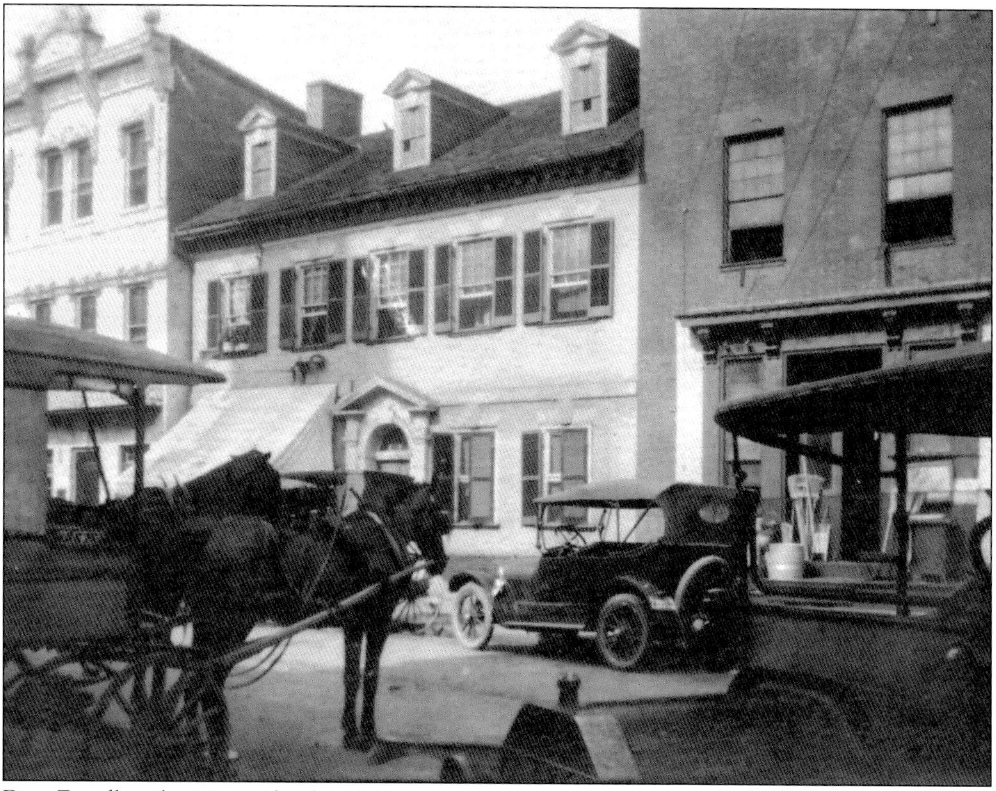

Durr Freedley, the curator for the newly planned American Wing of the Metropolitan Museum of Art, visited Alexandria as part of an effort to collect fine examples of early American architecture. He was directed to Gadsby's Tavern and learned about the tavern's association with George Washington. This photograph is thought to have been taken during Freedley's initial visit. (Courtesy of the American Wing, the Metropolitan Museum of Art).

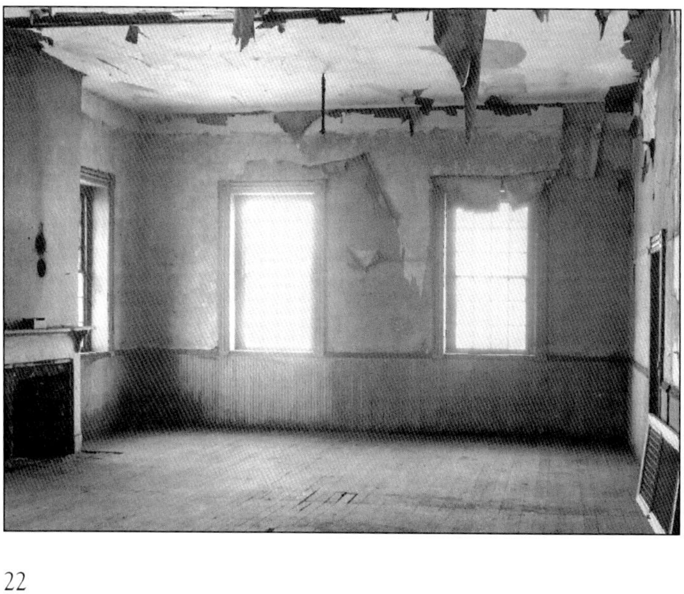

The May 21, 1917, sale of the Ballroom woodwork, original front door, and two dining-room mantels was brokered between Freedley and J.P. Ryan, on behalf of sisters Rebecca Irwin and Ruth Irwin Brook, who owned the buildings. The transaction did not include the Ballroom's window sashes or floor. This February 1936 photograph shows the room with temporary replacement woodwork. (HABS; photograph by Albert S. Burns.)

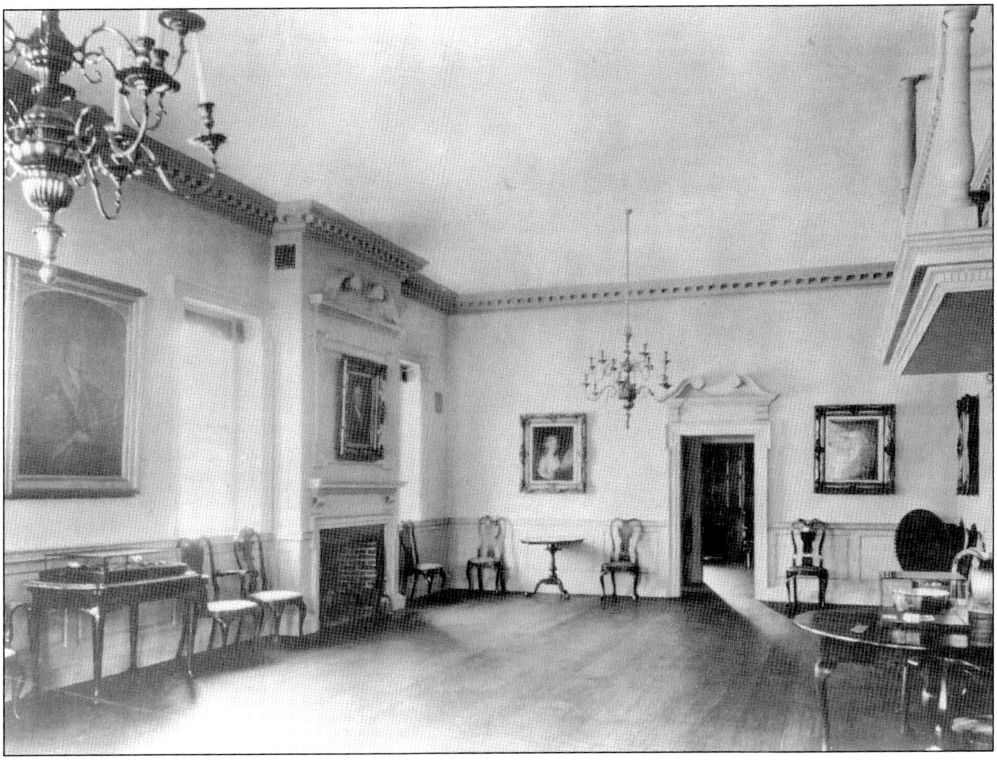

The American Wing of the Metropolitan Museum of Art opened in 1924. As part of the installation of the Ballroom woodwork, the entire room had been painstakingly stripped of its original paint layering to return the original crispness to the molding details. The room was painted gray-green, to match what was thought to be the original color, and furnished as a gallery of 18th-century antiques. (ALSC.)

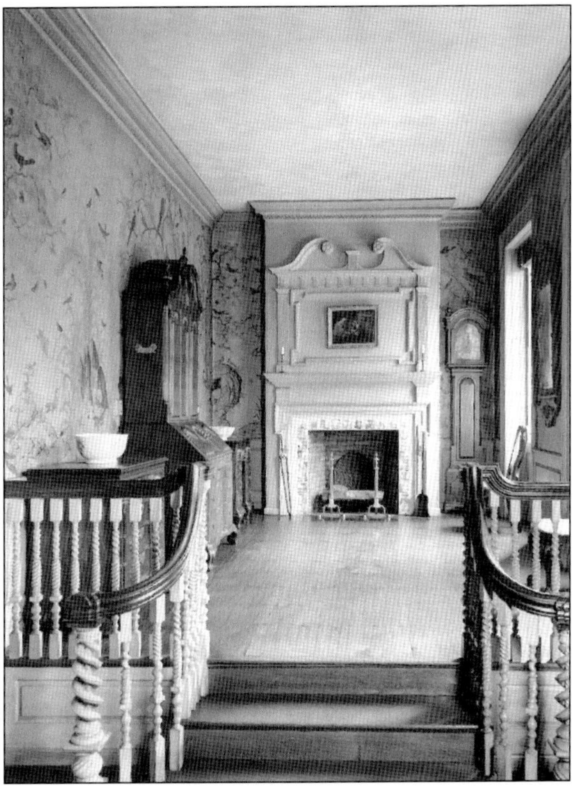

An original mantel from the main dining room of the City Hotel building was also featured in the American Wing. A second mantel, which was not used, was sold at auction through the Kende Galleries. This mantel was listed for sale for $650 with catalog entry, "#327 Painted Pine Chimney breast from Alexandria, Virginia. American 1792. Height 11' Width 7'." The location of this mantel is unknown today. (ALSC.)

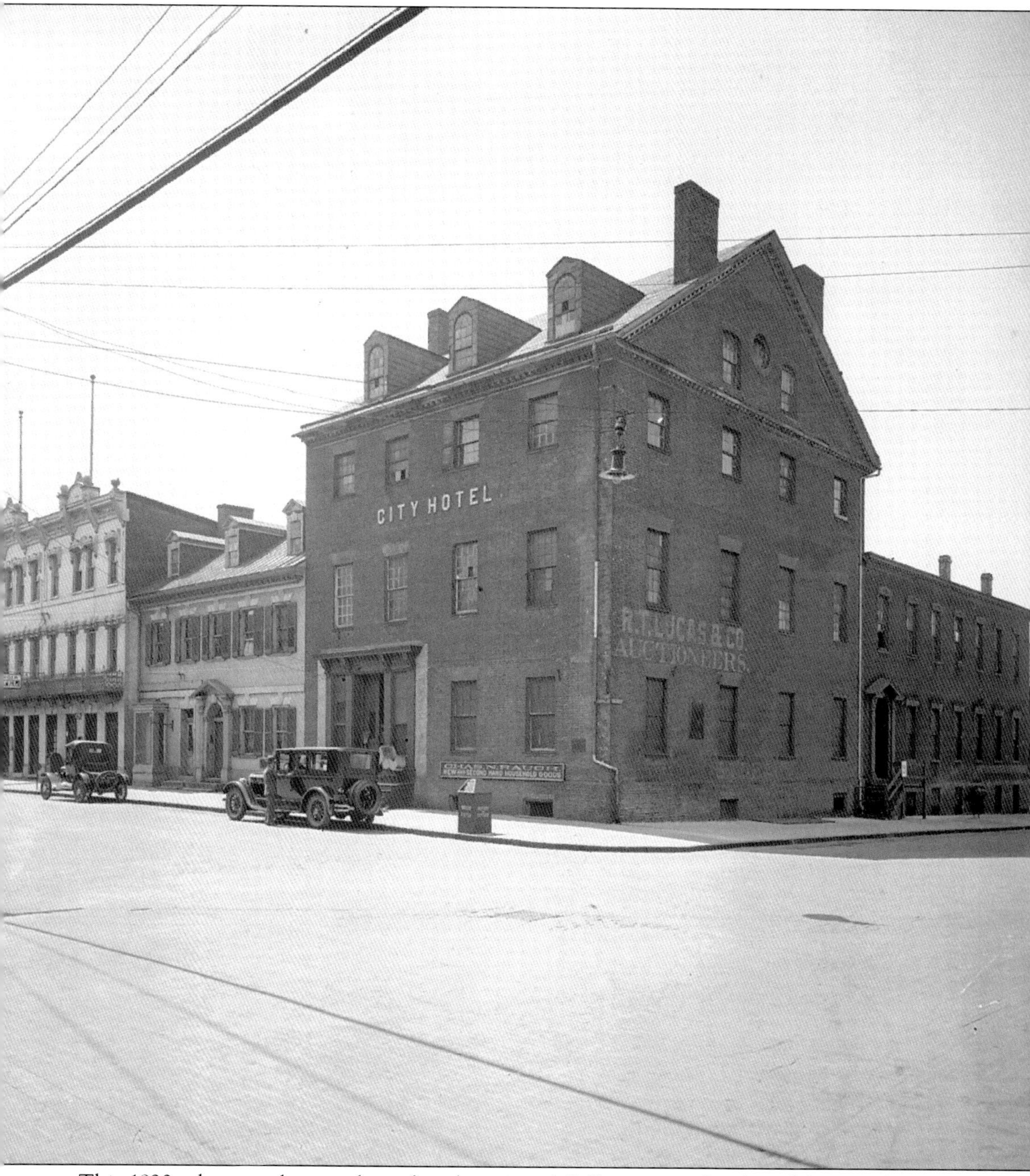

This 1920s photograph was taken after the original Ballroom woodwork and famous door had been purchased by the Metropolitan Museum of Art. The business of Charles N. Rauch, offering both new and secondhand household goods, operated out of the City Hotel between 1919 and 1926. This is thought to be a publicity photograph for the Ford Motor Company, featuring its latest car in front of the famous tavern buildings. Each historic building already had a plaque, emphasizing the importance of the structures to Alexandria. Ownership by this time had passed to Irwin descendants Thomas Fleming Jr., Robert F. Fleming, and William H. Irwin Fleming. The Flemings were exploring options to sell or tear down the buildings.

Two

THE SPIRIT OF PRESERVATION

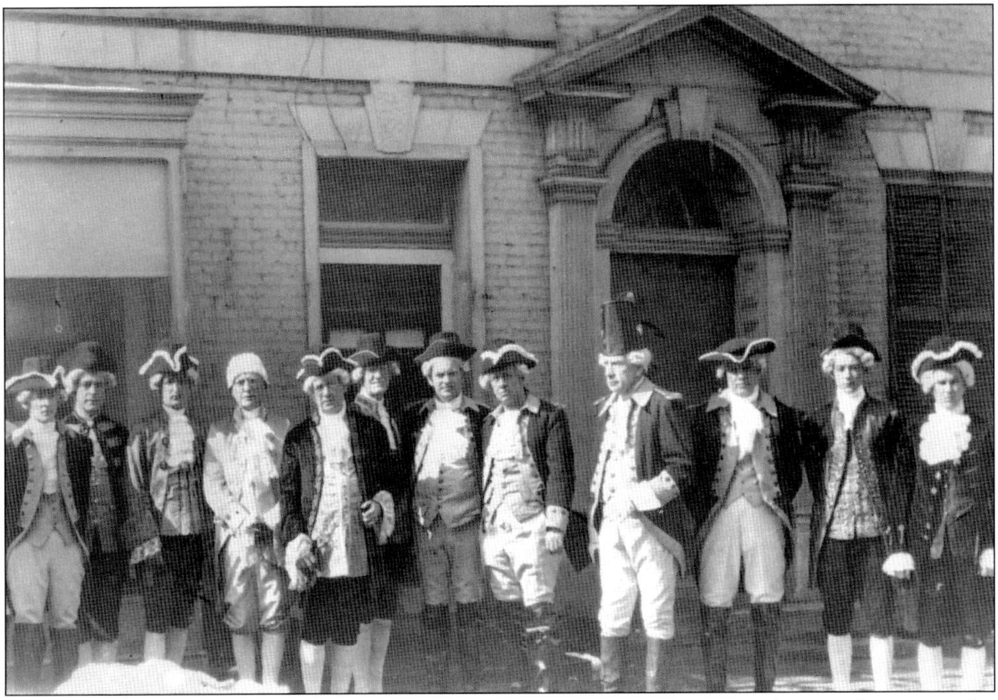

American Legion Post 24, founded in 1919, voted on June 24, 1927, to purchase and preserve the two historic Gadsby's Tavern buildings, saving them from demolition. The purchase price was $18,000, with an anticipated $22,000 needed to restore the buildings. The legion had been seeking a permanent home as well as a way to honor the veterans of World War I. The preservation of these important historic buildings, which had been a center of the community in their day, was determined to be a suitable living memorial to those who died in the war. On January 11, 1929, the legion formally purchased the buildings. Here, legion members pose in front of the newly purchased Gadsby's Tavern. They projected that thousands of visitors a year would pay 10¢ each to see the historic "shrine" on their way to Mount Vernon. (ALSC.)

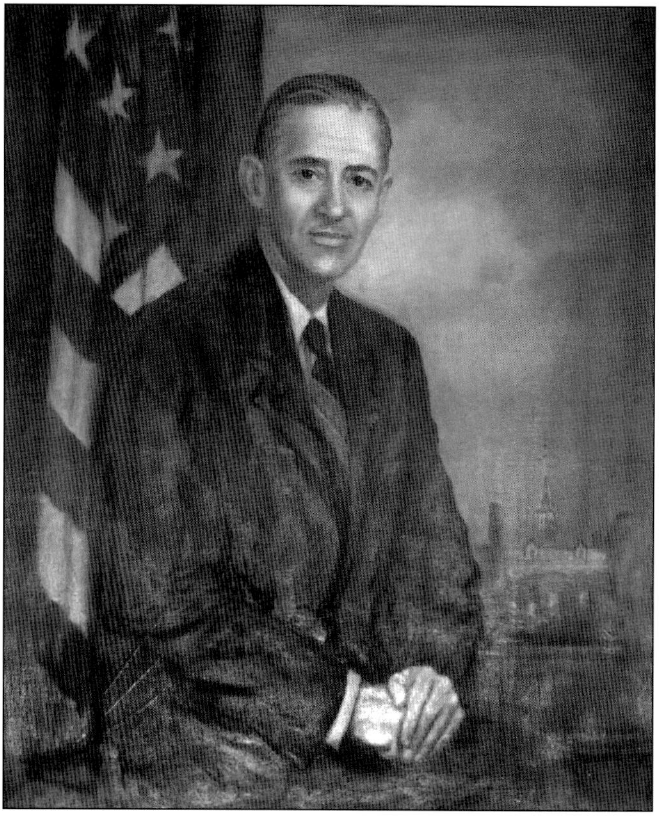

F. Clinton Knight was the post commander of American Legion Post 24 when the membership voted to purchase and preserve the Gadsby's Tavern buildings. He served in World War I, was elected to the city council, managed a family hardware business on King Street, and was active in state and national legion projects. He was referred to as "Alexandria's Mr. American Legion." (Collection of American Legion Post 24.)

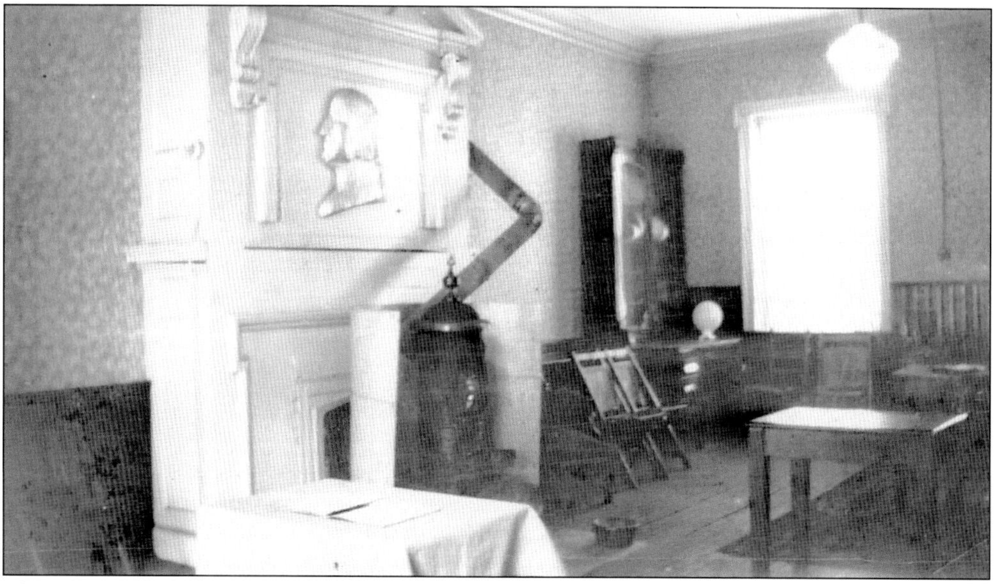

The Taproom of the smaller tavern served as a meeting room for the American Legion and planning headquarters for the restoration. Milton L. Grigg, a local architect working with the Colonial Williamsburg restoration, initially donated his consulting services to the tavern project. Almost immediately, local organizations, such as Daughters of the American Revolution (DAR), the Colonial Dames, and the Business and Professional Women's Club, signed on to help.

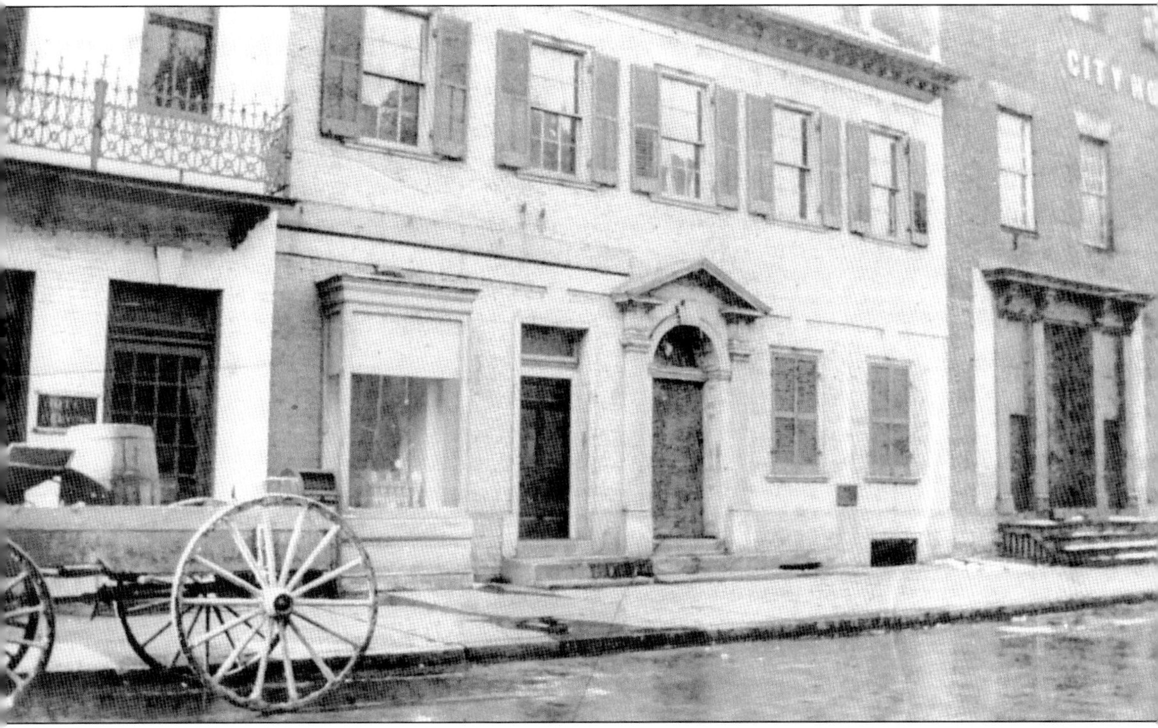

The American Legion called the three-story building "Gadsby's Tavern" and the four-story structure the "City Hotel." At the time, it was believed that the Gadsby's Tavern building was constructed in 1752 and was the former Mason's Ordinary, and that the City Hotel was built by John Wise in 1792. The true Mason's Ordinary was obscured by the more modern facade of the Belvoir Hotel. Note an architectural model of a restored Gadsby's Tavern in the shop window. The restoration was to occur in several phases, with the first-floor rooms in both tavern buildings being completed first. The interior woodwork was to be milled and installed by W.A. Smoot & Co. (Smoot Lumber) of Alexandria.

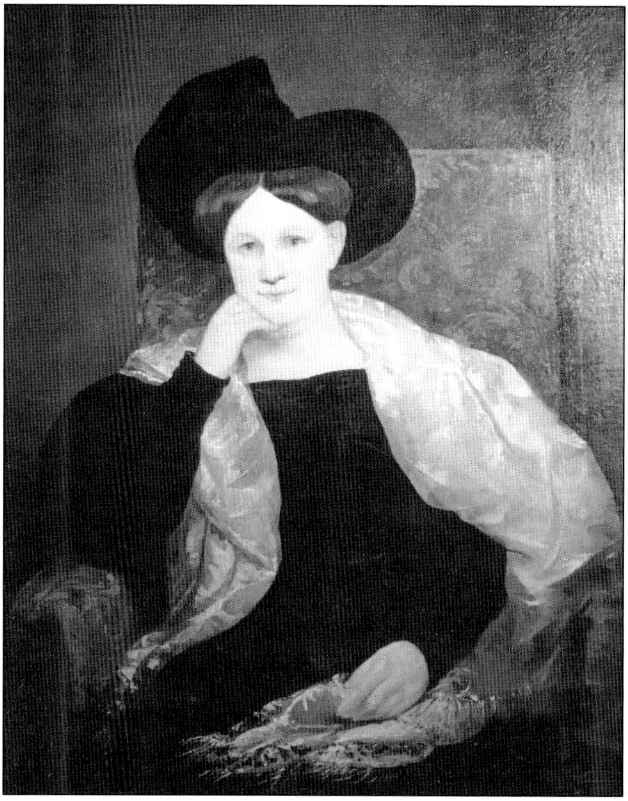

This portrait of Providence (Provey) Gadsby, the third wife of John Gadsby, along with the companion portrait of John Gadsby, were purchased at public auction in 1930 and donated to the American Legion. The portraits were purchased for $60 by Robert S. Jones, Charles C. Callahan, and George W. Zachary.

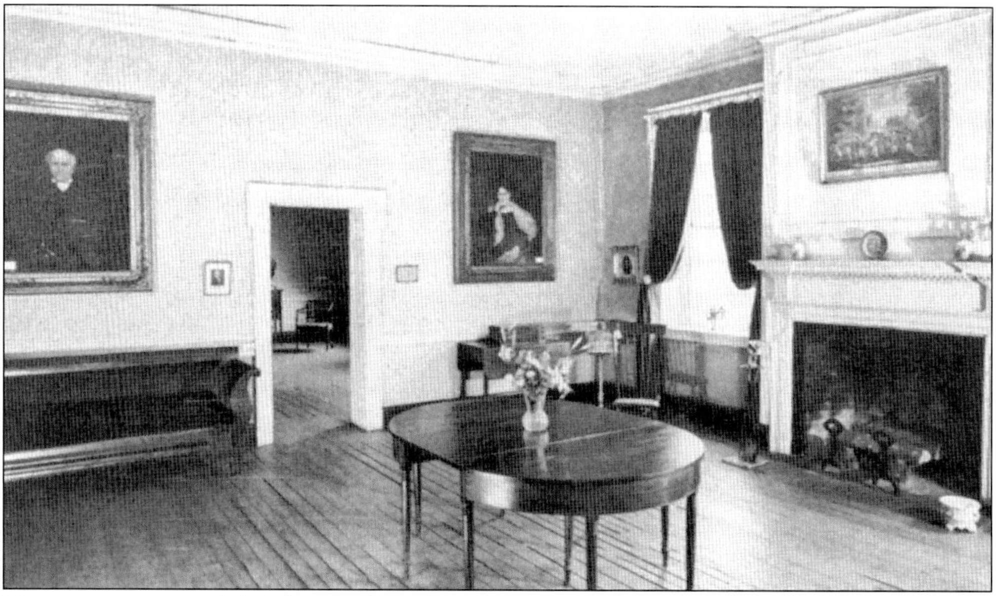

The portraits were exhibited in the front dining room of the City Hotel, along with antiques that were loaned or donated for display. This room, as well as the back dining room and Taproom on the first floor of the City Hotel, were restored with funds from the Colonial Dames, the Virginia chapters of the DAR, and the Washington Society of Alexandria. The buildings opened for tours in May 1930.

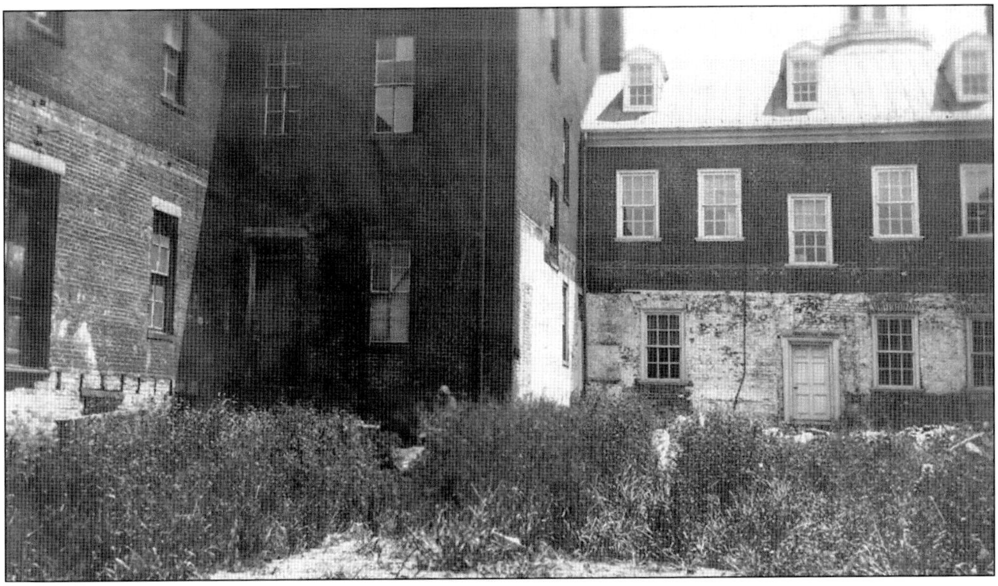

The courtyard is seen before (above) and after (right) its restoration. The courtyard project, sponsored by the Garden Club of Alexandria, was completed in 1931. The design incorporated bricks from the ruins of Abingdon, the birthplace of Eleanor "Nelly" Parke Custis Lewis, the step-granddaughter of George Washington. The Garden Club also reused cobblestones from old streets in Alexandria. The dedication included the unveiling of a plaque by the president of the Garden Club of Virginia, Mrs. Frank Mason Dillard. For the Alexandria club's work, it received the Massie Medal award from the Garden Club of Virginia for the best restoration completed that year. (Right, HABS; photograph by John O. Brostrup.)

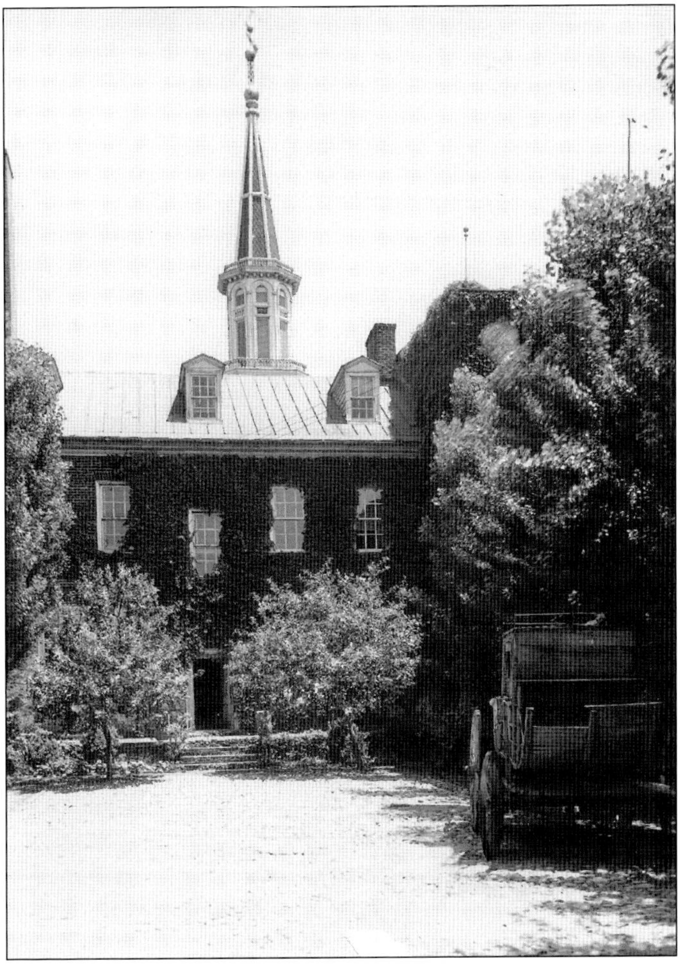

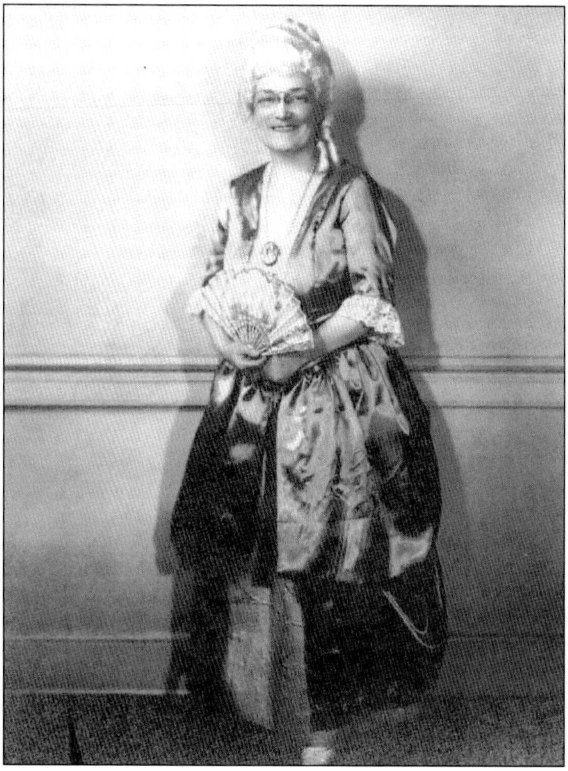

Rebecca Ramsay Reese was a major contributor to the fundraising and restoration effort. A member of the Mount Vernon Chapter of the DAR, she coordinated the restoration of the front facade of the City Hotel building as well as the Ballroom. According to the *Alexandria Gazette*, she had "studied the old tavern from cellar to garret." Here, she poses in her Colonial costume for the February 22, 1932, Birthnight Ball.

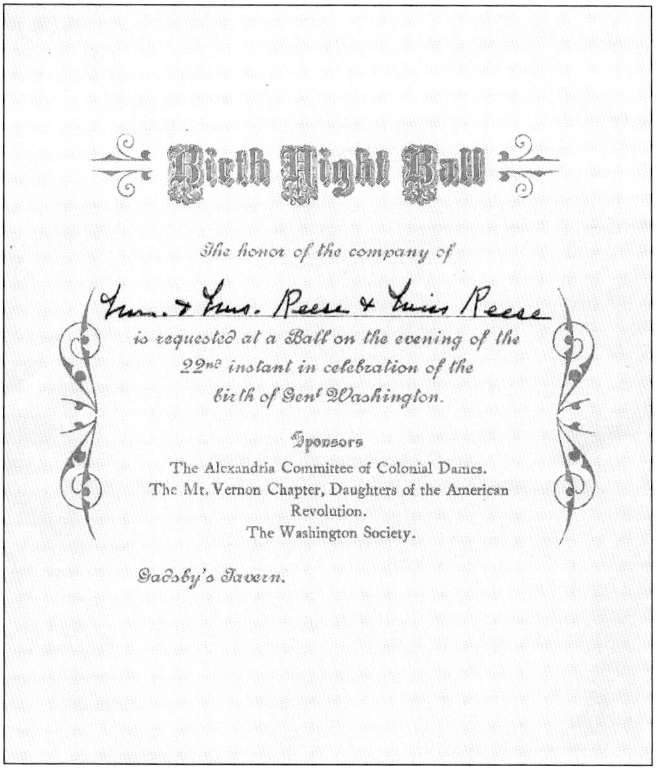

Birth Night Ball

The honor of the company of

Mr. & Mrs. Reese & Miss Reese

is requested at a Ball on the evening of the 22nd instant in celebration of the birth of Genl Washington.

Sponsors

The Alexandria Committee of Colonial Dames.
The Mt. Vernon Chapter, Daughters of the American Revolution.
The Washington Society.

Gadsby's Tavern.

The 1799 Birthnight Ball was re-created in 1932 as part of the bicentennial of George Washington's birth and the restoration of Gadsby's Tavern. Tickets to the gala event were $3 each, and Colonial attire was strongly encouraged. Many of the guests were descendants of those at the original 1799 ball, and a few wore antique gowns. NBC radio broadcast live from the milestone event.

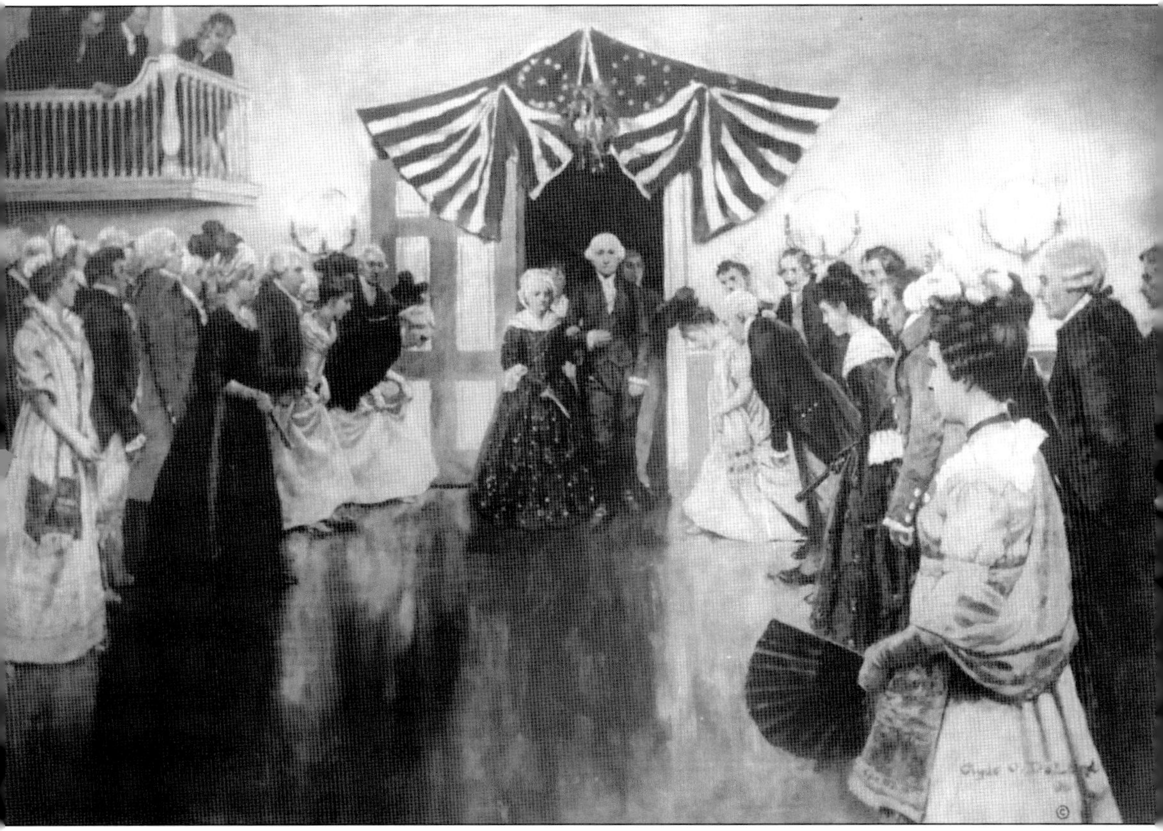

As part of the 1932 commemoration activities, Philadelphia artist Clyde O. Deland created a painting depicting General and Martha Washington entering the Ballroom of Gadsby's Tavern at the 1799 Birthnight Ball. The artist spent time in Alexandria learning about the history and proposed restoration of the tavern. He donated a print of the finished painting, *The Birthnight Ball in Gadsby's Tavern*, to the American Legion.

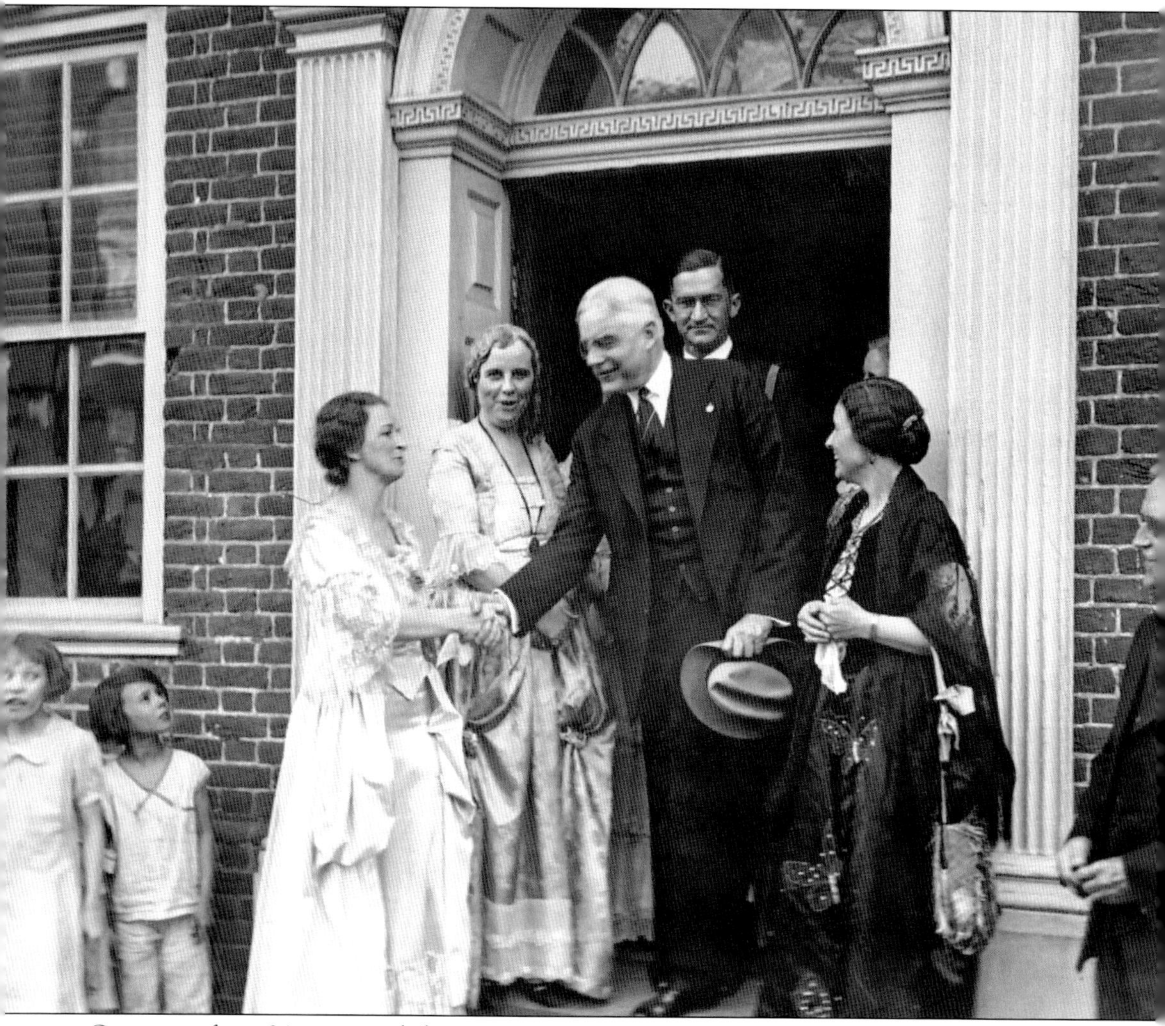

Governors from 24 states and their wives were entertained at Gadsby's Tavern on April 28, 1932. Georgia governor Richard B. Russell, the official spokesman for the delegation, praised the hospitality of "Old Virginia." It was noted in the newspaper that New York governor Franklin D. Roosevelt left the party to continue to Washington to attend a previous engagement. Roosevelt was elected president of the United States that fall. Here, Virginia governor John Garland Pollard shakes hands with a Mrs. Lindsey, one of the costumed committee members who received the group. (ALSC.)

In 1932, the Chesapeake & Ohio Railway launched *The George Washington*. It was accompanied by three dining cars, the *Gadsby's Tavern*, the *Raleigh Tavern*, and the *Michie's Tavern*. Referred to as *The George*, it ran until 1971. Dining Car No. 965, *Gadsby's Tavern*, is the last surviving car from that original 1932 train. It has been preserved by the Chesapeake & Ohio Historical Society, Inc., of Clifton Forge, Virginia.

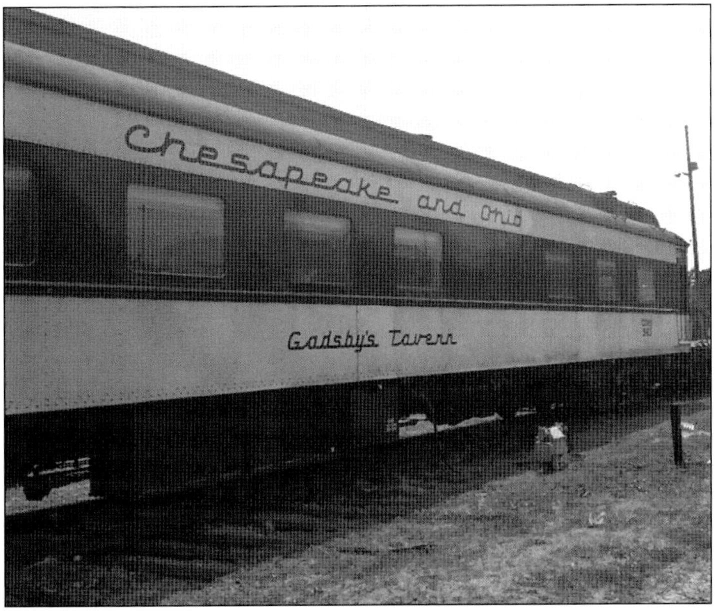

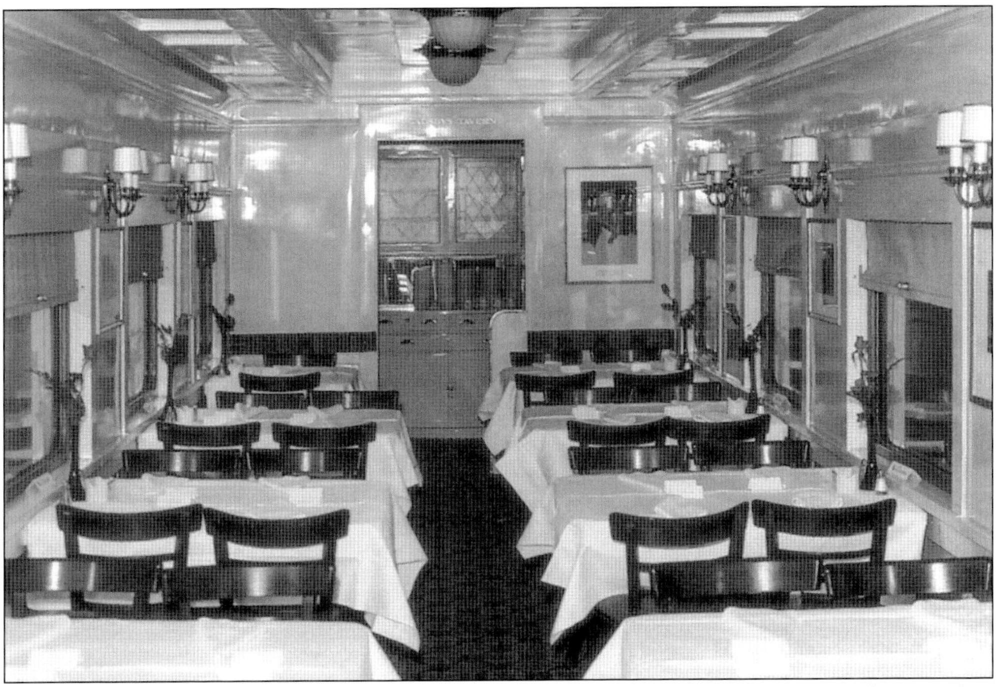

The *Gadsby's Tavern* dining car, which could accommodate 44 passengers, was decorated in the Colonial style with etchings from George Washington's life, a print of Gadsby's Tavern, and Duncan Phyfe–style chairs. The dining car china, which consisted of 33 different pieces, featured a portrait of Washington. Special menus included a short history of Gadsby's Tavern and offered choices such as the "Mount Vernon Dinner" or the "Tavern Dinner."

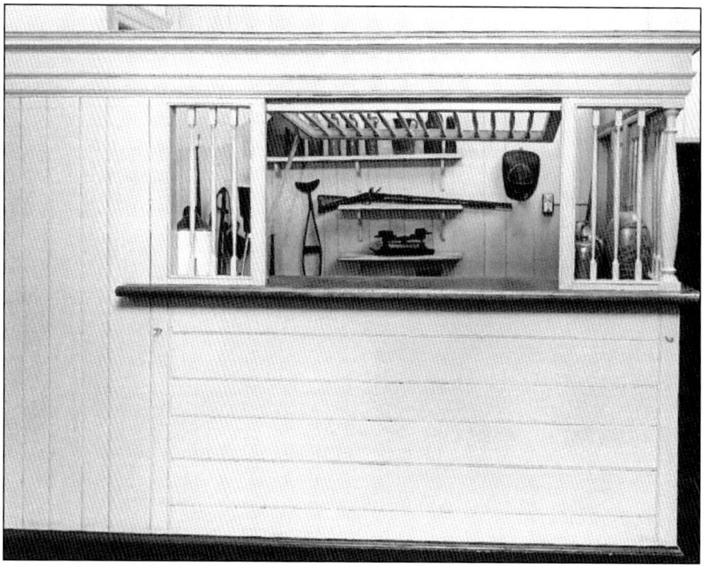

By 1933, the interior restoration of the first floor of the City Hotel and the first and second floors of Gadsby's Tavern were nearing completion. The iconic Taproom bar was designed by Milton Grigg and fabricated by the Charlottesville Lumber Company. The bar was scheduled to be shipped in two sections on June 1, 1933, requiring installation and painting.

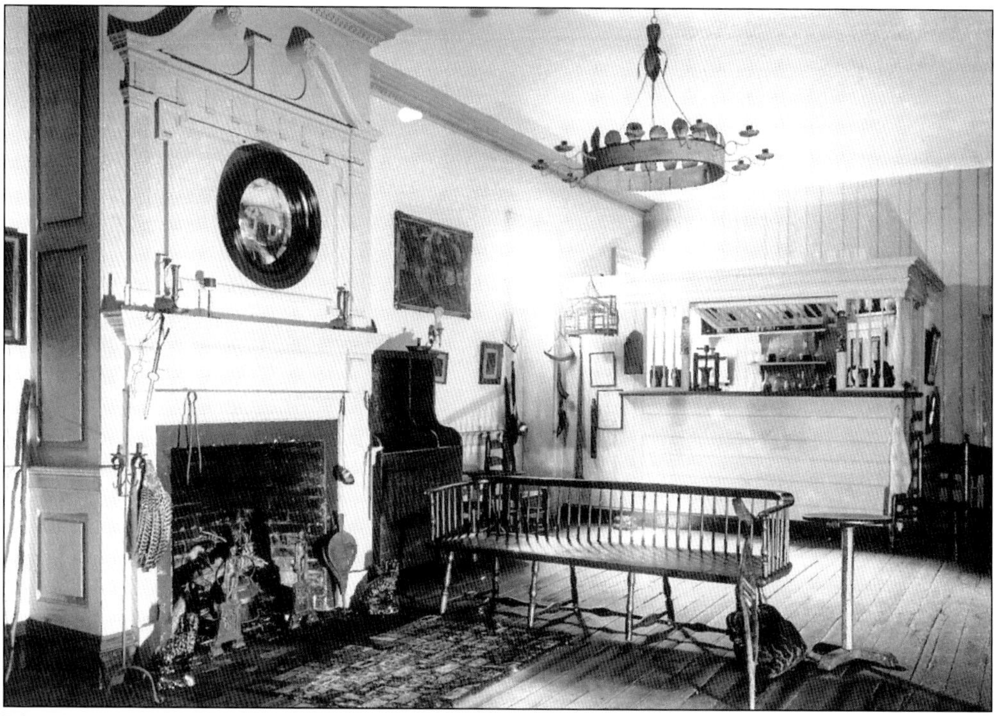

The American Legion turned to Mrs. Mark H. Henderson from Charlottesville and her large collection of antiques to furnish Gadsby's Tavern. Her collection, which had been on view at Michie Tavern, featured early American furniture, including a set of six chairs formerly owned by Henry "Light Horse Harry" Lee and a dining table that had belonged to Pres. James Monroe. (HABS; photograph by John O. Brostrup.)

First Lady Eleanor Roosevelt was the guest of honor at a preview of the Henderson Collection on June 14, 1933. The *Alexandria Gazette* noted that Roosevelt enjoyed her tour of the collection and her conversation with restoration architect Milton Grigg. Here, Roosevelt poses with Eleanor Selden Washington, the great-grandniece of George Washington and the last person born at Mount Vernon. (Underwood & Underwood/Corbis.)

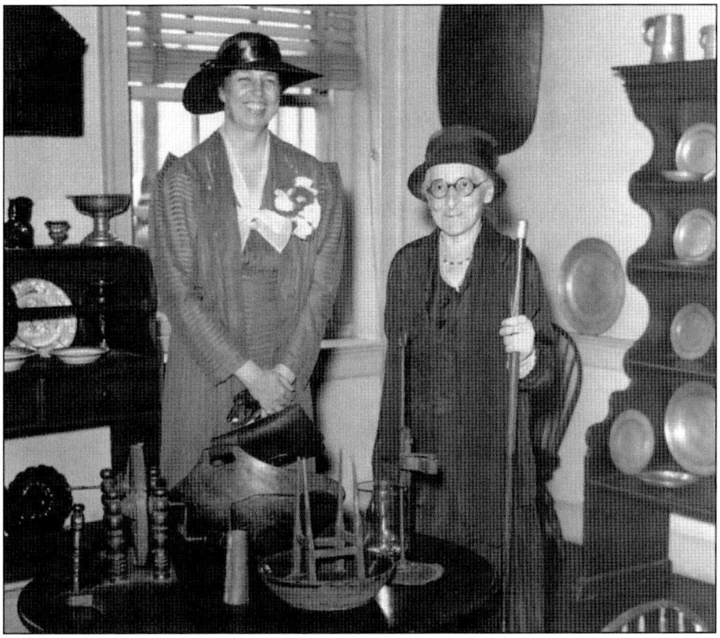

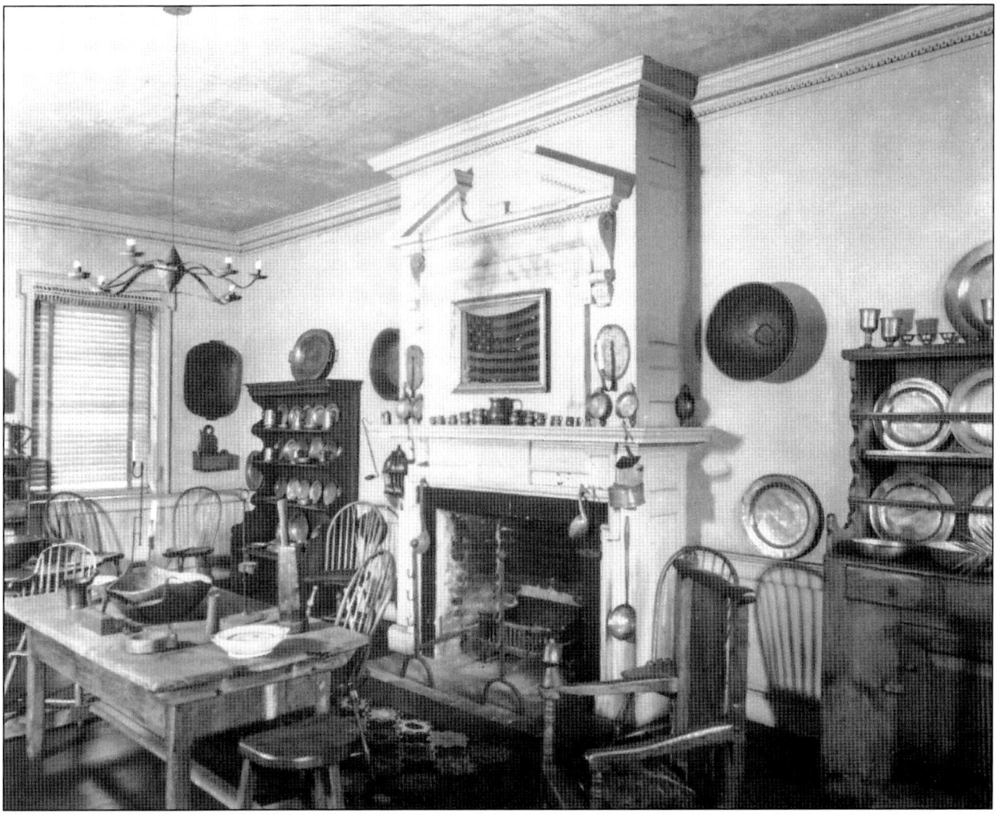

The collection went on view to the public beginning on June 16, 1933, and attracted 5,400 visitors in just one year. The exhibit was open weekdays and Sundays, and admission was 25¢. Residents of Alexandria were required to pay admission on their first visit, but subsequent visits were free.

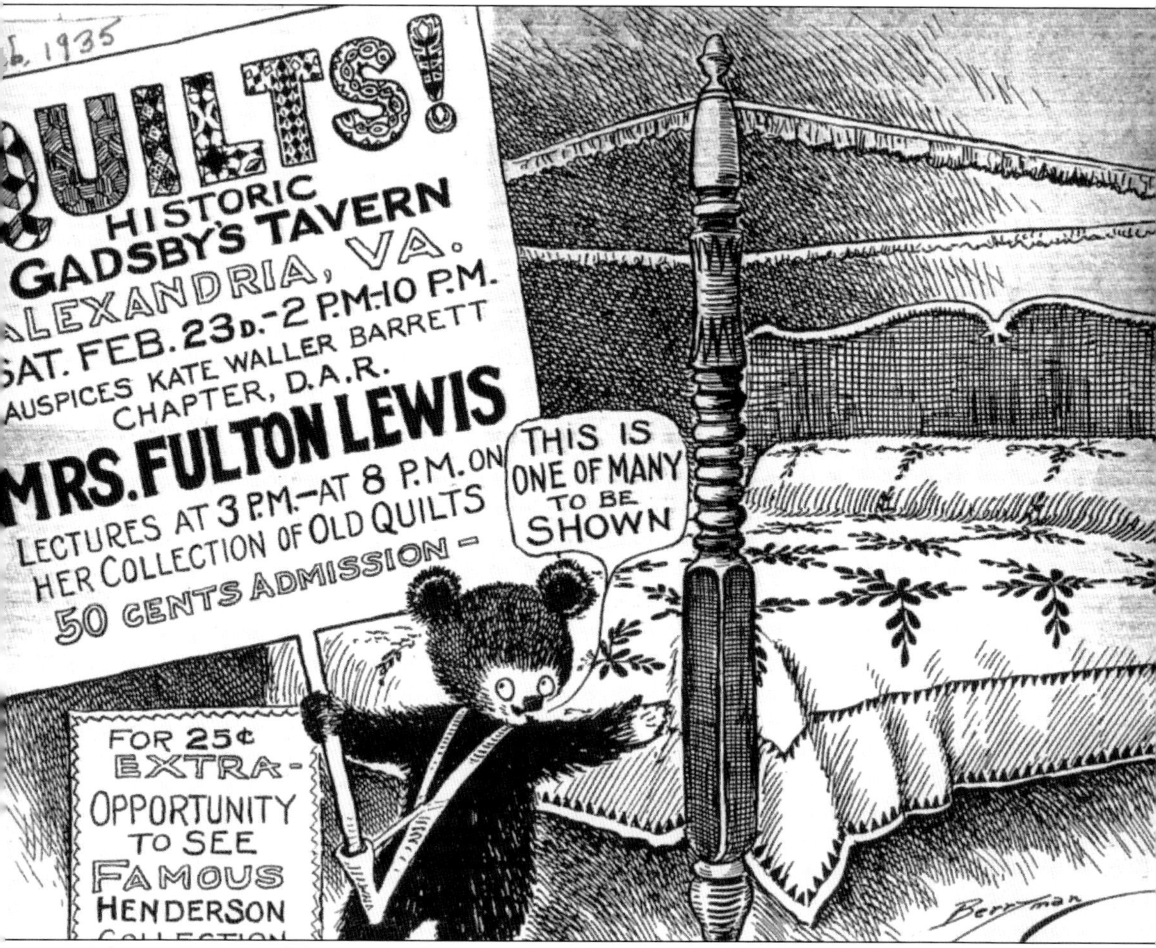

The involvement of the Kate Waller Barrett Chapter of the DAR with Gadsby's began in 1928 and was the chapter's first project following its organization in 1925. The chapter pledged its support to the legion and held a variety of fundraisers to assist the restoration. While the Henderson Collection was on view, the chapter sponsored an exhibition of quilts owned by Mrs. Fulton Lewis of Georgetown, DC, in February 1935.

The Assembly Room, furnished as a lady's parlor, or the "mistress' bed room," was featured extensively in regional newspapers and magazines. The *Washington Sunday Star* magazine's front-page article about Gadsby's Tavern and the exhibit announced, "Famous Colonial Tavern of Alexandria now contains notable collection of antiques rated as one hundred percent authentic . . . a treasure trove for antiquarians and a shrine for visitors."

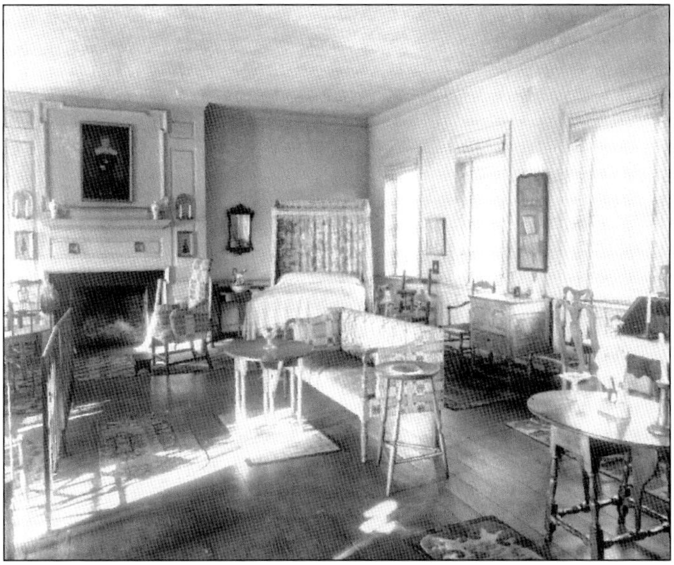

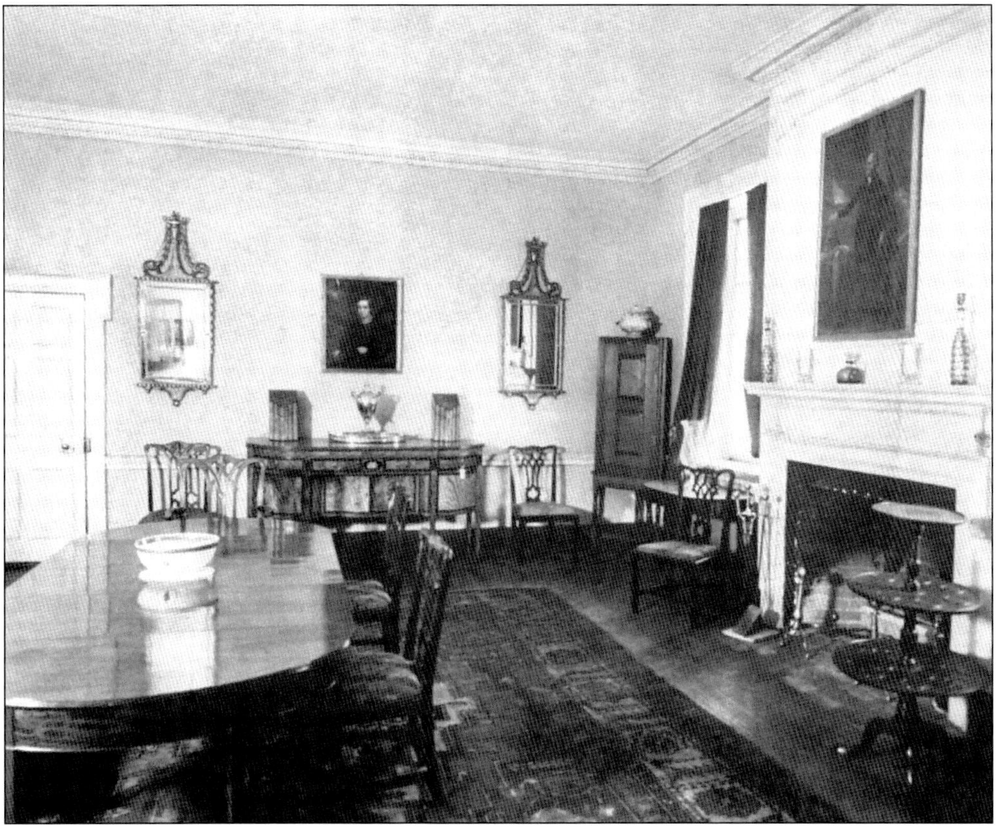

Despite efforts to make the exhibition permanent, the collection of antiques was removed from Gadsby's Tavern over an insurance dispute and shipped to New York City for public auction. The collection was sold on April 23, 1938, through Parke-Bernet Galleries, Inc. With this turn of events, the Alexandria Association started a drive to collect "famous" pieces owned by Alexandrians who were willing to lend them to the tavern.

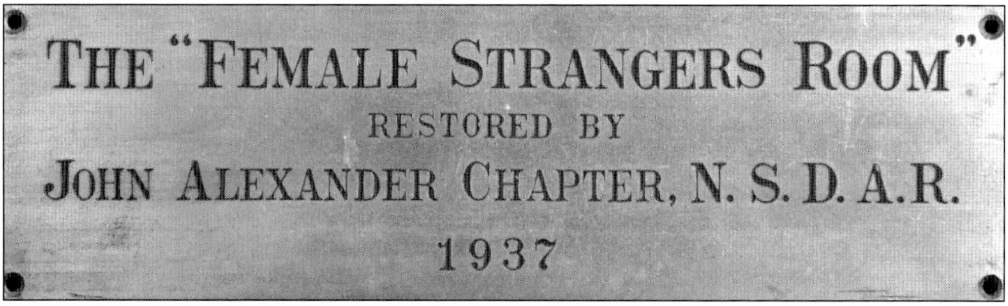

With the loss of the Henderson Collection, furnishing the historic landmark became the new challenge. Alexandria chapters of the DAR and the National Society of the Children of the American Revolution stepped up to sponsor individual rooms. These groups were able to fundraise within their own organizations to support their chosen rooms.

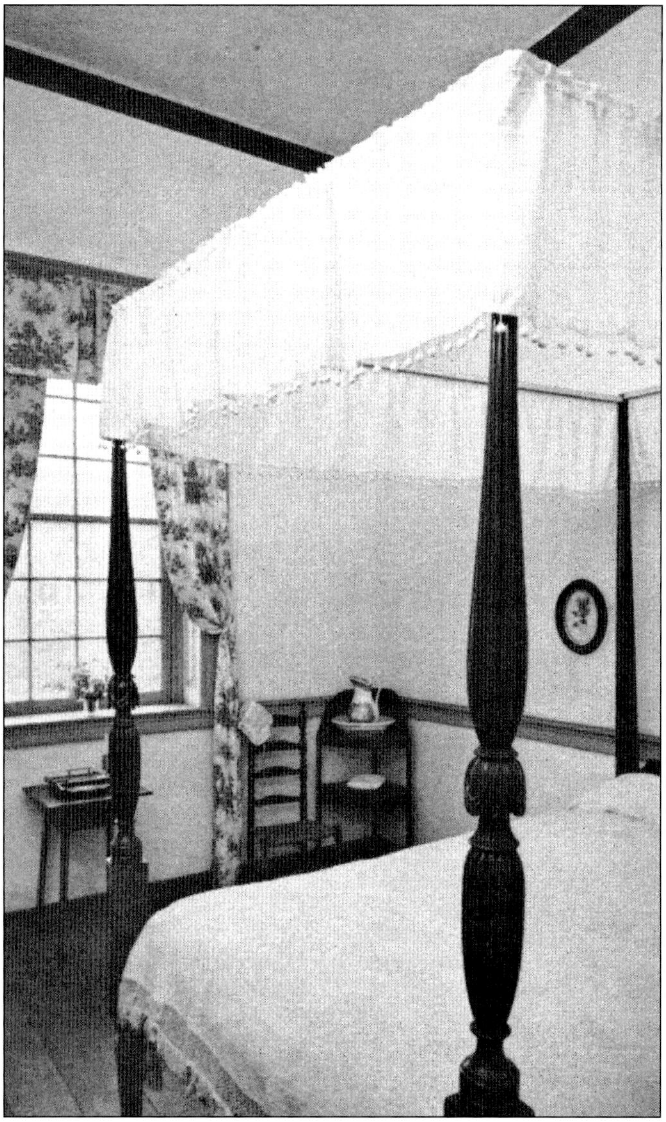

Members of the John Alexander Chapter of the DAR sponsored the east bedchamber of the City Hotel as a memorial to its deceased members. The chapter held a variety of fundraisers, including lectures, to acquire appropriate objects. The room was named the "Female Stranger Room," after its association with the tale of a mysterious woman who came to Alexandria and was believed to have died in the room.

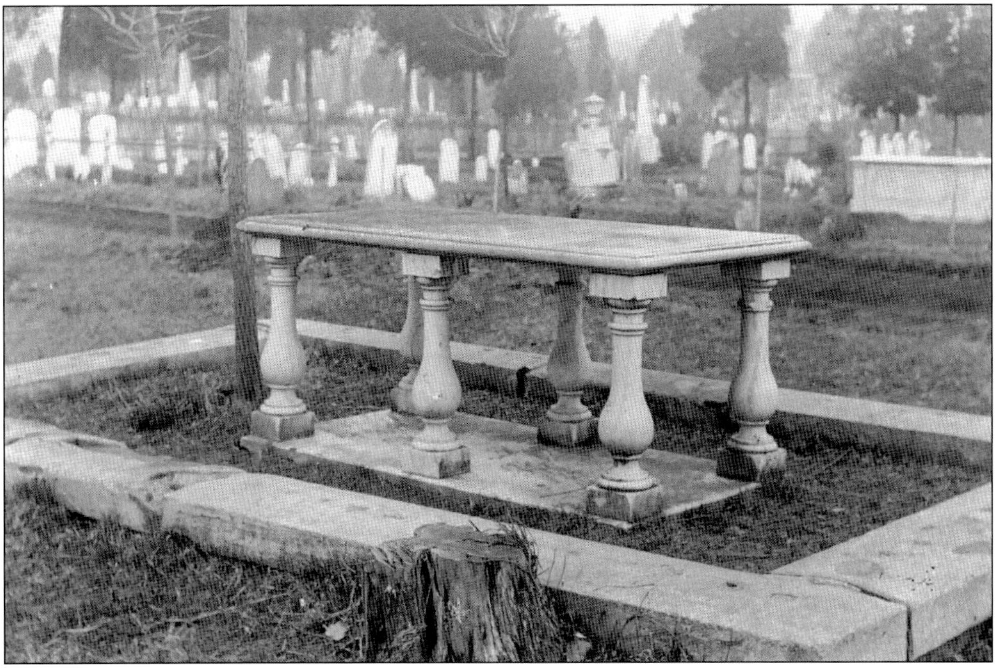

The "Female Stranger" story is a romantic legend associated with Gadsby's Tavern. The story, with many versions, involves a couple who arrived by ship from the West Indies into the port of Alexandria in 1816 and took a room at Gadsby's Tavern, the finest establishment in town. The woman was gravely ill. The doctor and two nurses hired to care for her were promptly sworn to secrecy about her identity. The woman's condition progressively worsened, and she died at the tavern. Her disconsolate companion commissioned an expensive tabletop tomb and buried her at St. Paul's Cemetery in Alexandria. The engraving on the tomb begins, "To the memory of a Female Stranger whose mortal sufferings terminated on the 14th day of October 1816." (Above, ALSC.)

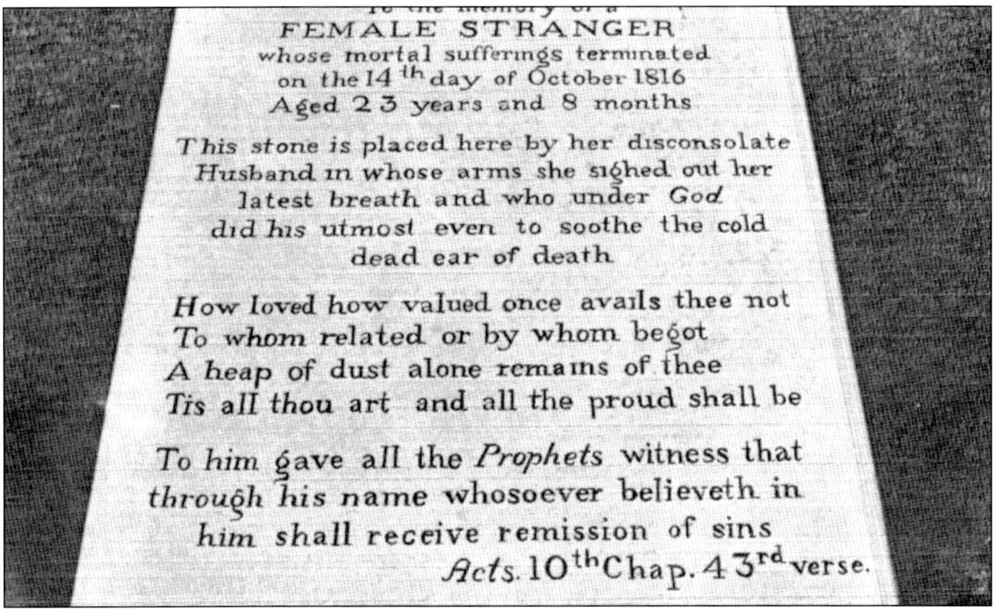

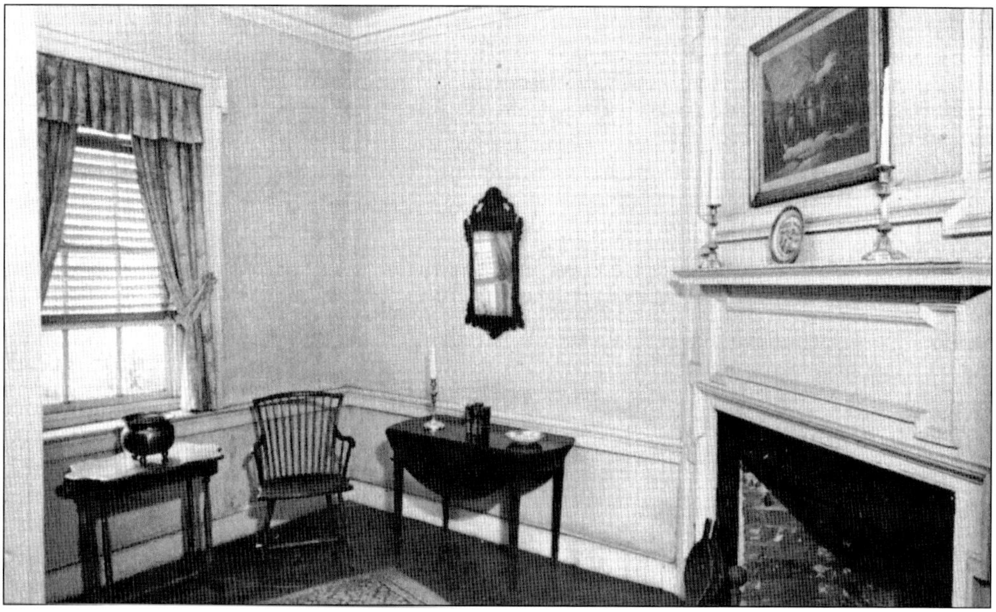

The Kate Waller Barrett Chapter of the DAR restored and furnished the small dining room, which had been called the Lafayette Room when the Henderson Collection furnished the tavern. The chapter started purchasing objects for the room in November 1938, beginning with a Pembroke table. The room was finished and formally dedicated in 1941.

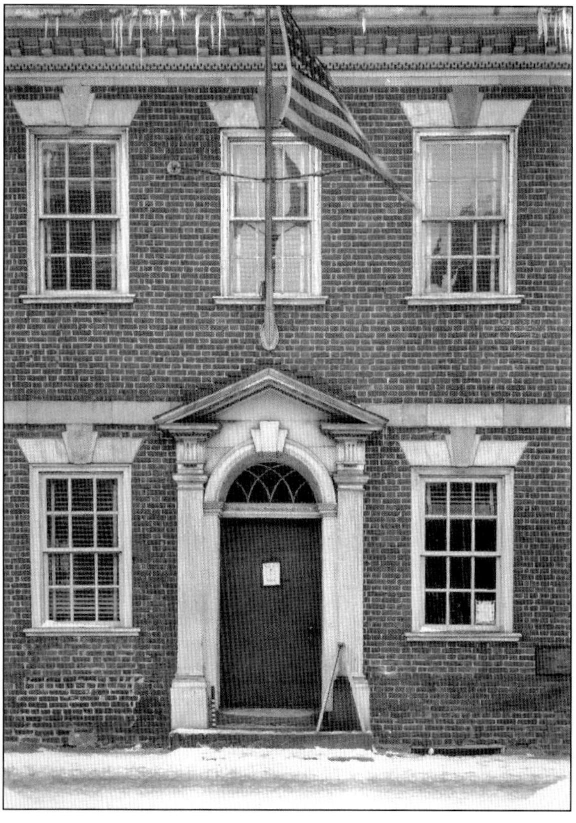

The facade of the newly restored Gadsby's Tavern building is seen here in February 1936. A sign on the steps advertises that tours are available. The two buildings were documented in 1936 as part of the Historic American Buildings Survey by local architect Thomas Tileston Waterman. Photographs, measured drawings, a history, and a description of the site were included in the report. (HABS; photograph by Albert S. Burns.)

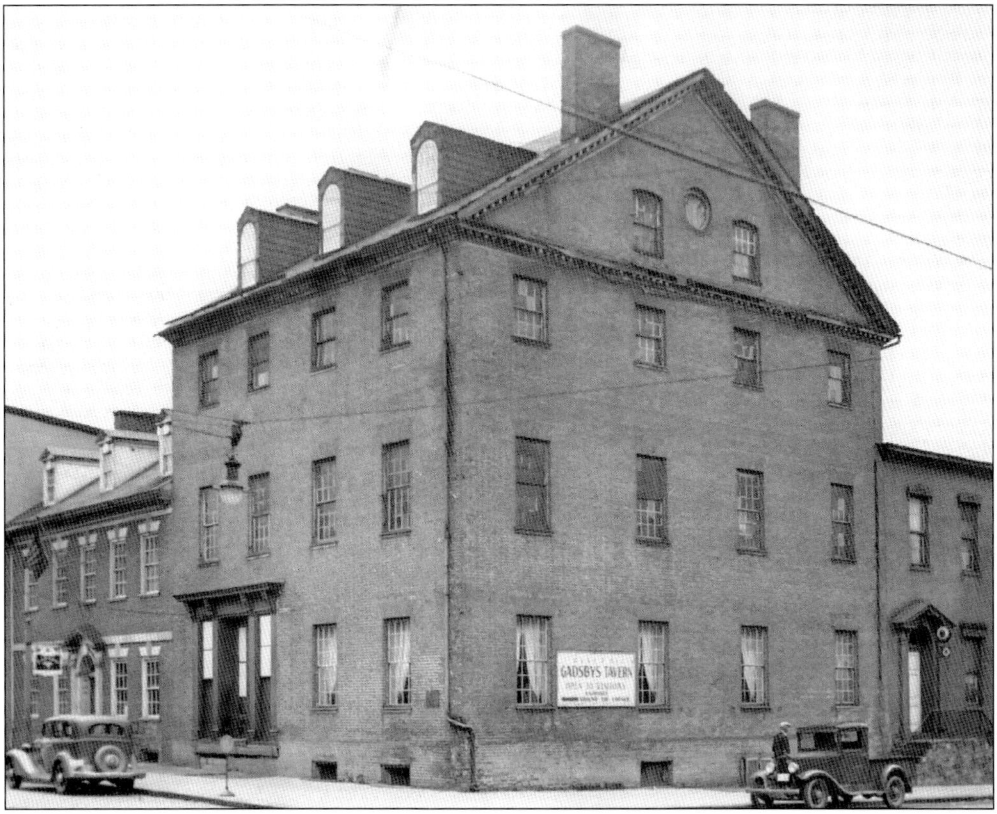

The beginning of the restoration of the front facade of the City Hotel building is seen here in the mid-1930s. The steps have been detached from the front of the building to prepare for the removal of the Italianate door. A sign at the corner of the building advertises that Gadsby's Tavern is open to the public and that the entrance is around the corner. (Historical Society of Washington, DC.)

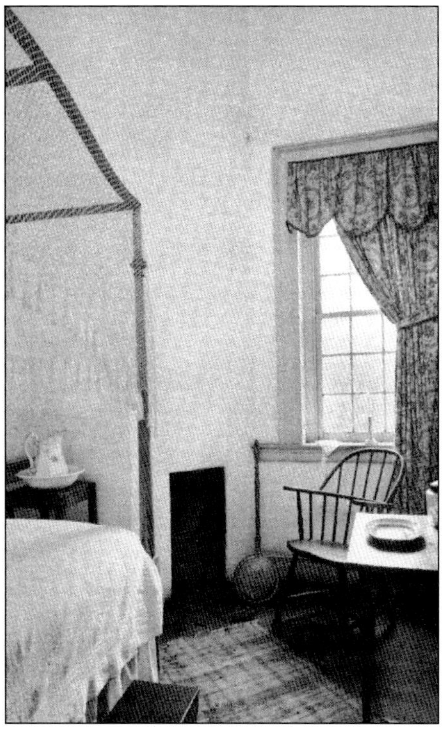

The west bedchamber, or Swann Room, was restored by 1938. Both the middle and west bedchambers were sponsored by the National Society of the Children of the American Revolution (NSCAR). The organization referred to the bedchambers as the Pouch Room and the Swann Room, named after Mrs. William H. Pouch (NSCAR president general, 1941–1944) and Mrs. Charles A. Swann Sinclair (NSCAR president, 1933–1937).

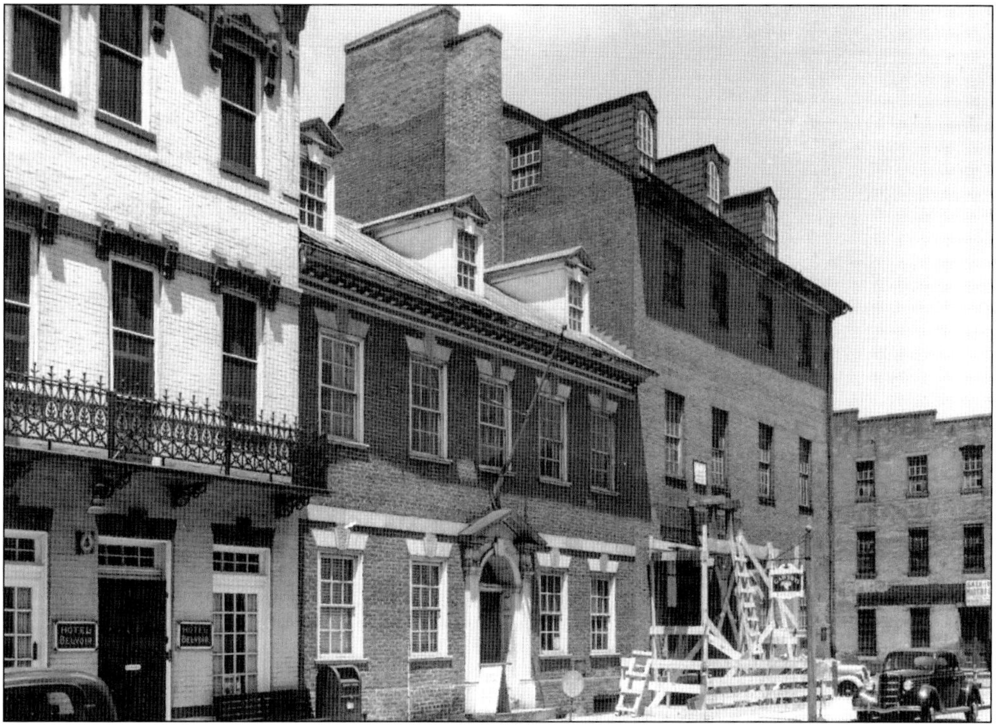

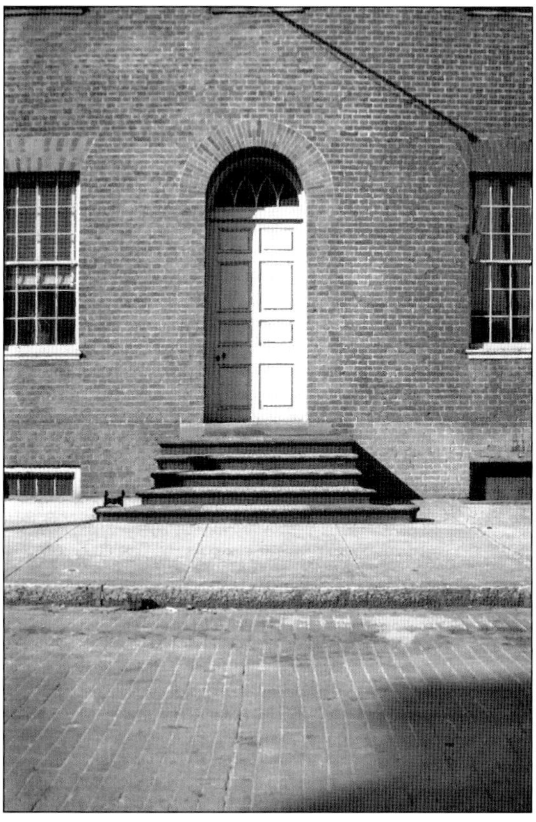

Scaffolding was in place over the facade of the City Hotel's Italianate door by June 15, 1936. The plan was to remove the Victorian doorway, replace the missing bricks, re-create the removed window, and prepare the entrance for the return of the original 1792 door. This work was overseen by local architect Delos H. Smith and funded by the Mount Vernon Chapter of the DAR. (HABS; photograph by John O. Brostrup.)

The completed restoration of the front facade of the City Hotel building is seen here. This project cost $1,700 and included the restored doorway and wall, a window, stone steps, and a boot scraper. At this point, Rebecca Ramsay Reese had almost given up hope of being able to repurchase the original door from the Metropolitan Museum of Art. Instead, plans were in place to duplicate the original. (ALSC.)

The Alexandria Association funded the restoration of the City Hotel roof, the building's cornices, and the dormer windows. The total cost was $2,500. According to its minutes, the Alexandria Association supported the work so that the "interior restoration might go forward in this historic building." (ALSC.)

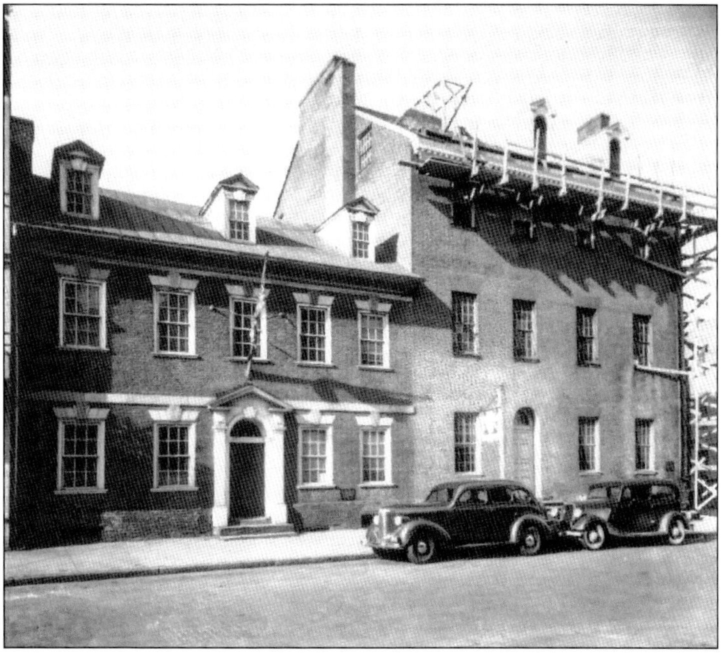

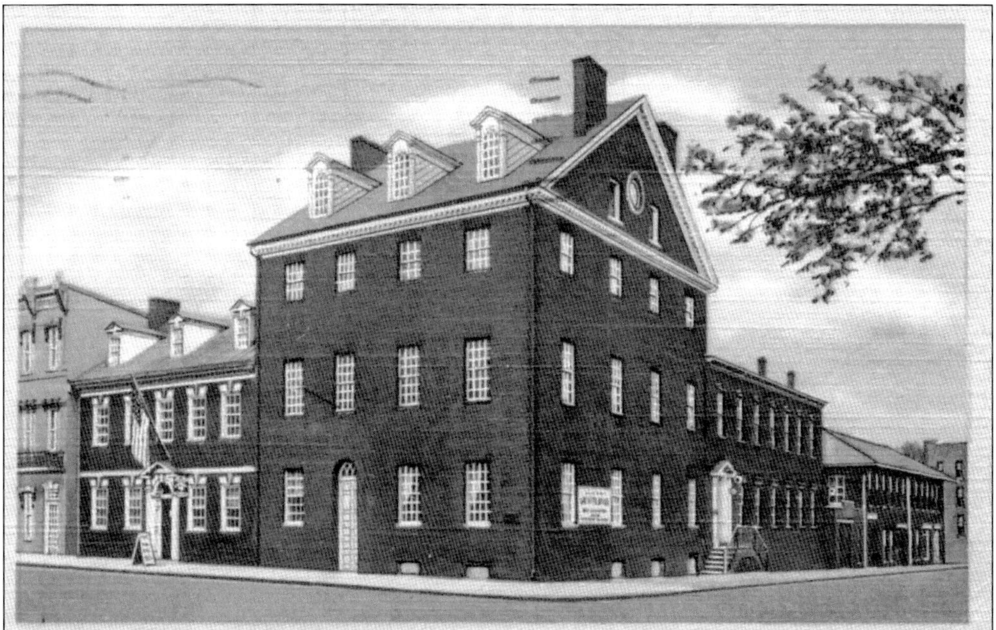

This postcard, produced by B.S. Reynolds Co. of Washington, DC, shows the City Hotel building restored and ready for the return of the original door. In 1939, American Legion Post 24 created a separate entity, Gadsby's Tavern and City Hotel, Inc., to support the historic buildings. The corporation's board consisted of nine members, five from American Legion Post 24 and four citizens at large.

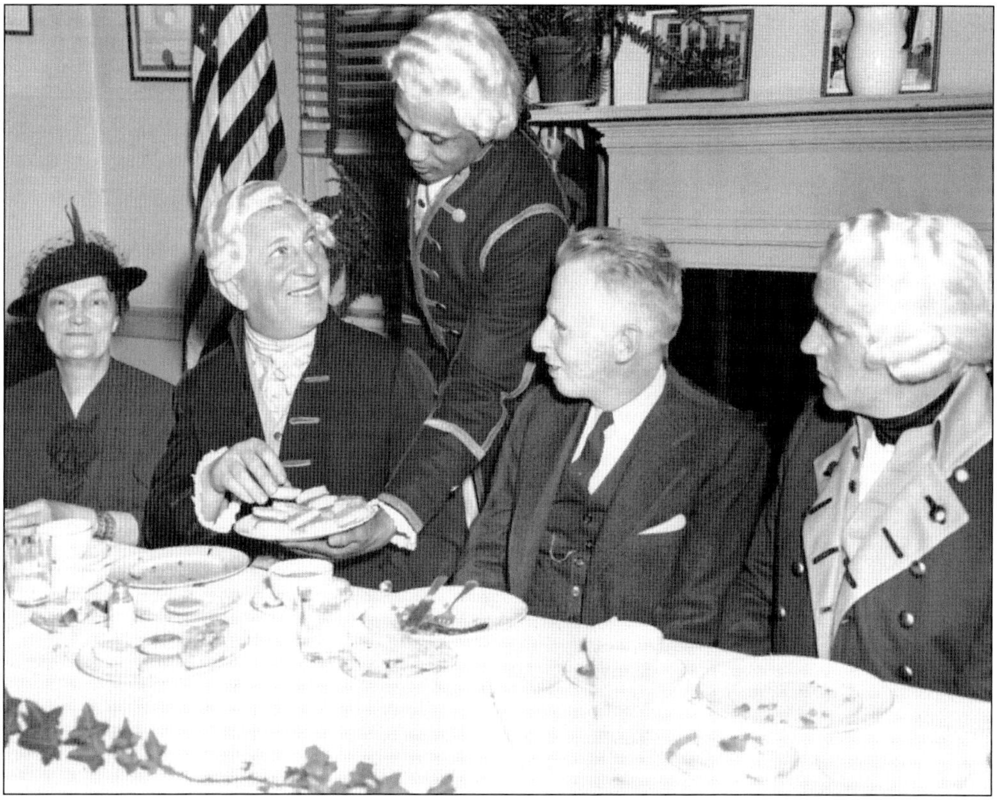

On April 16, 1939, a reenactment lunch was held to commemorate the 150th anniversary of Washington's ride from Mount Vernon to New York City to take his oath as president. Pictured here are, from left to right, Rebecca Ramsay Reese (great-granddaughter of town founder Dennis Ramsay), Denys Wortman (portraying George Washington), an unidentified costumed waiter, Mayor Richard L. Ruffner, and Laurens M. Hamilton (portraying Col. David Humphreys).

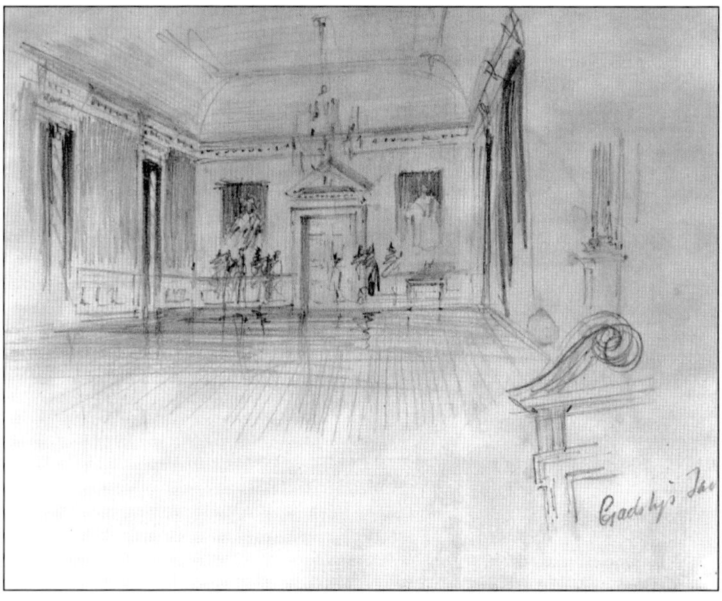

Thomas Tileston Waterman created this architectural drawing of the ballroom of the Governor's Palace in Colonial Williamsburg. Note the sketch of a pediment from Gadsby's Tavern's Ballroom at lower right. Waterman was hired by Rebecca Ramsay Reese to duplicate the Ballroom woodwork from the original, located in the Metropolitan Museum of Art. (LOC.)

The Virginia State Chapters of the DAR adopted the restoration of the Ballroom as their golden jubilee project and appointed a committee at their March 1939 conference. Almost immediately, they received $1,015 in pledges from 32 Virginia chapters. The woodwork was milled, installed, and painted to replicate the original. This English mirror, which matched the woodwork, was purchased to honor Rebecca Ramsay Reese. A celebration was held on October 10, 1940.

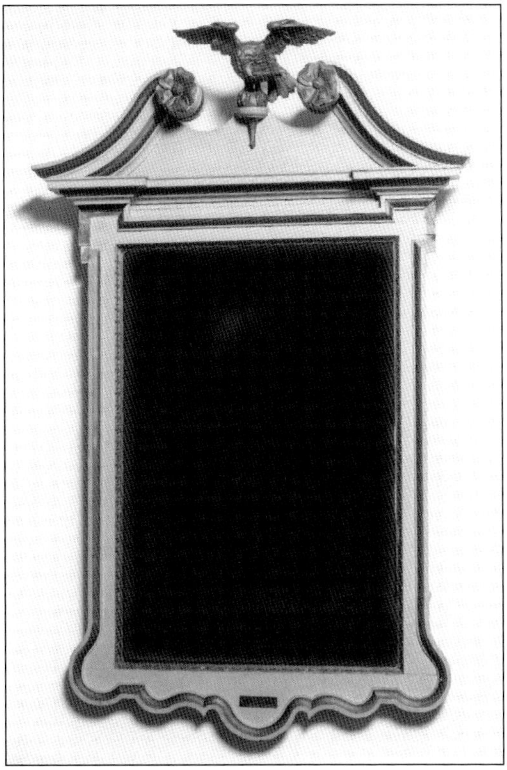

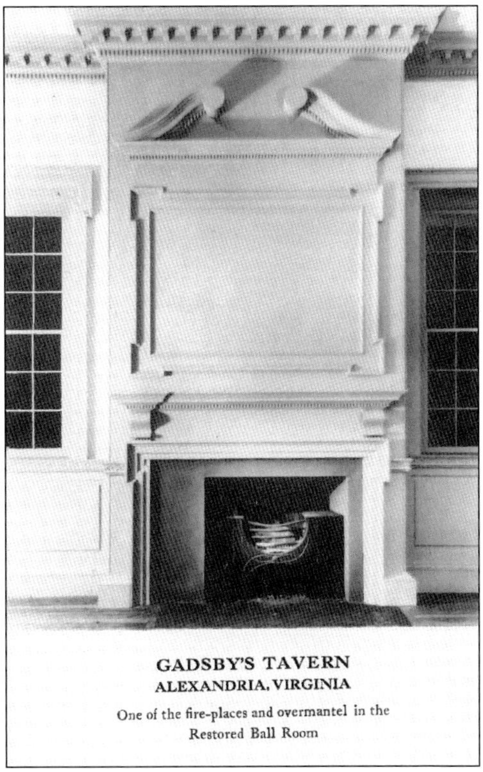

This postcard features the newly reproduced woodwork for the historic Ballroom. The coal grate is thought to be the only object original to the tavern. Because of its heavy weight and utilitarian nature, it had never been sold with other furnishings. When the building was constructed in 1792, many of the fireplaces were installed to burn coal rather than wood. This coal grate is on view today in the Ballroom. (ALSC.)

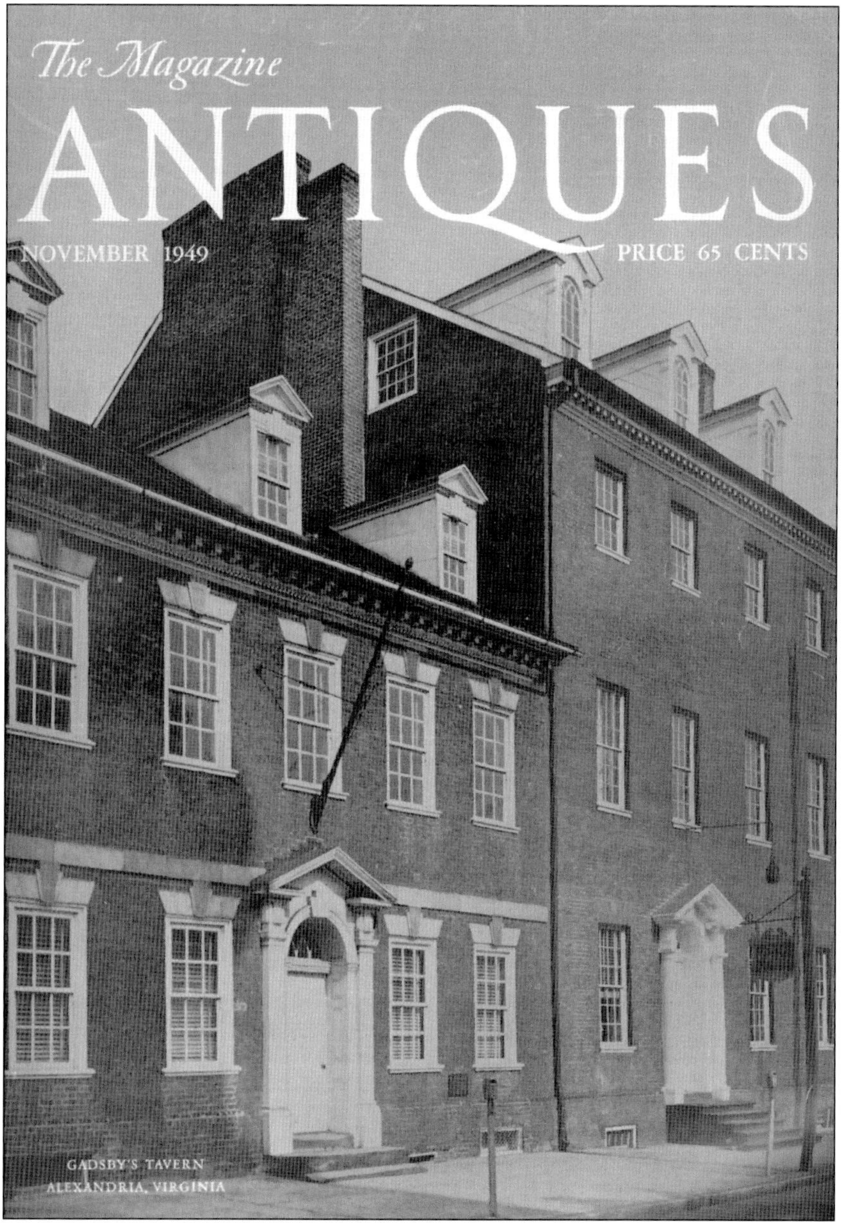

Gadsby's Tavern was the cover story of *The Magazine Antiques* in November 1949. The article featured the return of the original front door from the Metropolitan Museum of Art in New York City. Col. and Mrs. Charles Beatty Moore successfully negotiated the purchase after several prior attempts had failed. The Moores presented the door to the Alexandria Association, which funded its installation. The dedication ceremony took place on November 11, 1949, and the doorway was officially presented to George Giammittorio, commander of American Legion Post 24. The program included the "The Star-Spangled Banner" played by a US Army band and an invocation by Rev. Norman Roberts, chaplain of the legion post. Edward Boykin, noted historian and director of the National Capital Sesquicentennial Commemoration, was the principal speaker for the ceremony, attended by more than 500 people. Mrs. Woodrow Wilson was the first to pass through the doorway at the event.

In 1949, Scalamandre of New York wove and donated fabric for curtains to be made by B. Altman for the Ballroom. The curtains were installed in time for the November 11, 1949, celebration of the return of the original City Hotel door. In an October 1949 display in its Fifth Avenue store window, B. Altman promoted Gadsby's Tavern, the new Scalamandre curtains, and the important door.

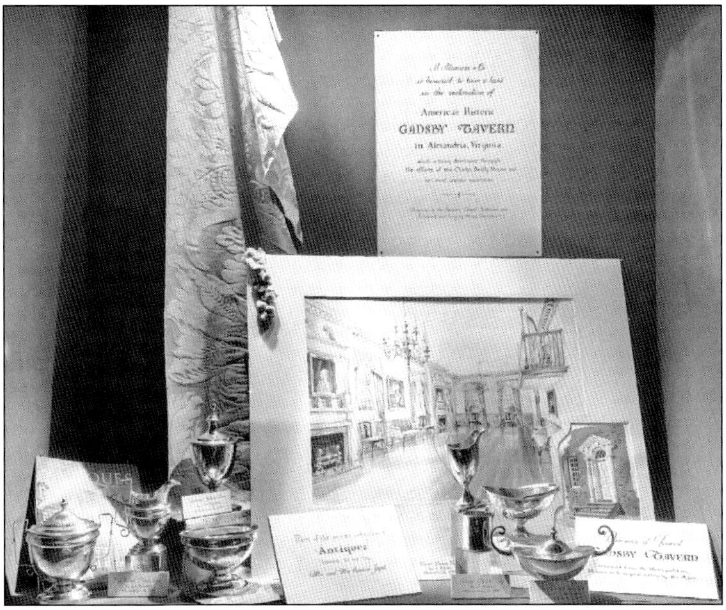

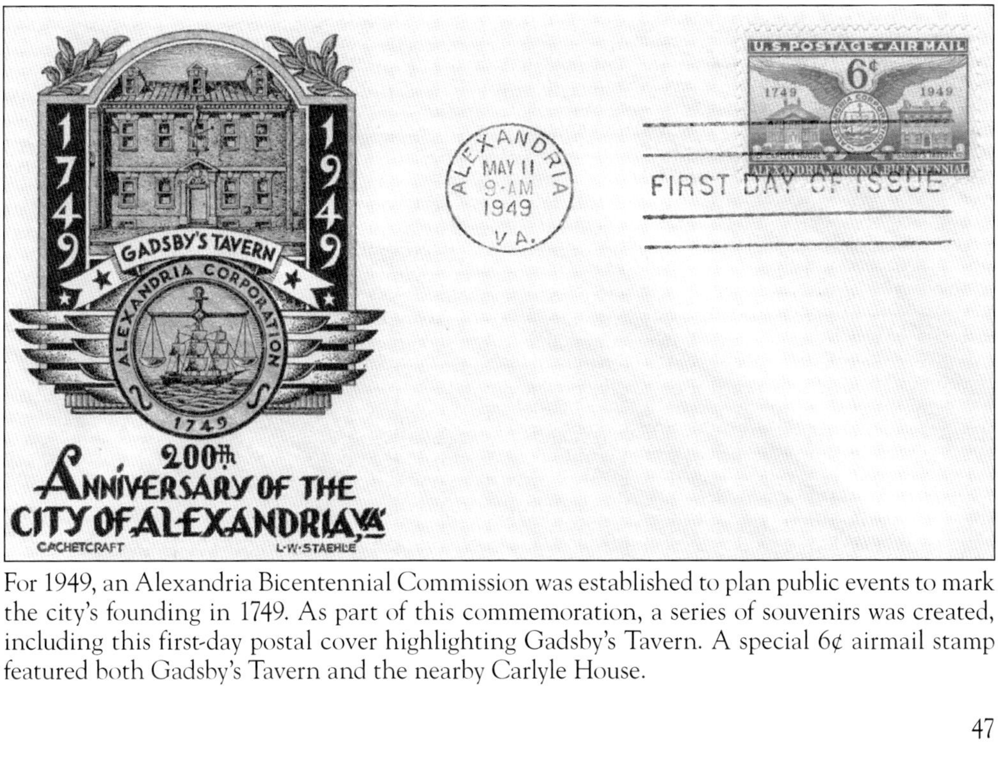

For 1949, an Alexandria Bicentennial Commission was established to plan public events to mark the city's founding in 1749. As part of this commemoration, a series of souvenirs was created, including this first-day postal cover highlighting Gadsby's Tavern. A special 6¢ airmail stamp featured both Gadsby's Tavern and the nearby Carlyle House.

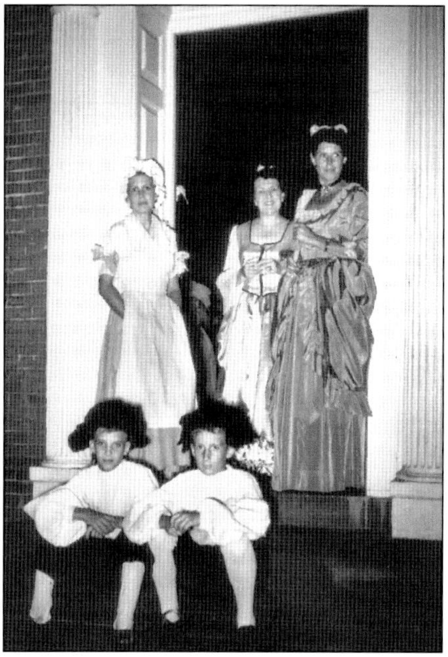

Between 1946 and 1969, the Little Theatre of Alexandria called Gadsby's Tavern its home. The tavern hosted 24 theatrical seasons, known as the Gadsby Plays. These plays quickly became a social event in Alexandria and helped the tavern recapture its past. Here, costumed hostesses and "link boys" wearing tricorn hats wait for guests to arrive at the front door to see *The Jealous Wife* in 1950.

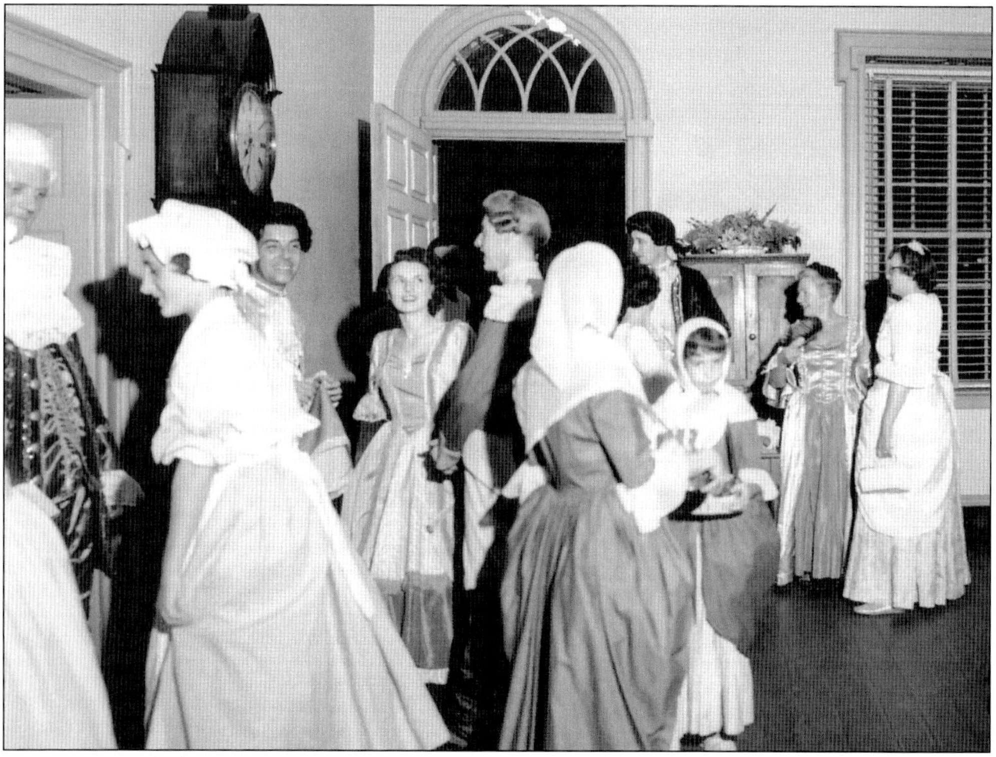

Guests entered the tavern and were greeted by costumed serving girls offering oranges with peppermint sticks. The guest list was a who's who in Washington and included Mrs. Woodrow Wilson, Gen. Omar Bradley, and Pres. Harry Truman. Special nights were held for local groups, such as the National Society of the Children of the American Revolution, who helped in the preservation of the tavern. (Little Theatre of Alexandria.)

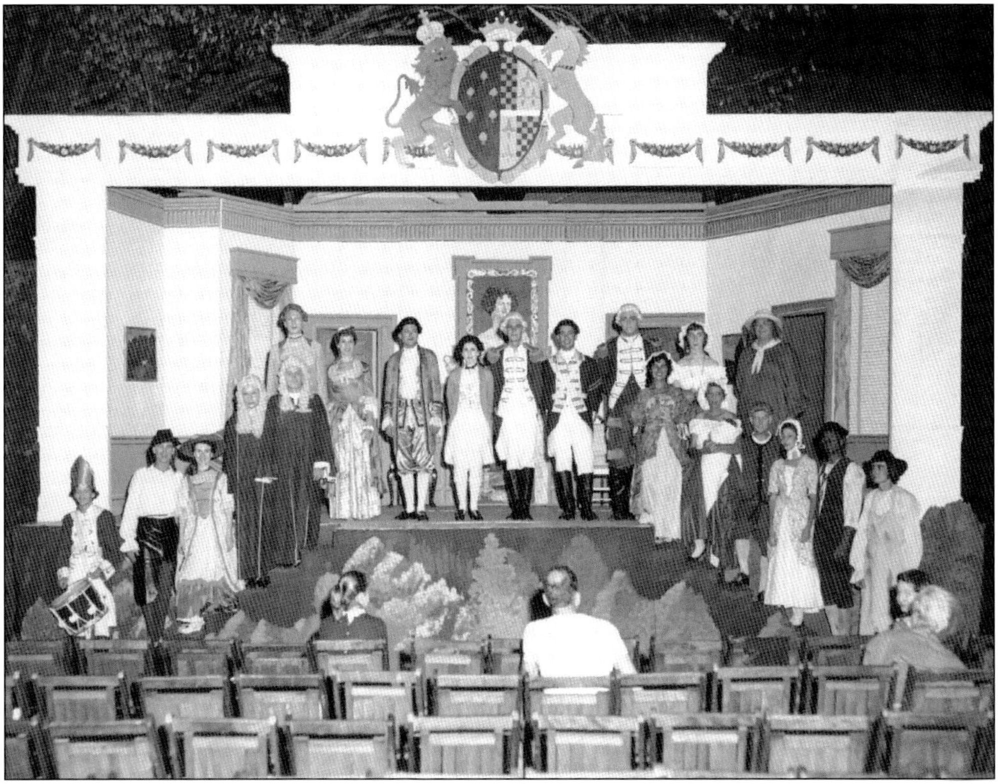

Performances were originally held in the Ballroom, which seated 135 patrons. Soon, audiences outgrew the space, and performances were moved to the tavern's courtyard. The large, outdoor space was ideal except for the airplane noise and the uneven seating caused by the courtyard's cobblestone surface. This is the cast of George Farquhar's *Recruiting Officer*, which was produced nightly in September 1957, Tuesday through Saturday. (Little Theatre of Alexandria.)

For the *Merry Wives of Windsor* in 1960, actors portraying George and Martha Washington were on hand to greet visitors. The front-of-the-house cast, which included link boys, hostesses, serving girls, John Gadsby, the major domo, and the Washingtons, played an integral role in creating the historical atmosphere for guests attending a play. From the moment a guest entered the tavern, history came to life. (Little Theatre of Alexandria.)

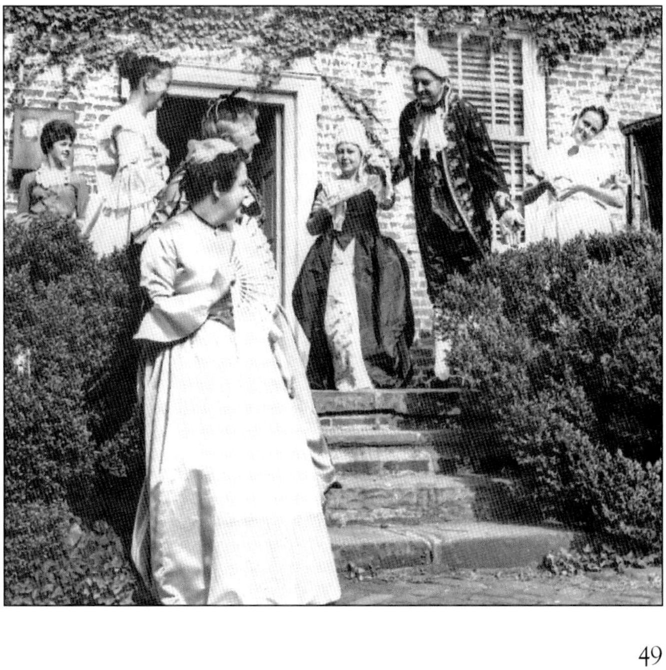

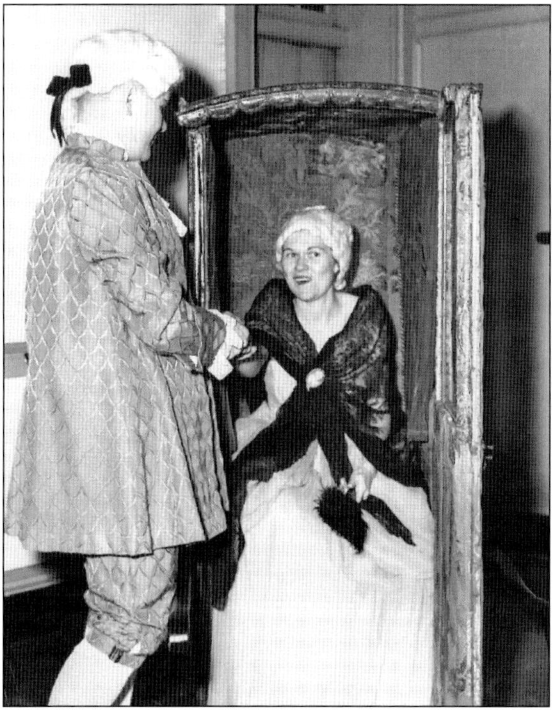

Dressing up in Colonial attire was part of the Gadsby's Tavern experience. American Legion post commander Bill Glasgow assisted his wife, Catherine, out of a sedan chair that was on display in the Taproom in 1951.

Post commander Bill Glasgow pointed out a secret compartment in a tavern desk to costumed guests at an American Legion event. (ALSC.)

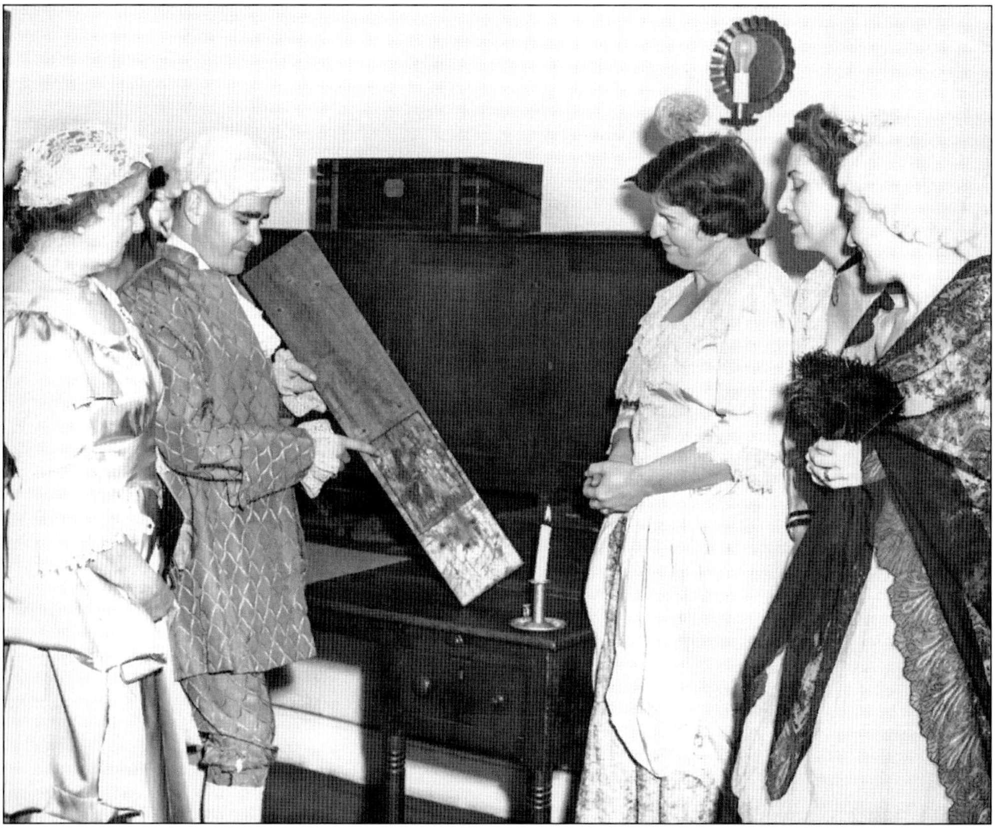

Guests pose at the 1954 Birthnight Ball. At left is 14-year-old Patrisia Carroll Owens. Her dress was made by her aunt Catherine Otley and was worn to the 1954 and 1955 Birthnight Balls.

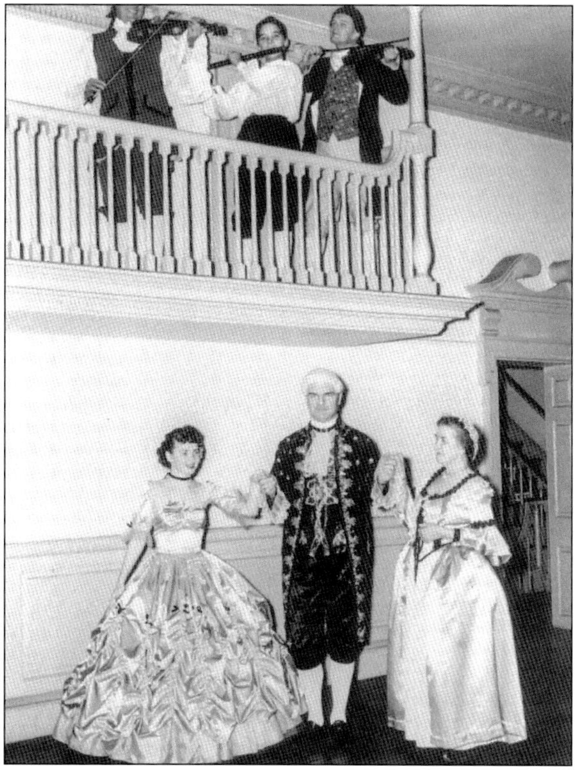

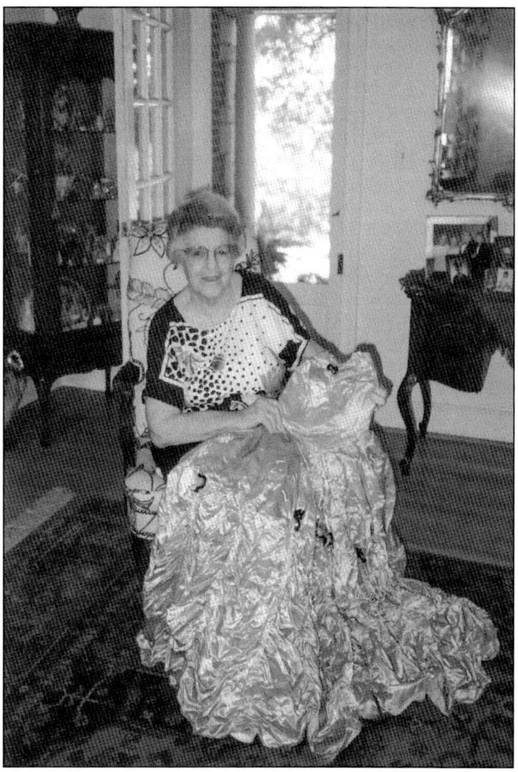

Catherine Otley poses with the ball gown she made for her niece Patrisia in 1954. The dress was donated to Gadsby's Tavern Museum in 1993, along with photographs of the events at which the dress was worn.

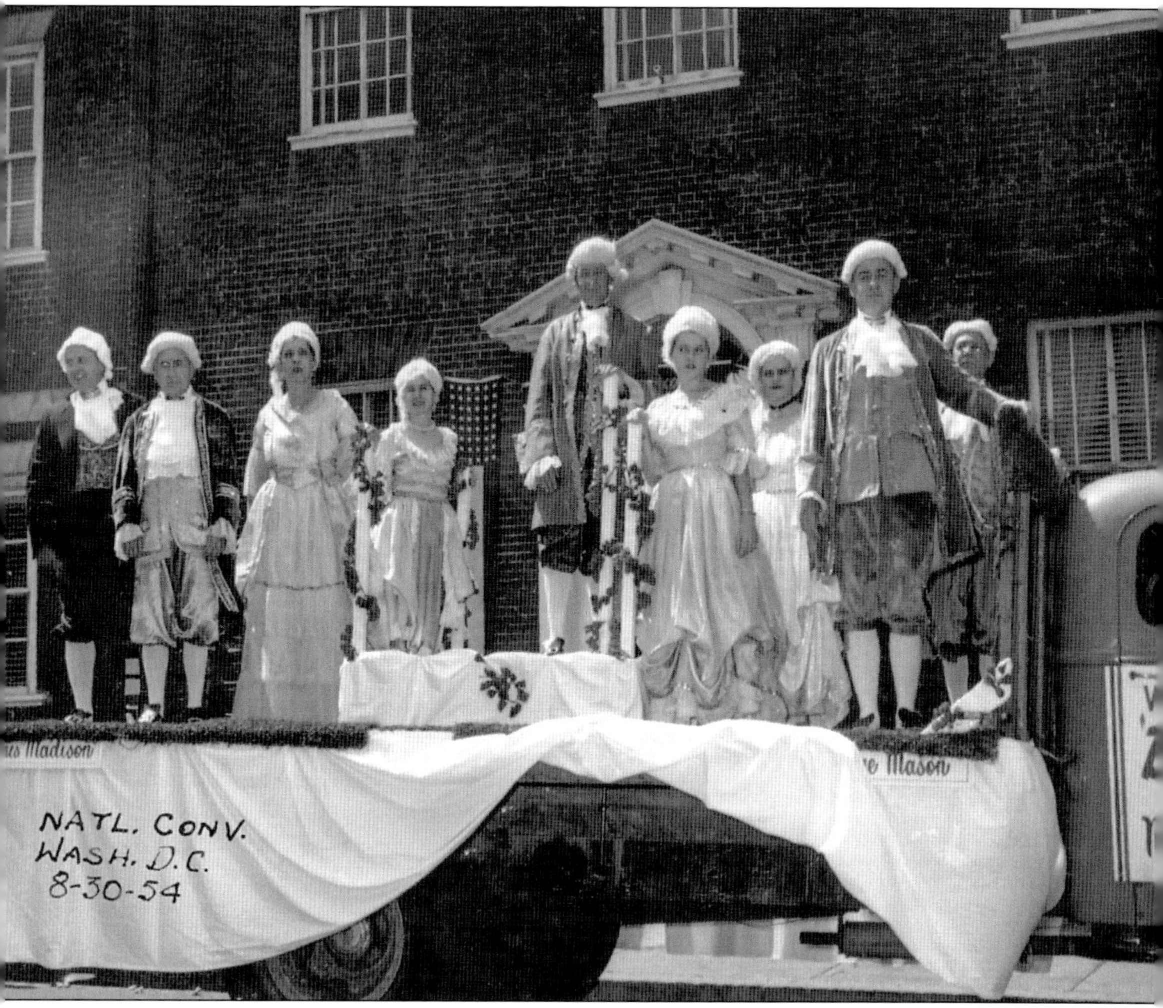

American Legion Post 24 created a float and participated in the American Legion National Convention Parade in Washington, DC, on August 30, 1954. Members of American Legion Post 24 portrayed Founding Fathers such as George Washington and James Madison. (ALSC.)

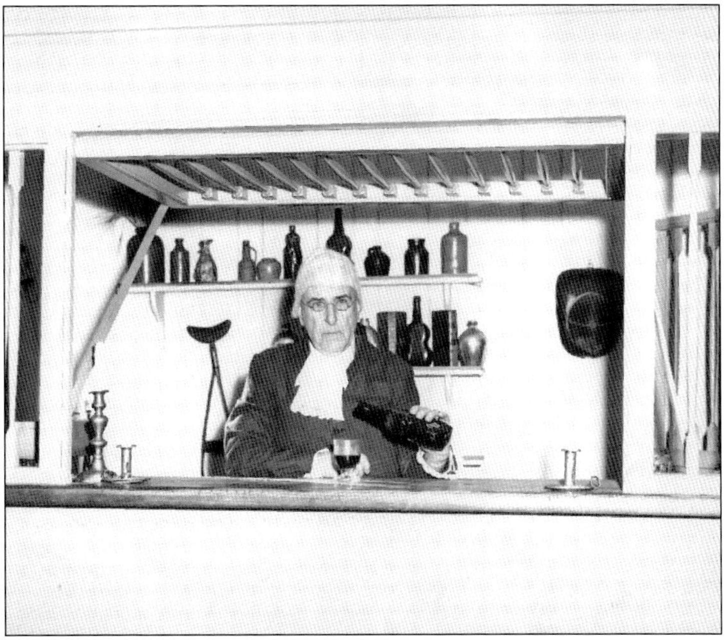

A past post commander, W. Milton Glasgow, tended bar for the Birthnight Balls in the 1950s. Architect Milton Grigg responded to a question about the bar's accuracy in a 1955 letter. He wrote, "There was nothing remaining of the bar but there was structural evidence of where it had been. . . . Heavy wear and abuse in the interval since its installation 25 years ago has given a false impression of originality." (ALSC.)

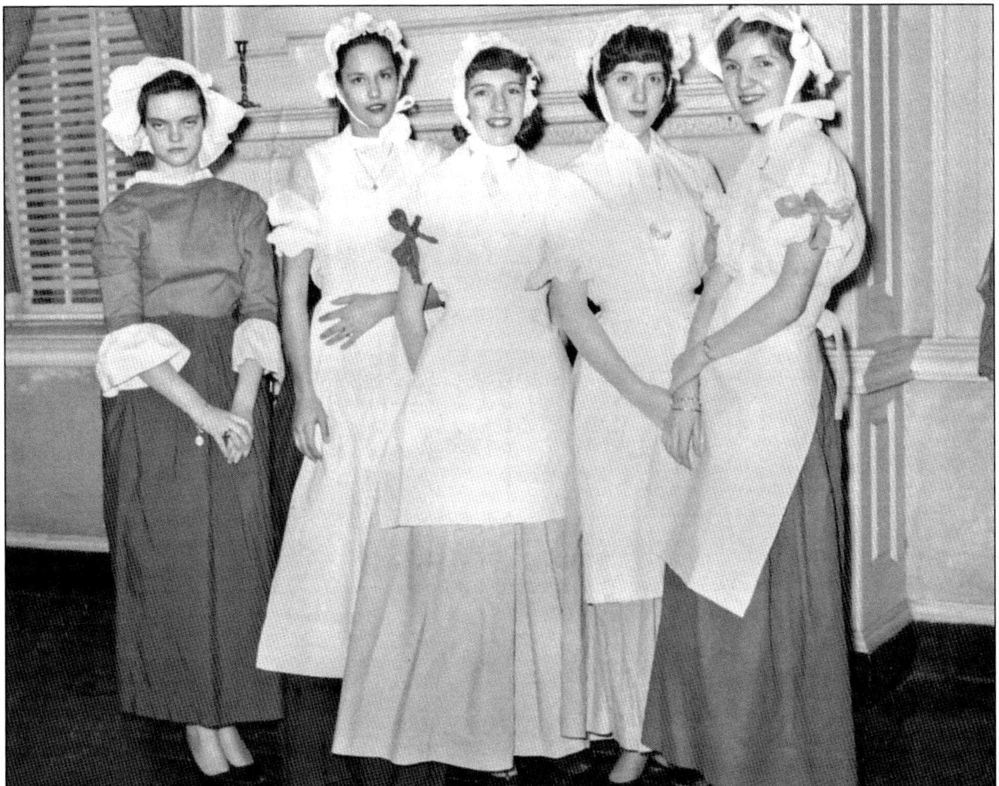

Costumed young ladies, often the daughters of legion members, were on hand to assist with greeting guests and checking coats at the annual Birthnight Ball and other American Legion social events.

OUR TOWN:

1749-1865

Likenesses of This Place & Its People Taken from Life

BY

ARTISTS KNOWN AND UNKNOWN

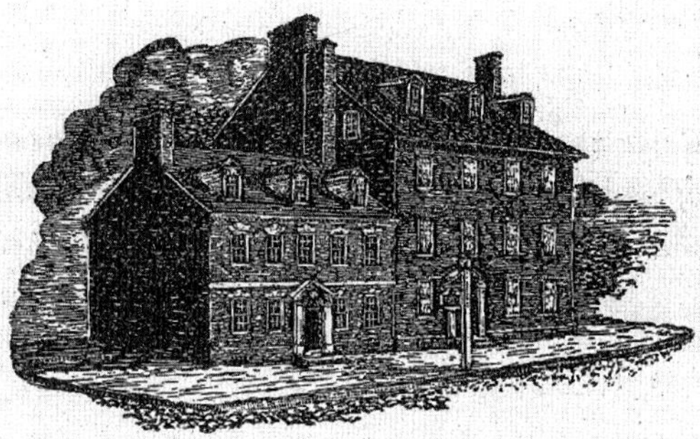

Sponsored by the ALEXANDRIA ASSOCIATION

Member National Trust *for* Historic Preservation

AT

GADSBY'S TAVERN

April 12-*May* 12, 1956

Our Town: 1749–1865, an exhibit held at Gadsby's Tavern, was the first time portraits of Alexandrians were displayed together. This exhibit, curated by members of the Alexandria Association, was accompanied by a catalog. Many of the people whose portraits were included in the exhibit were contemporaries of John Gadsby and may have been patrons of the tavern.

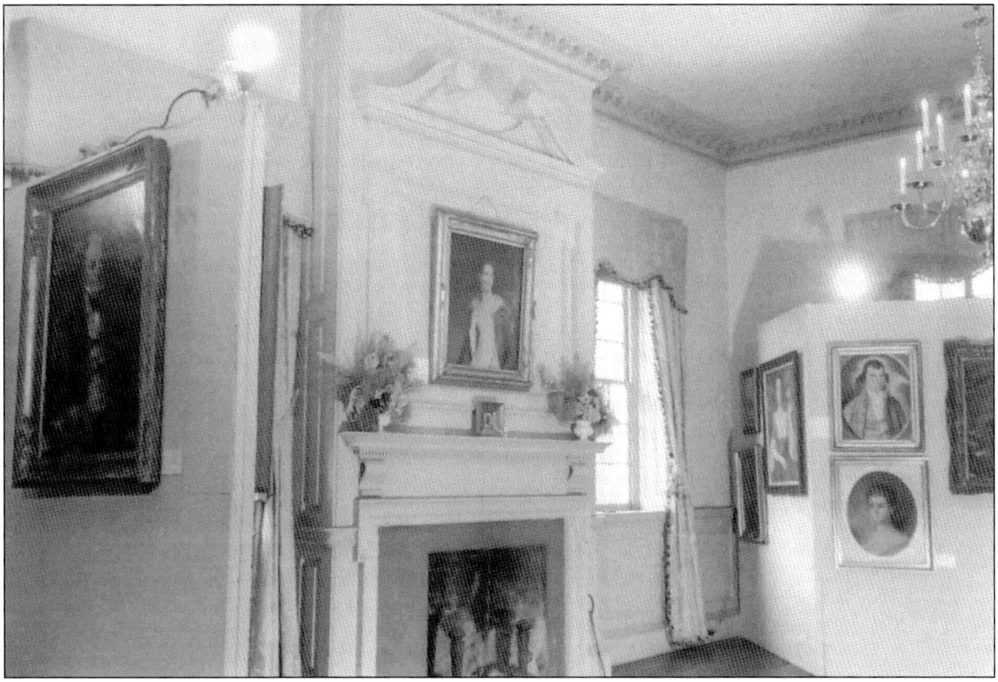

The Our Town: 1749–1865 exhibit was displayed in the historic Ballroom from April 12 to May 12, 1956. The exhibition included 200 portraits and miniatures from more than 100 private owners in 10 states. Paintings by John Gadsby Chapman, the grandson of tavern keeper John Gadsby, were featured in the show, including the portraits of John and Provey Gadsby. (Both, ALSC.)

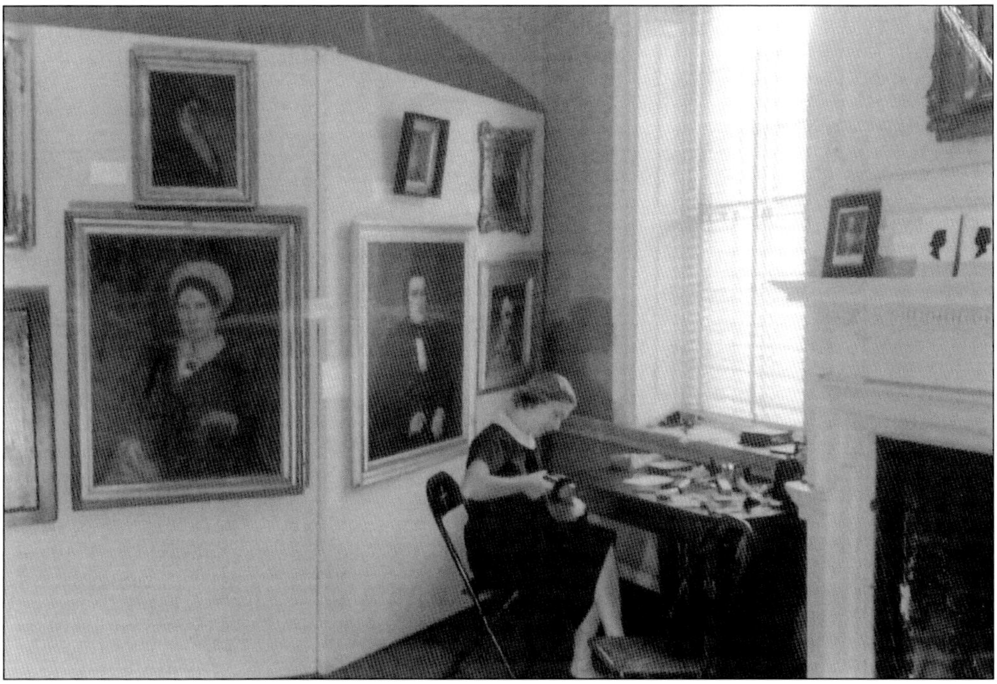

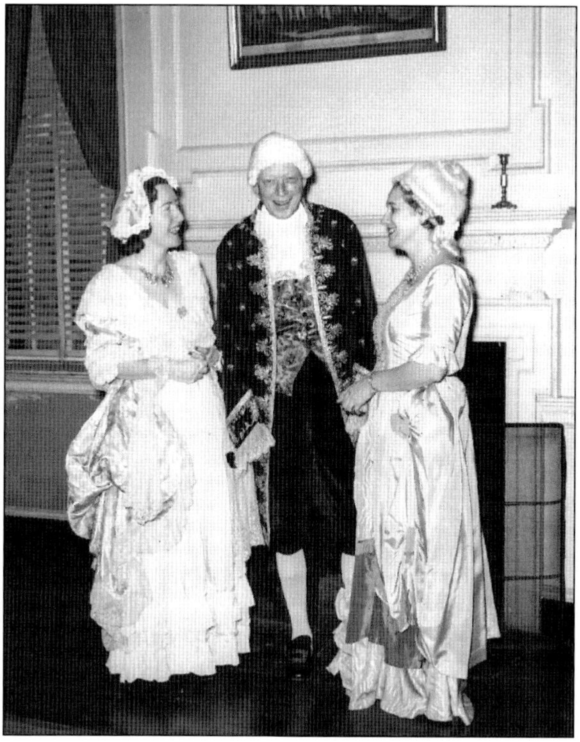

Plans for the February 22, 1958, Birthnight Ball were published in the January 29 *Alexandria Gazette*. The committee was led by F. Clinton Knight, and patrons included Sen. and Mrs. Harry F. Byrd and Congressman and Mrs. Joel T. Broyhill. The Birthnight Ball featured portrayals of George and Martha Washington, Dr. Craik, and John Gadsby. The dress code for the event called for Colonial attire or formal wear.

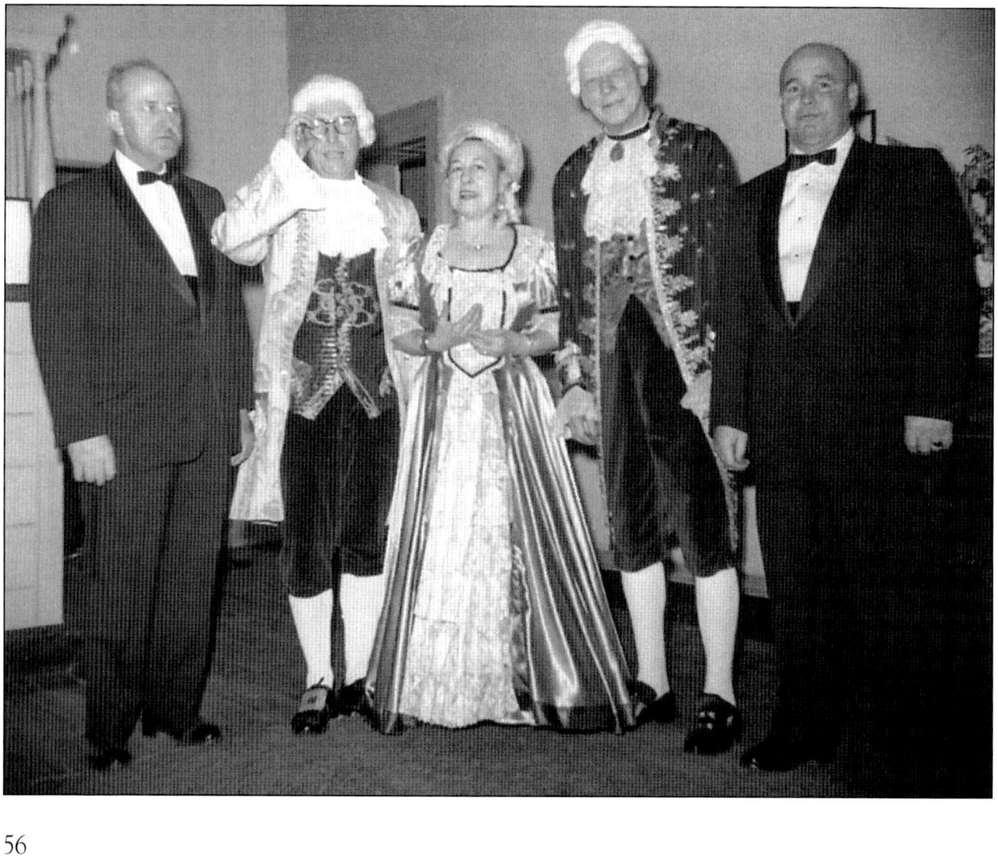

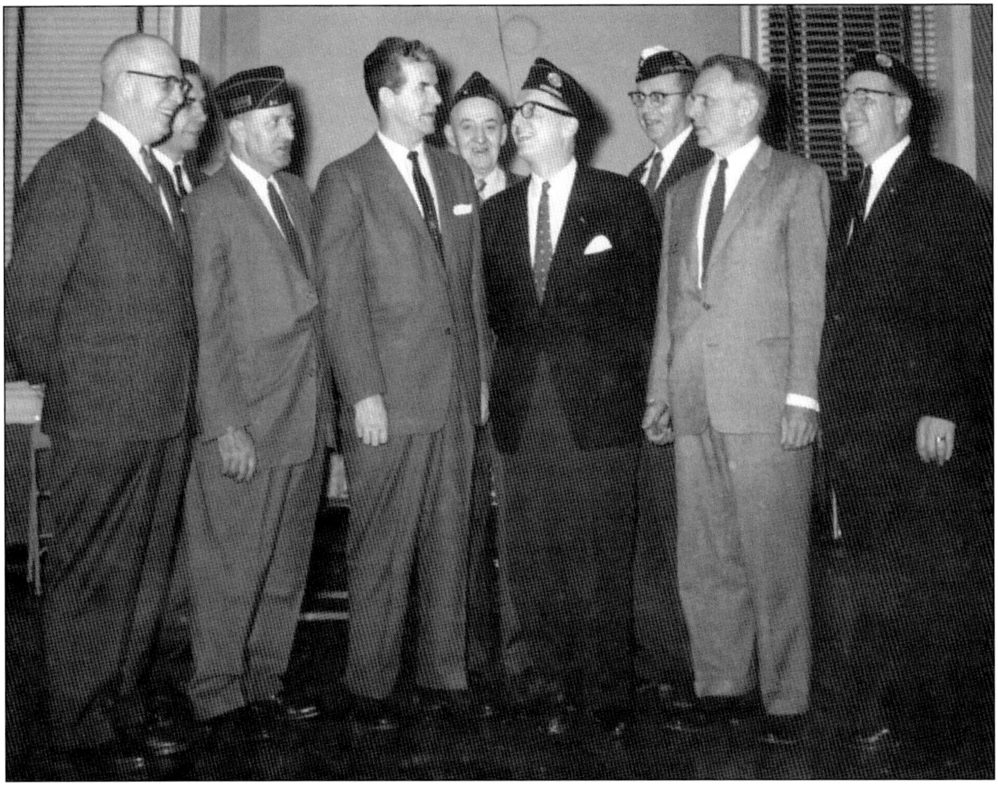

Wilbur Clarence (Dan) Daniel, fourth from the left, was welcomed at an American Legion Post 24 Executive Committee meeting. Post commander Clayton T. Mills (third from left) and F. Clinton Knight (fifth from left) flank Daniel. Dan Daniel was state commander of the American Legion in 1951 and national commander in 1956. He went on to be elected to the Virginia House of Delegates and to Congress from the 5th District. (Collection of Linda Mary Mills.)

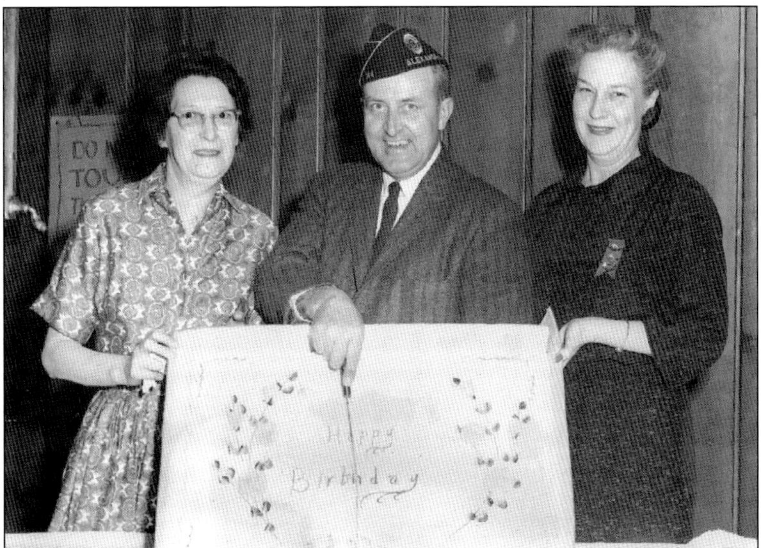

Post commander Clayton T. Mills poses with members of the American Legion Auxiliary, Hazel Crown Boran (left) and Vivian Egan (right), in 1958. They cut and served a birthday cake to honor the anniversary of American Legion Post 24's charter, on August 1, 1920. (Collection of Linda Mary Mills.)

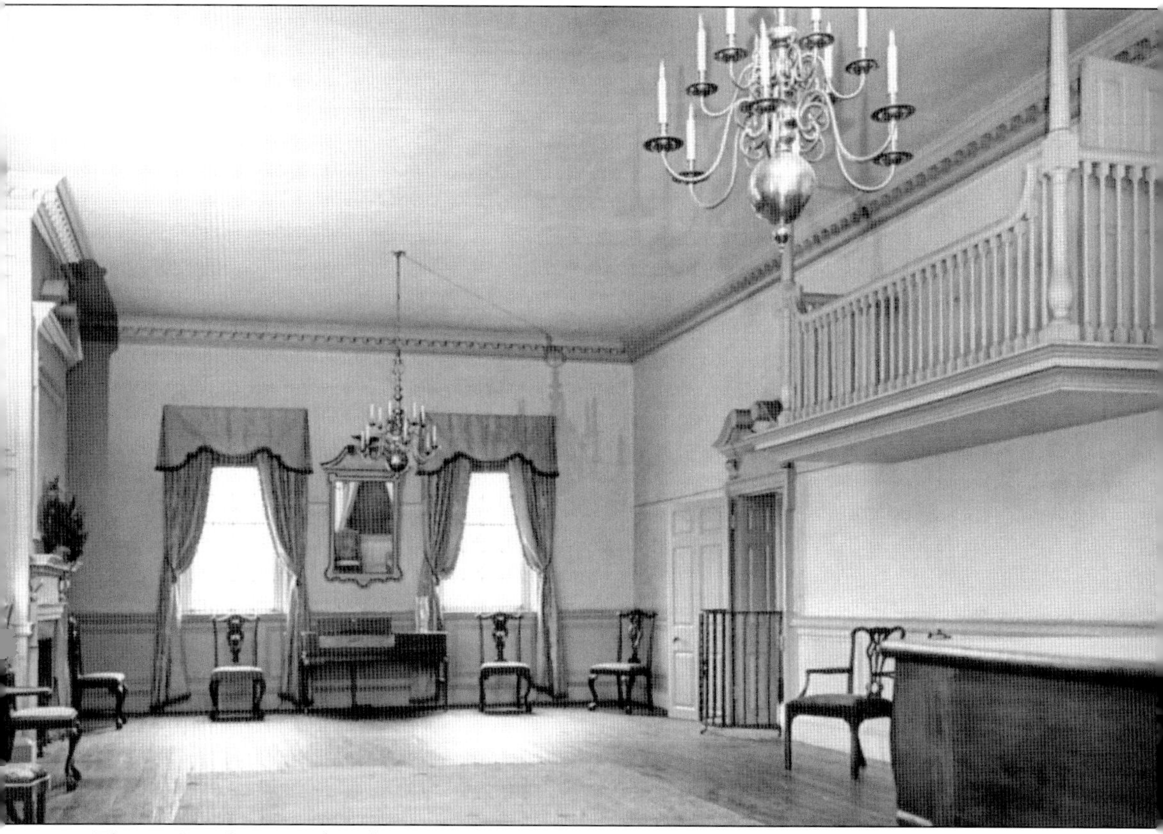

This 1960s photograph, taken 20 years after the Ballroom restoration, illustrates the work of the Virginia State Chapters of the DAR. The woodwork was copied by Thomas Waterman and reproduced locally by Smoot Lumber. The curtains were produced and donated by Scalamandre and B. Altman. Purchased in an antique store in London, the mirror was donated by the Mount Vernon Chapter of the DAR, as were the two chandeliers.

Kevin Marvin Glasgow and a costumed guest pose in the small dining room, sponsored by the Kate Waller Barrett Chapter of the DAR. The occasion was the annual Birthnight Ball.

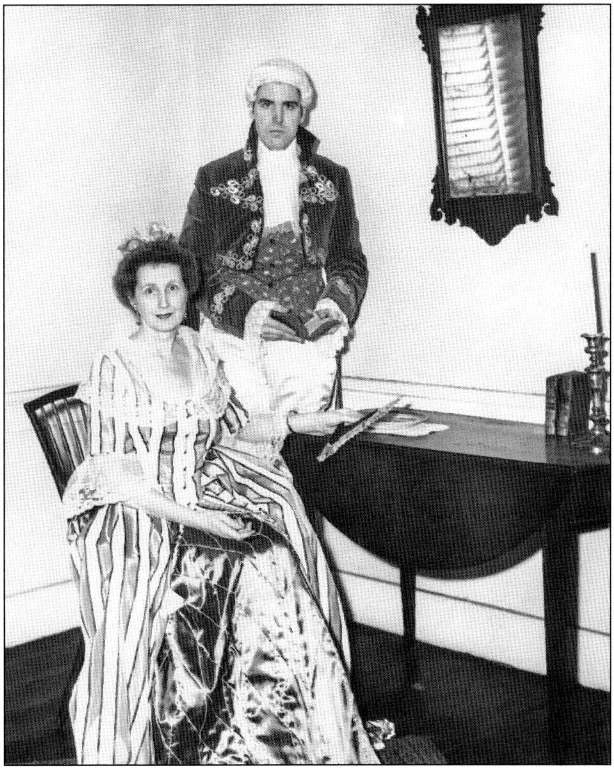

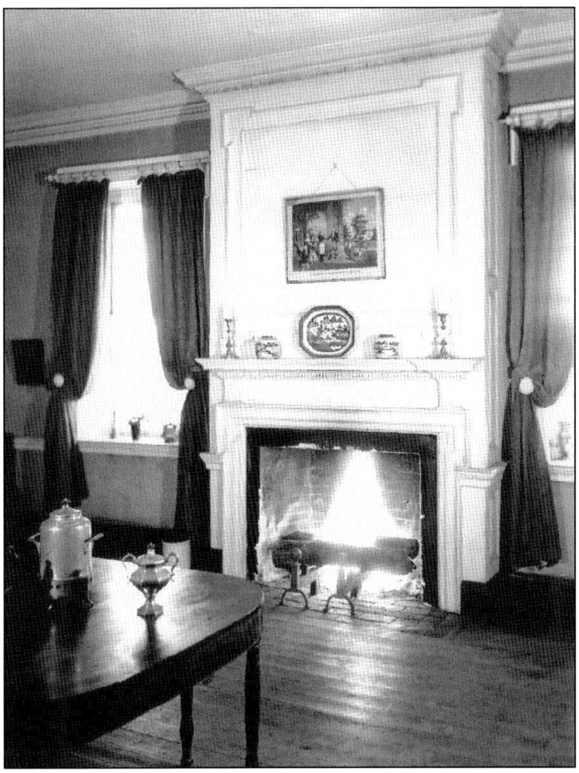

This is an early-1960s view of the main dining room of the City Hotel building. The fireplaces throughout the tavern buildings were operable and provided the only source of heat during events. Many Alexandrians recall the lovely atmosphere of the firelit tavern.

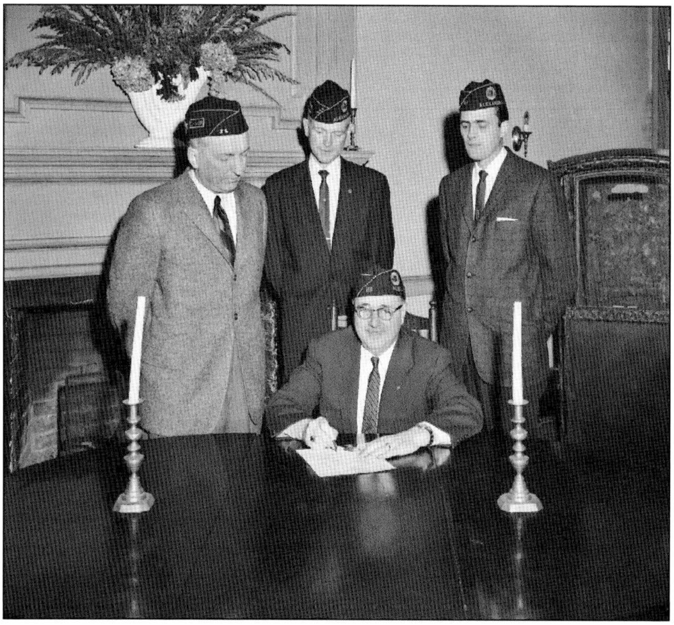

Mayor Leroy S. Bendheim (seated) signed a city proclamation honoring the 42nd anniversary of American Legion Post 24 at Gadsby's Tavern on March 16, 1961. Bendheim, also a member, praised the service of American veterans, the work of the American Legion, and the accomplishments of Post 24. Standing behind Bendheim are, from left to right, Dr. W. Morgan Delaney (post commander), Kenneth M. Taylor (vice commander), and William F. Sanow (third vice commander). (ALSC.)

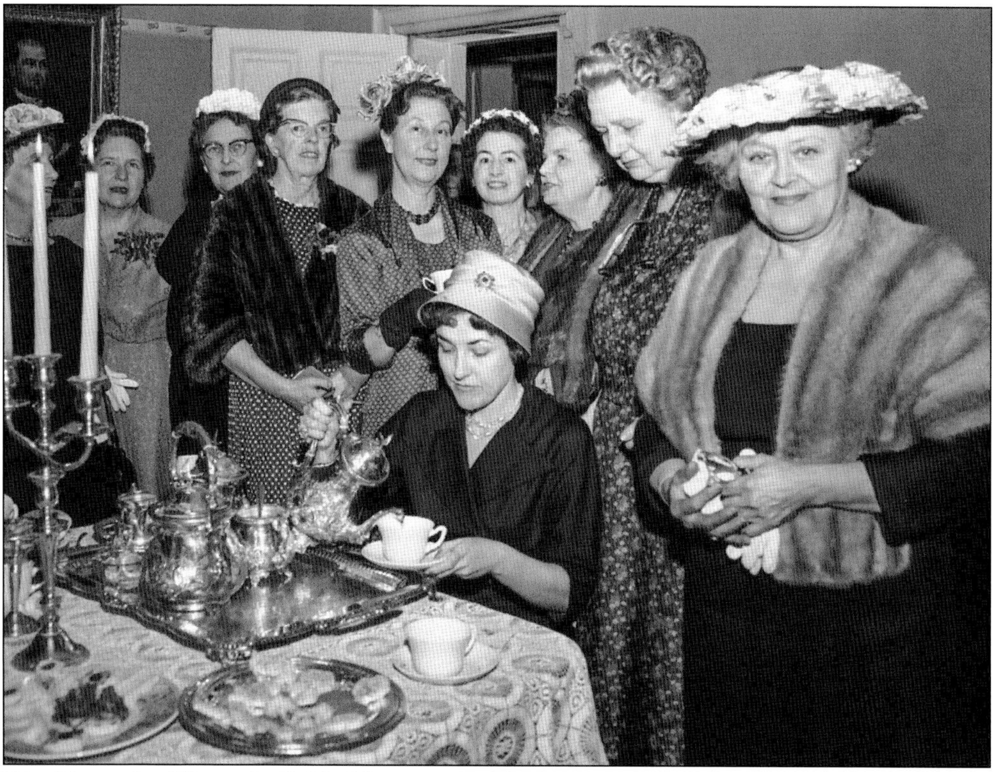

The Alexandria Women's Club held a tea at Gadsby's Tavern on April 6, 1961, to honor members who joined the club during Mrs. Waldo Moore's term as president. Pouring for the members is Mrs. William Donlon. Standing are, from left to right, Mrs. Burchell Leachman, Mrs. Robert Stamps, Mrs. Elmer Smith, Mrs. William Auman, Mrs. Harrison Thornton, Mrs. James Somerville, Mrs. William Smith, Mrs. Waldo Moore, and Mrs. Harry Kirk. (ALSC.)

On November 1, 1963, three members of the John Alexander Chapter of the DAR finalized plans for the 15th annual Alexandria Antiques Show. The show was held at the Alexandria Recreation Center on Cameron Street, and the proceeds benefited the chapter and work on Gadsby's Tavern. Shown here are, from left to right, Mrs. Raymond Cromley, Mrs. Eugene Zimmerman, and Mrs. Russell Holcomb. (ALSC.)

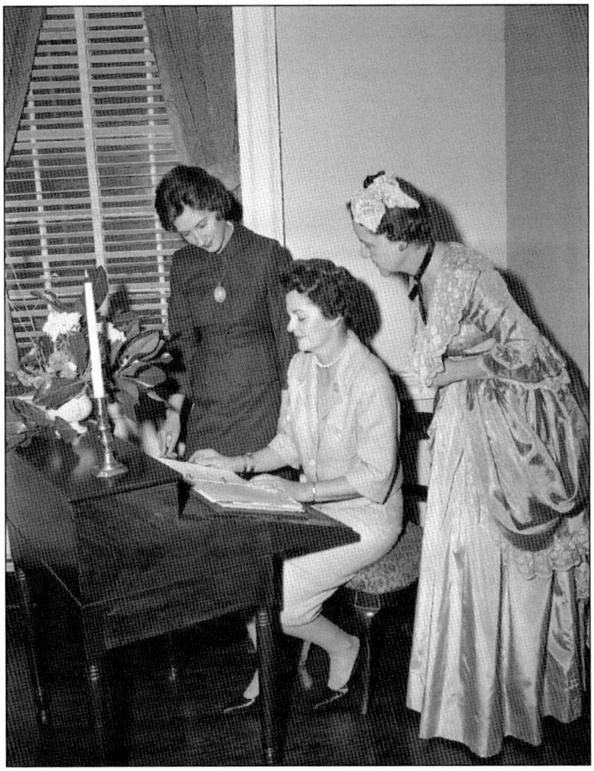

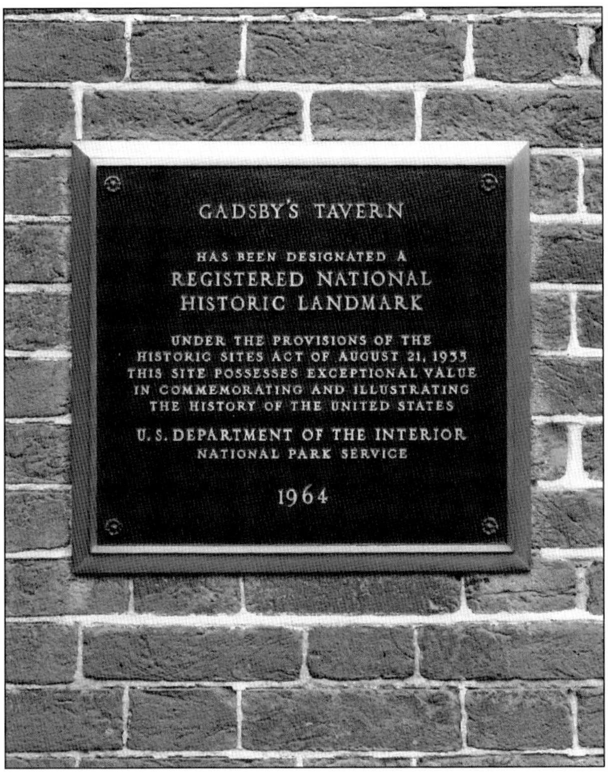

Gadsby's Tavern was designated a National Historic Landmark on November 4, 1963. The formal unveiling of the plaque took place on September 17, 1964. Charles S. Marshall of the National Park Service presented the marker to H. Warden Foley, commander of American Legion Post 24. Mayor Frank E. Mann offered remarks to the large crowd. The ceremony included Colonial-dressed military units and a fife-and-drum corps.

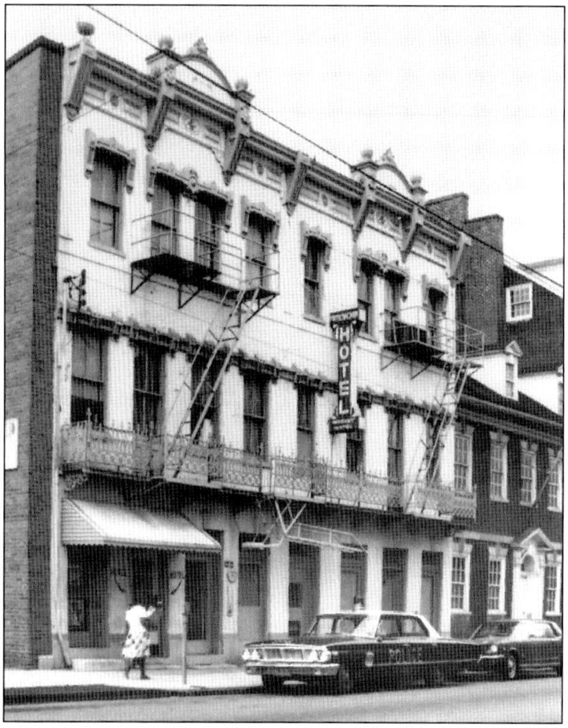

This 1964 photograph shows the Belvoir Hotel and the two historic Gadsby's Tavern buildings to the right. The Belvoir Hotel, formerly the Rammel Hotel, was three stories tall and had 36 sleeping rooms. According to recollections in the *Washington Star* newspaper, "the hotel once served the best oysters in the Washington area. Representatives and senators made special trips to Alexandria to try the seafood."

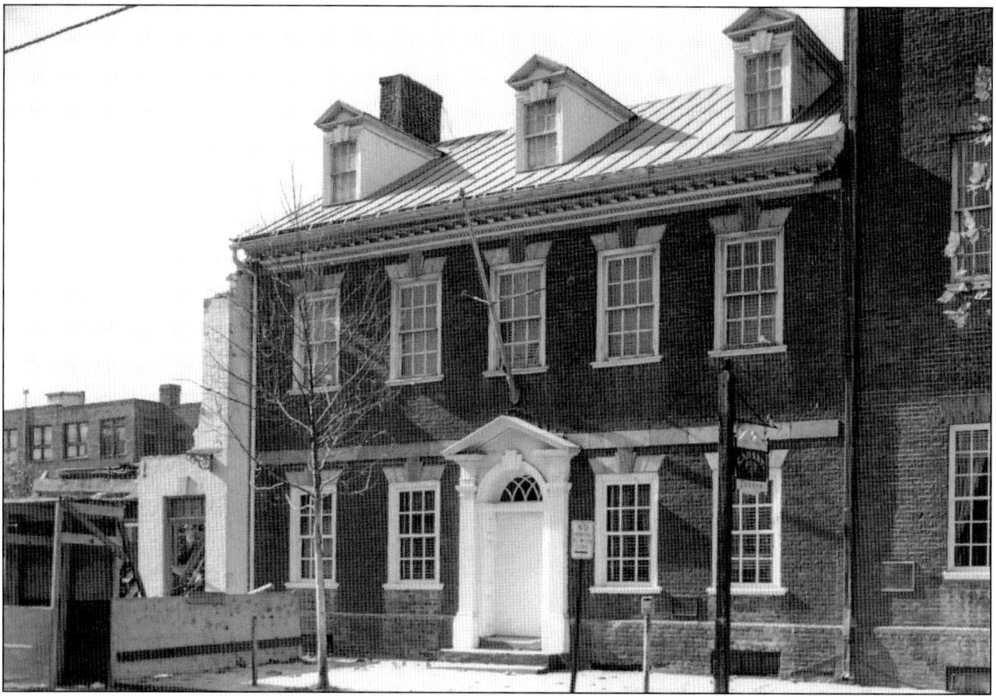

As part of the urban renewal of Alexandria, the Belvoir Hotel was torn down. Because of its Victorian facade, it had long been forgotten that the building incorporated an 18th-century structure. Once demolished, it was determined that this was the original Mason's Ordinary built on the lot by 1752. (ALSC.)

This photograph of the south facade of the tavern building was taken after the demolition of the original Mason's Ordinary. Every care was taken to protect the brick wall of the historic Gadsby's building that adjoined the Belvoir Hotel. Gadsby's Tavern was the cornerstone of the City of Alexandria's urban renewal project. (ALSC.)

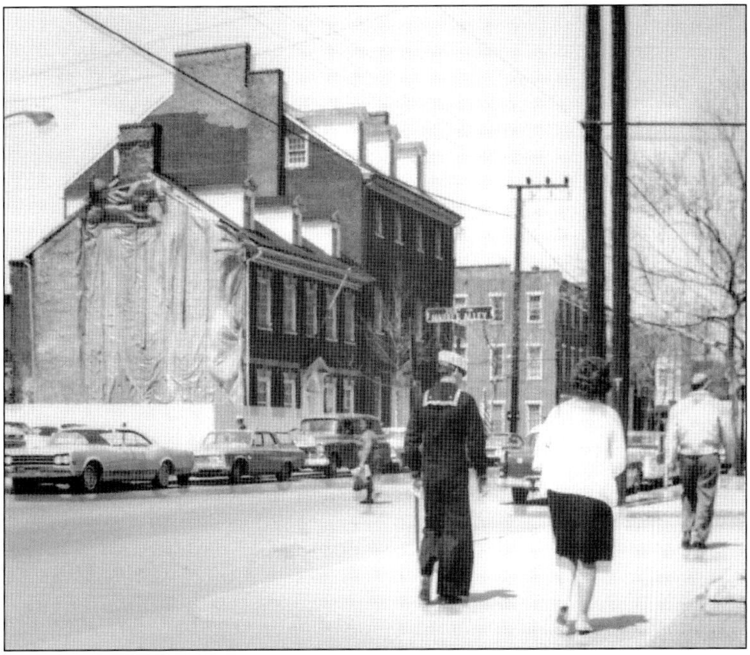

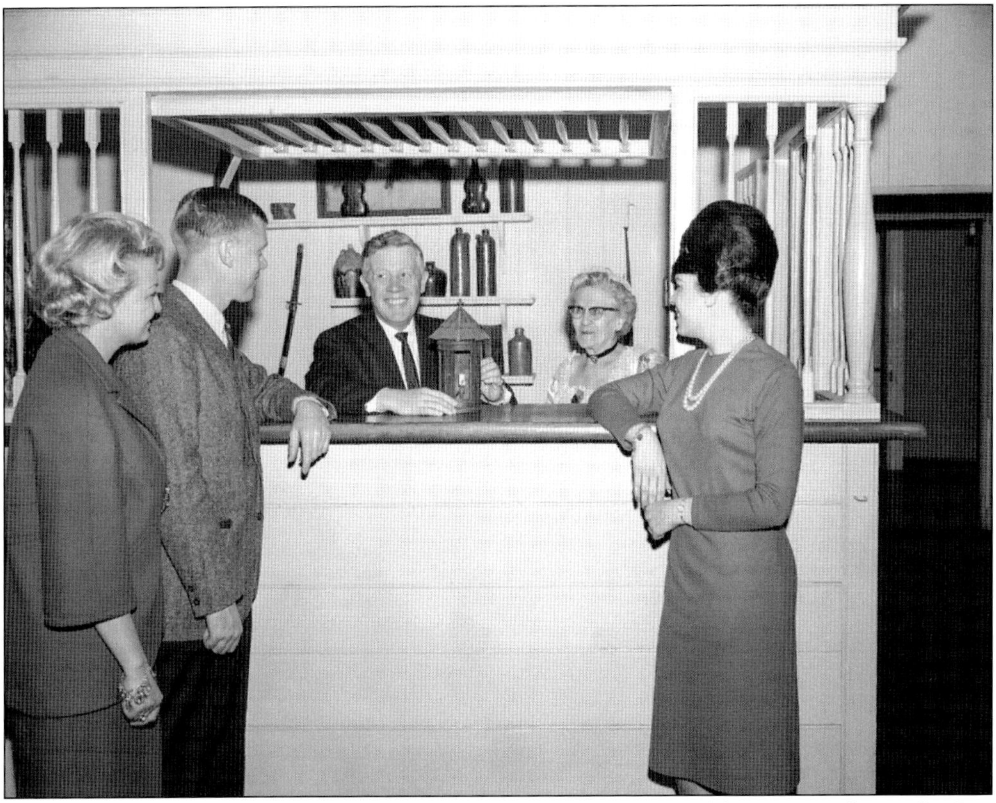

This photograph, captioned "California tourists," was taken in front of the Taproom bar in the City Hotel by the *Alexandria Gazette* on April 8, 1965. Throughout the legion's ownership of the buildings, it marketed the tavern buildings as a "must-see" historic attraction in Alexandria. (ALSC.)

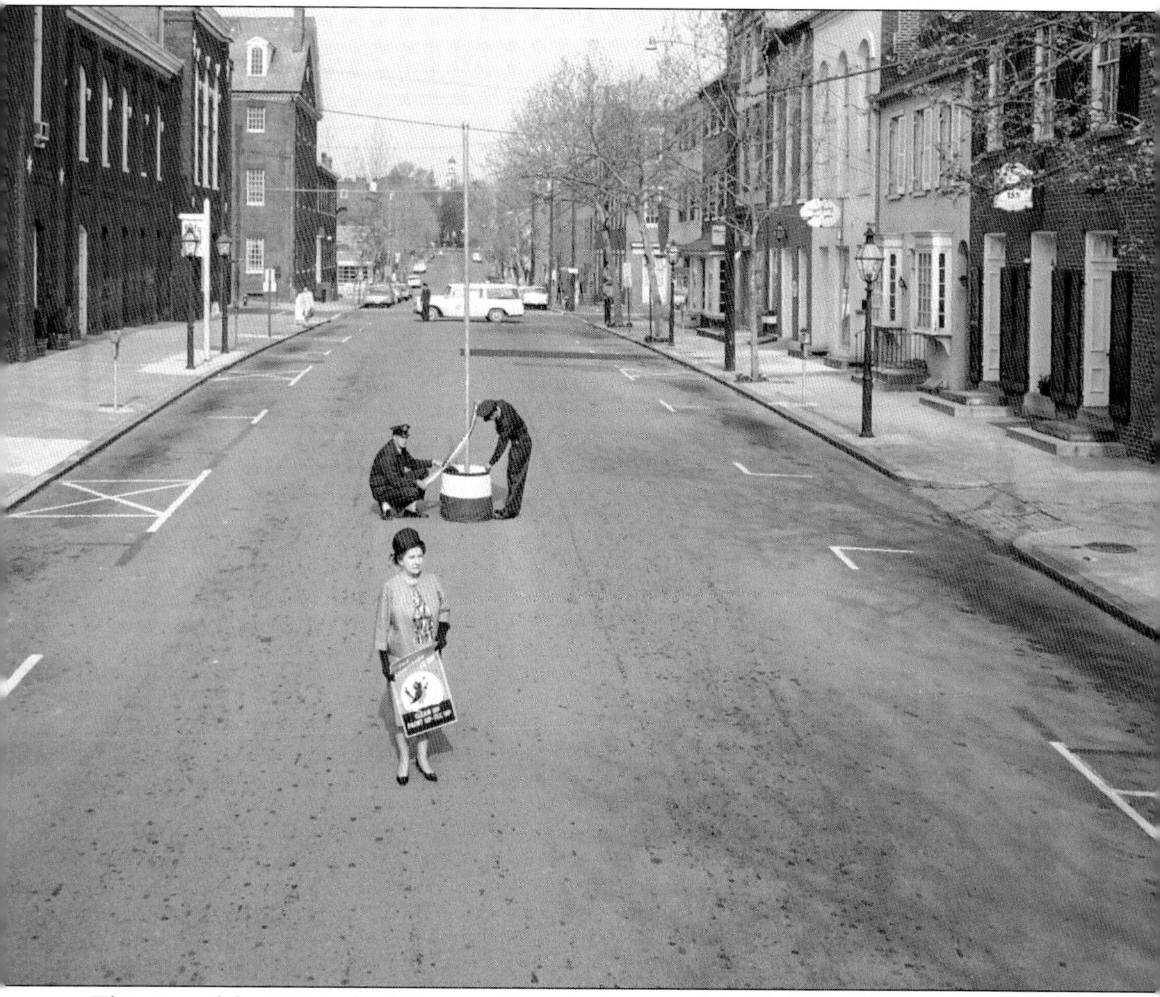

This view of the 300 block of Cameron Street looks toward Gadsby's Tavern at the intersection of Royal and Cameron Streets. On April 29, 1965, city employees William Wilkinson (left) and Clifton Haines (right) constructed a maypole for the City Beautification Festival. Mary B. Crowder carried a poster promoting the urban renewal program. It reads, "The Campaign Is On. Clean Up, Paint Up, Fix Up." (ALSC.)

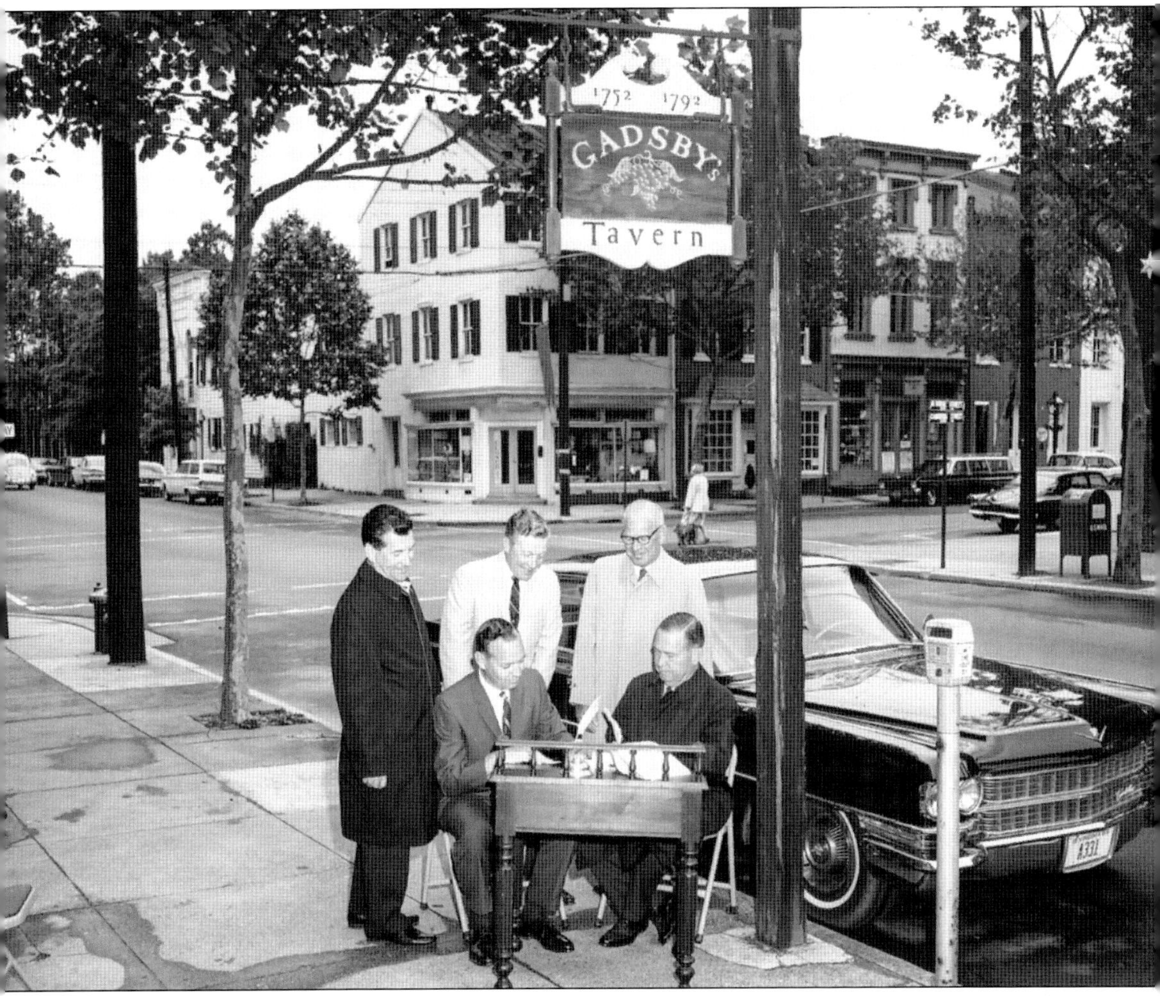

The signing of the urban renewal contract, after months of study, took place in a ceremony under the Gadsby's Tavern sign. Urban renewal developers and city officials gathered around an antique desk and used an antique pewter inkwell and a quill pen to formalize the project agreements. Shown here are, from left to right, (seated) Donald F. Simpson, president of the developers, and David S. Haddock, chairman of the housing authority; (standing) Harland K. Heumann, assistant redevelopment and housing administrator; Mayor Frank E. Mann; and Clarence Simpson, member of the Eugene Simpson & Bro., Inc., contracting firm. This photograph was published in the June 3, 1965, *Alexandria Gazette*. (ALSC.)

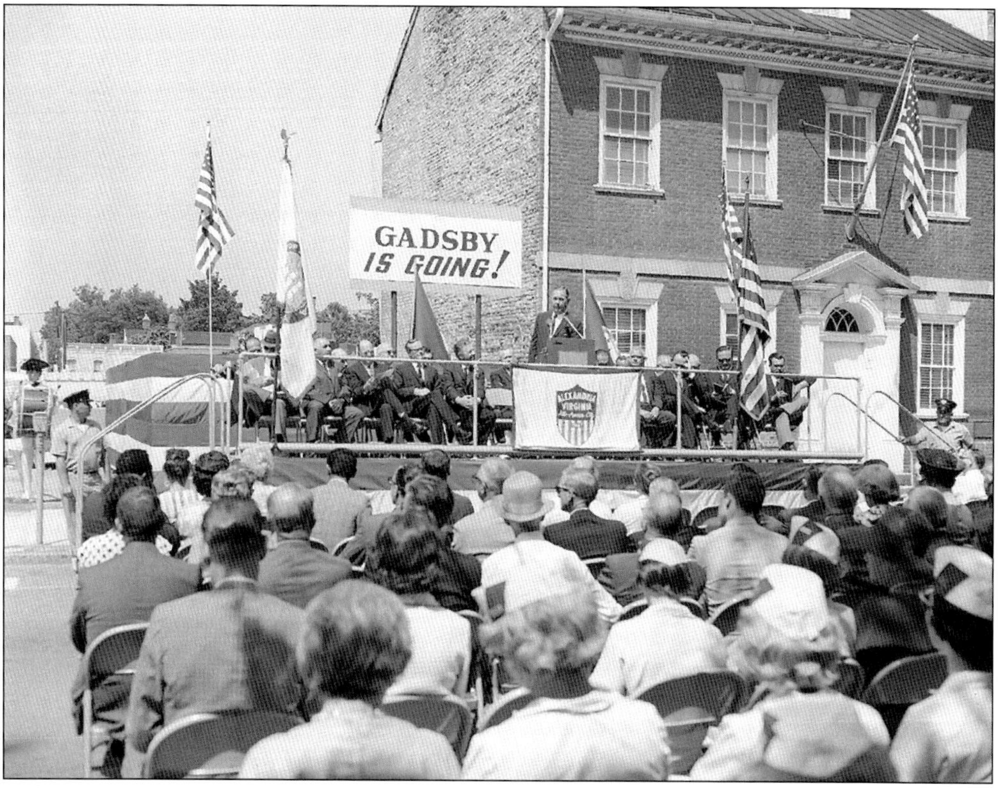

William L. Slayton, US Urban Renewal Commissioner, spoke at the August 12, 1965, launch of the City of Alexandria's urban renewal program. Seated behind him were dignitaries representing the city, urban renewal, and housing authority. The big sign, "Gadsby Is Going," did not mean that Gadsby's Tavern was the next building to be torn down. Rather, it meant that the actual work of renewal had started. (ALSC.)

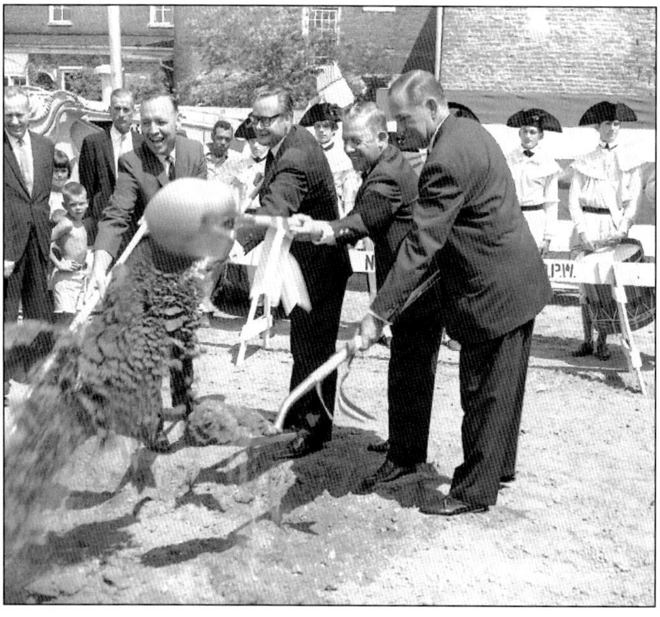

The official groundbreaking ceremony for urban renewal took place on August 12, 1965. According to the *Alexandria Gazette*, "Top urban renewal figures wielded power behind the shovel at the groundbreaking. Dirt flew in a specific direction—forward, since that was the way they said they were going." Pictured here are, from left to right, Donald F. Simpson, William L. Slayton, Mayor Frank E. Mann, and David S. Haddock. (ALSC.)

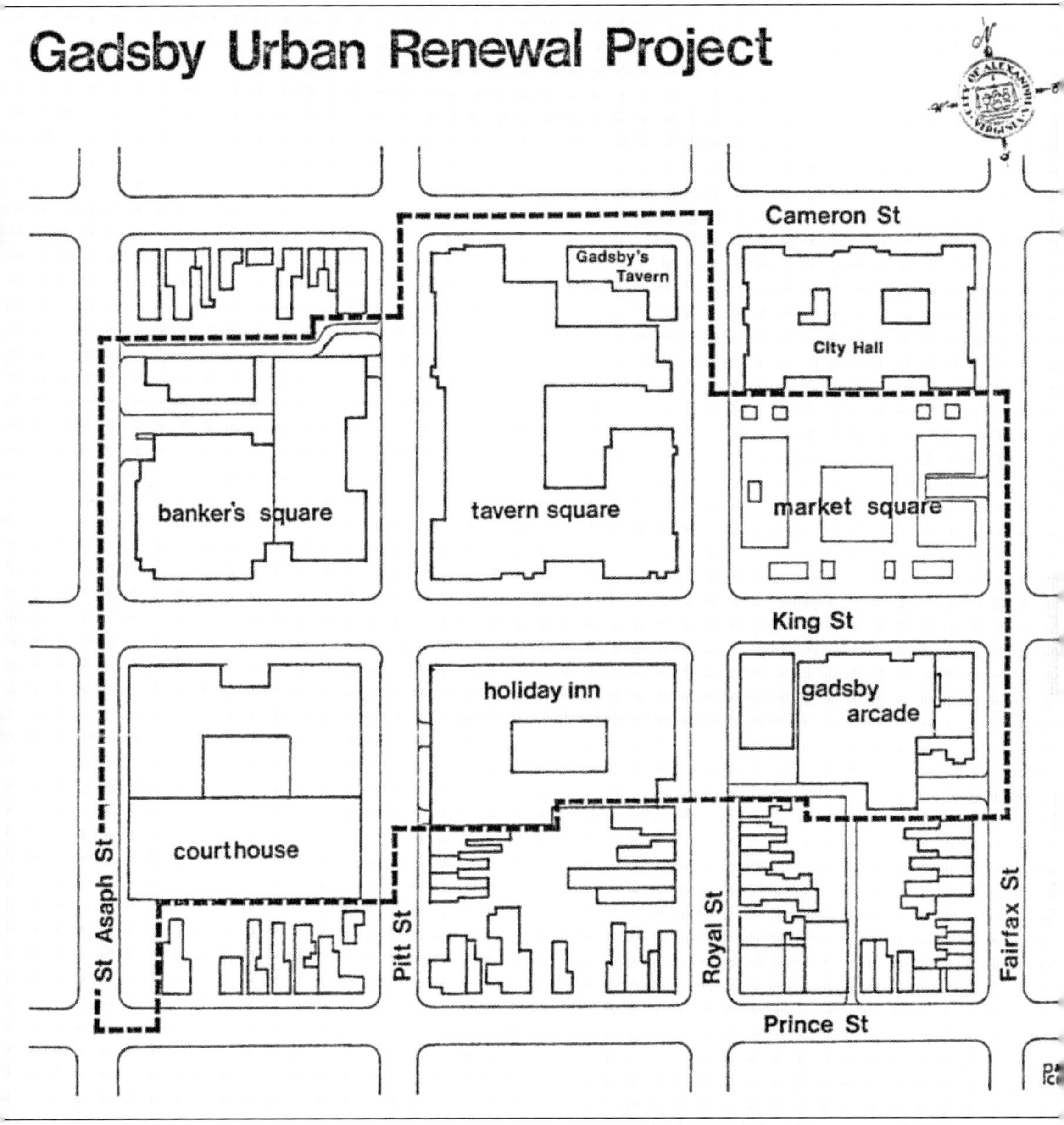

In November 1961, the Alexandria City Council approved the Gadsby Commercial Urban Renewal Project. Tavern Square and Market Square were the first two blocks to be completed. Bankers Square, the Gadsby Arcade, the Holiday Inn, and the courthouse blocks followed. Tavern Square and the Gadsby Arcade were named after historic Gadsby's Tavern. The Gadsby Arcade block preserved the historic Apothecary Shop, a family-owned business that operated from 1796 until 1933. It had been saved as a museum in 1938 by the Landmarks Society. Originally, a larger, 10-block plan of downtown Alexandria called for closing portions of Pitt, Royal, and King Streets for a pedestrian mall. The project was reduced to six blocks for economic reasons.

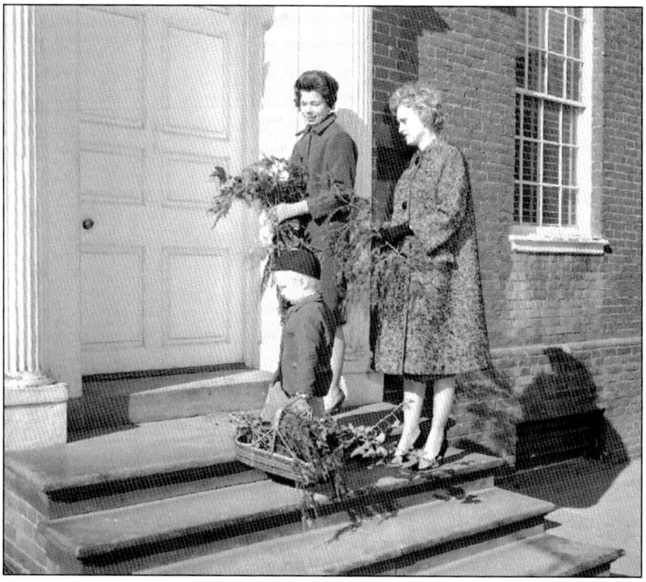

Despite urban renewal construction, normal activities continued. The *Alexandria Gazette* captured three-year-old Dillard Green helping his mother, Mrs. Samuel Green (left), and Mrs. Norris Harbold (right) carry fresh holiday decorations into the tavern. The women cochaired a black-tie Christmas Ball planned for December 11, 1965, at Gadsby's Tavern. The Junior Auxiliary of the Alexandria Hospital used the proceeds of the event to purchase two infant resuscitators for the hospital. (ALSC.)

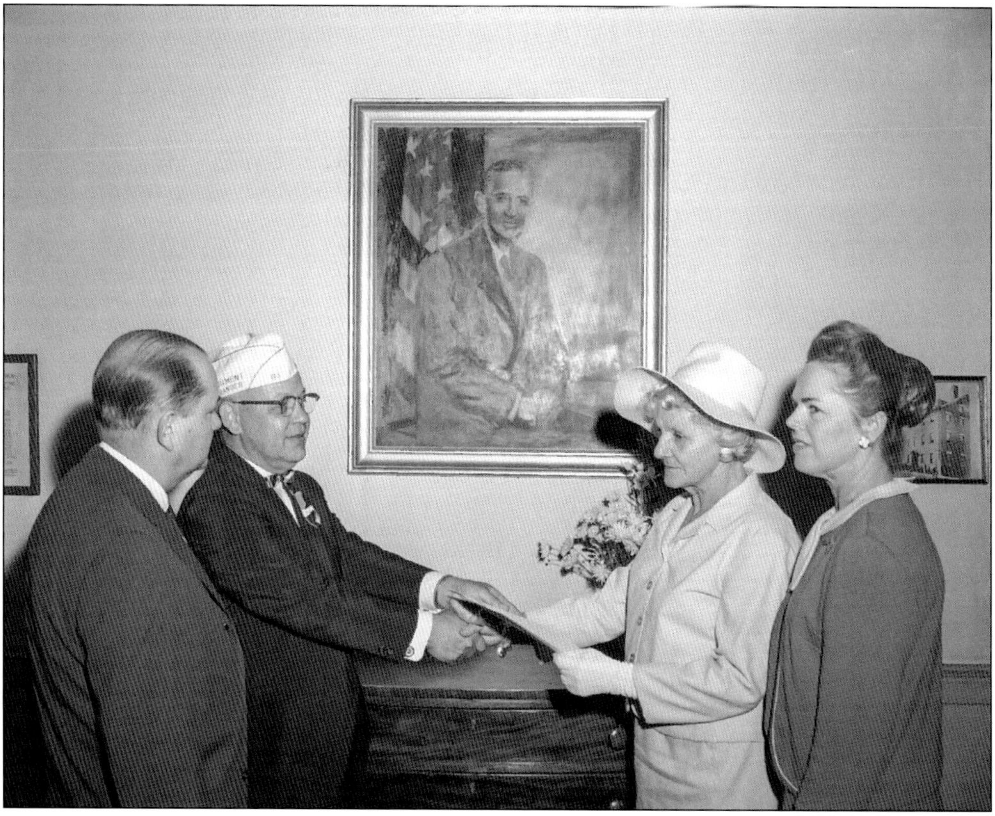

On Memorial Day 1966, American Legion Post 24 honored the late F. Clinton Knight for his dedication to the legion and the preservation of Gadsby's Tavern with a portrait. Judge George Giammittorio (far left) unveiled the painting as artist Mrs. Cyellen Carr (far right) looked on. Mrs. Clinton Knight accepted a special commendation of merit awarded to her husband from Ralph P. Mayo, commander of the Virginia Department of the American Legion. (ALSC.)

This view of the urban renewal construction next to Gadsby's Tavern shows the excavation for the two-story underground parking garage planned for the neighboring Tavern Square office building. Members of the American Legion closely monitored the work to ensure the safety of the historic buildings.

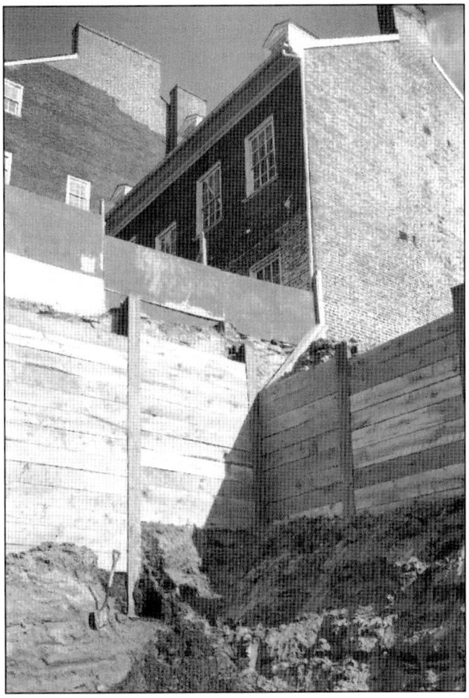

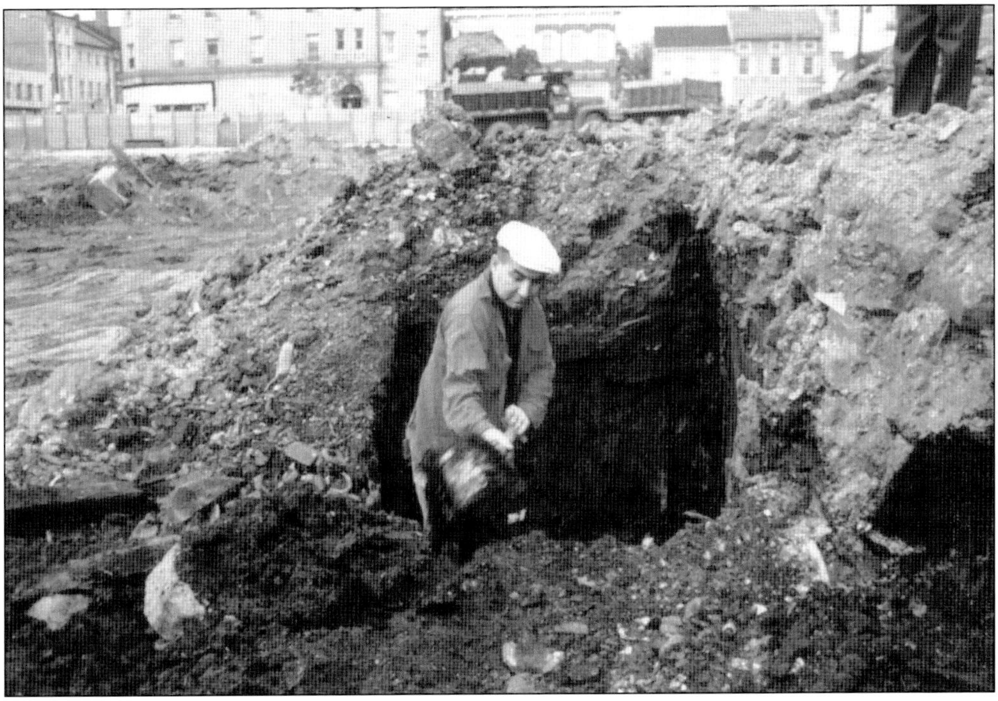

Richard J. Muzzrole, an archaeological aide with the Smithsonian Institution, conducted salvage archaeology at the request of the Alexandria Redevelopment and Housing Authority. For four months, he excavated the remains of eight wells and two privies uncovered in the demolition of the Tavern Square block. The importance of the archaeological material led to the 1975 creation of the Alexandria Archaeology Commission. A city archaeologist was hired in 1977. (ALSC.)

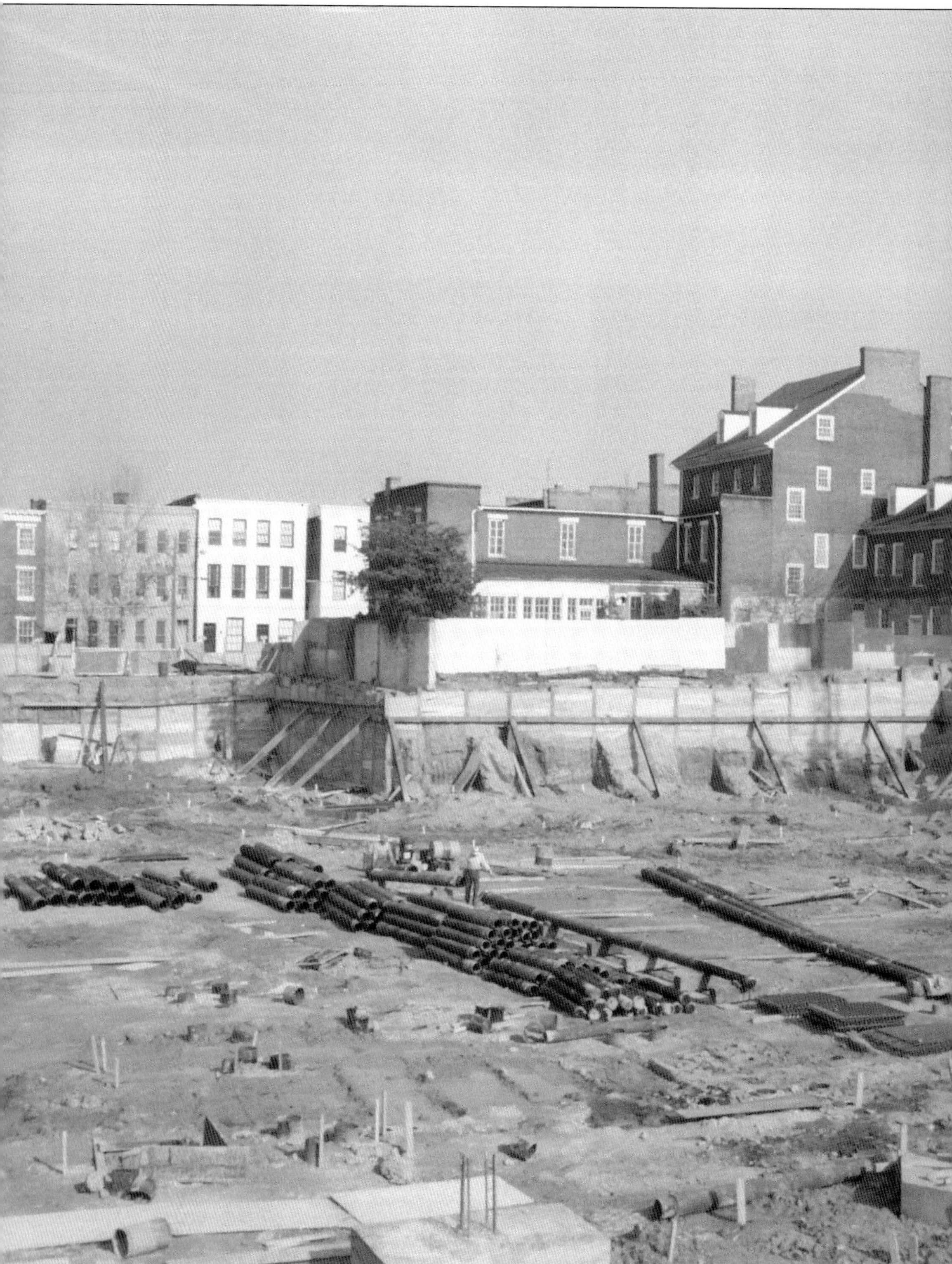

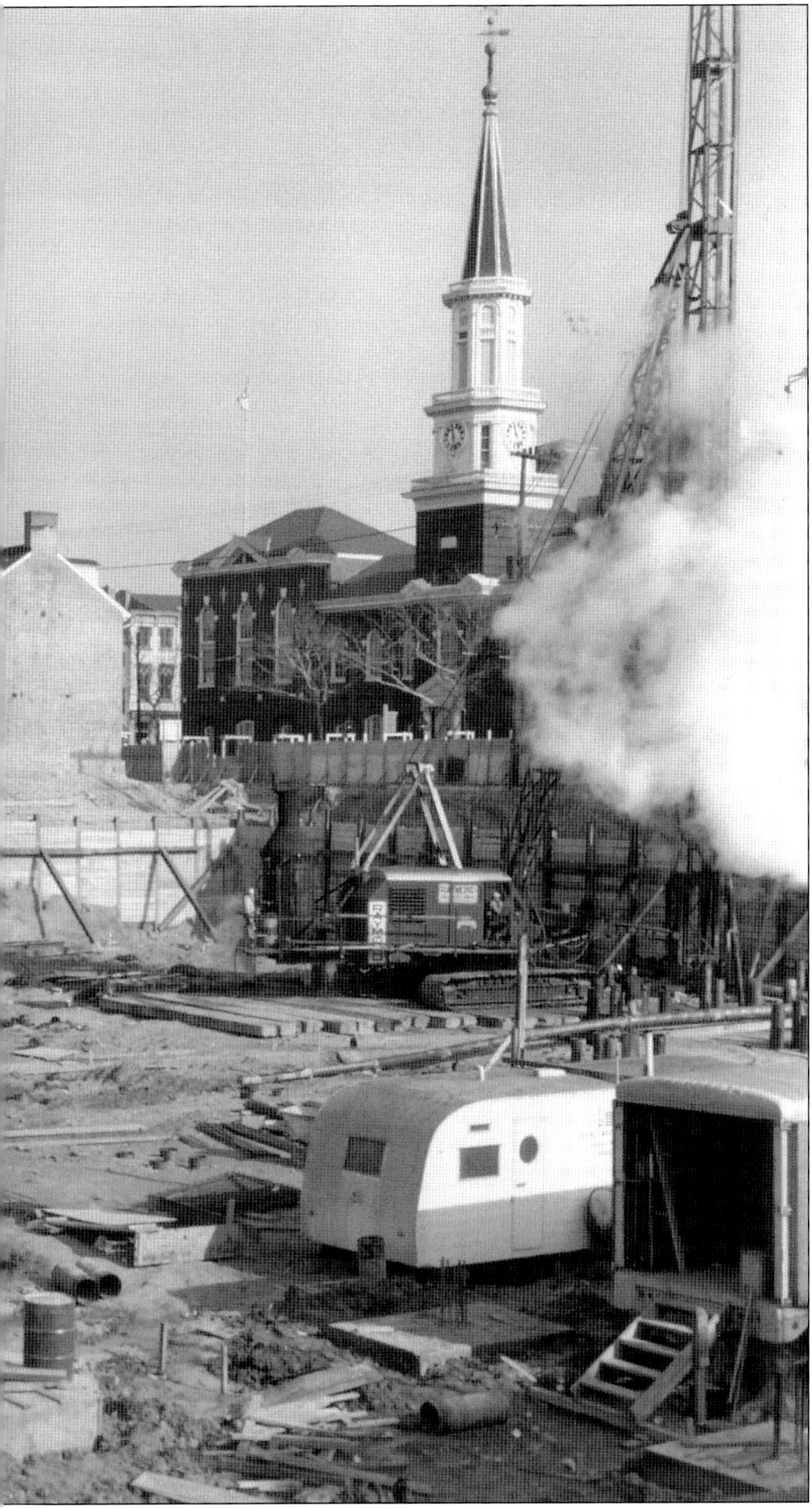

This photograph shows the demolished 100 block of North Royal Street and the 400 block of King Street, or Tavern Square. The Gadsby urban renewal redevelopment was in full swing. Note that the Gadsby's Tavern buildings, the icons of the renewal, are the only remaining structures on the block.

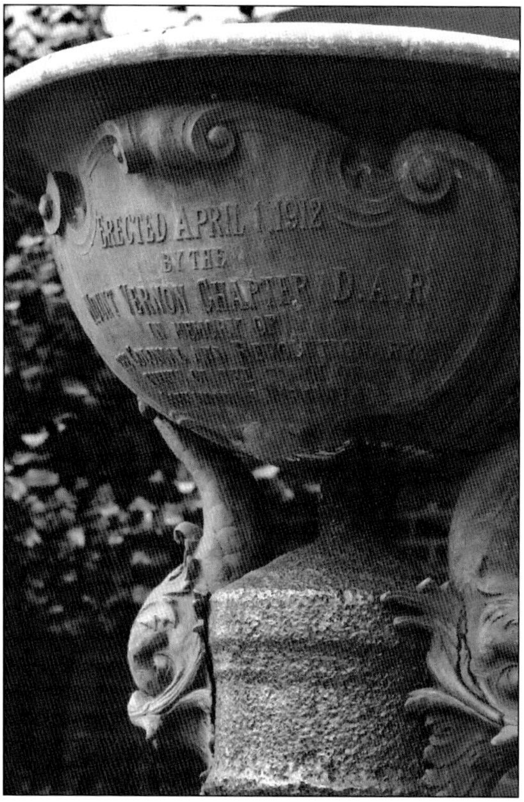

In 1912, the Mount Vernon Chapter of the DAR commissioned a bronze fountain to commemorate patriotic events associated with Alexandria. This sculpture, made by J.E. Caldwell & Company of Philadelphia, incorporated an iron cannon used by Gen. Edward Braddock's forces in the French and Indian War.

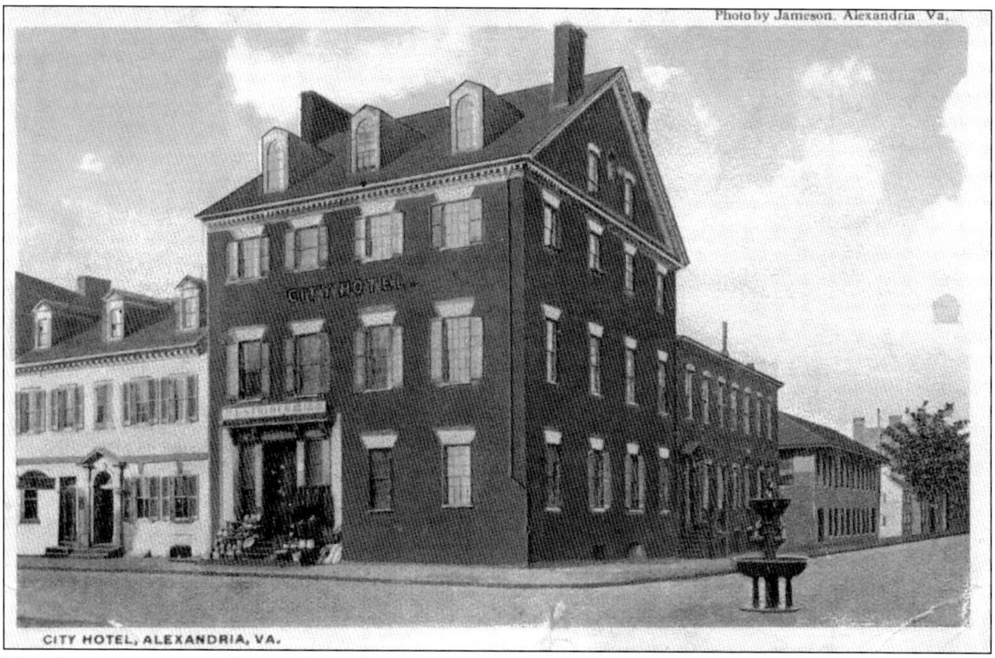

The fountain originally stood in the intersection of Royal and Cameron Streets. After being struck several times by passing vehicles and sent back to the company for repair, the fountain was relocated in 1923 to the southwest corner of Fairfax and Cameron Streets.

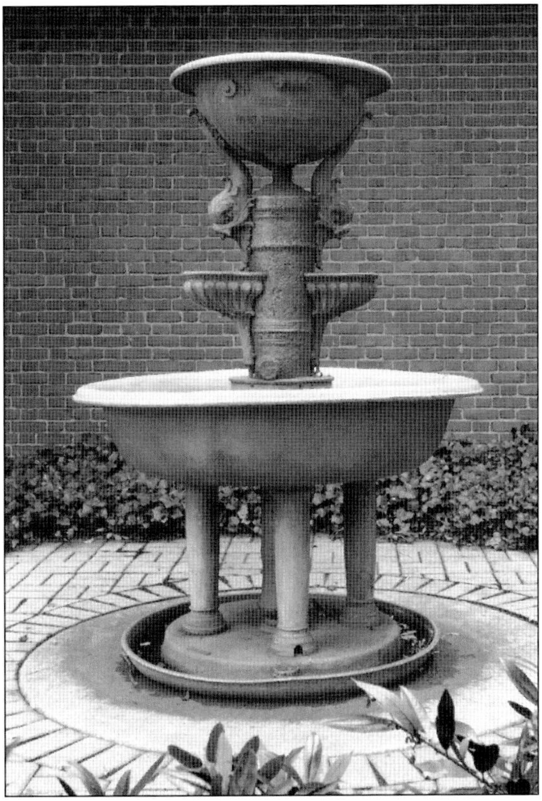

The fountain was designed with five bowls to provide drinking water. The top bowl was for birds, two small side bowls were for thirsty people, the large one was for horses, and the low one was to be used by small animals. With the redevelopment of Tavern Square, a small garden area was created next to Gadsby's Tavern. On June 2, 1967, the fountain was dedicated in this new setting, and it remains there today.

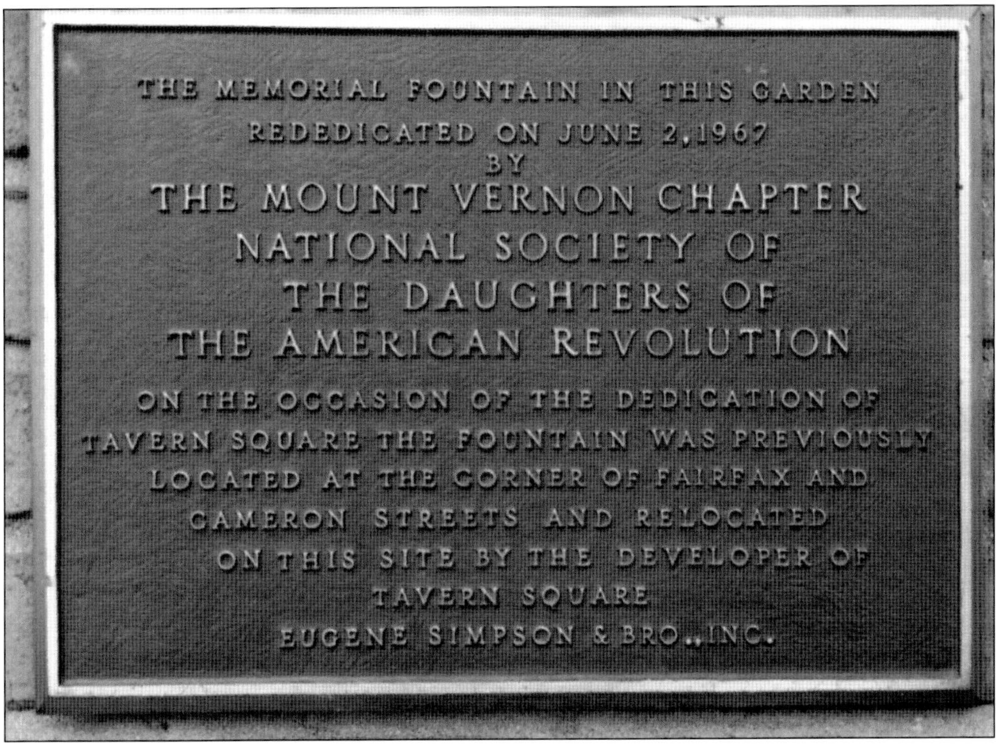

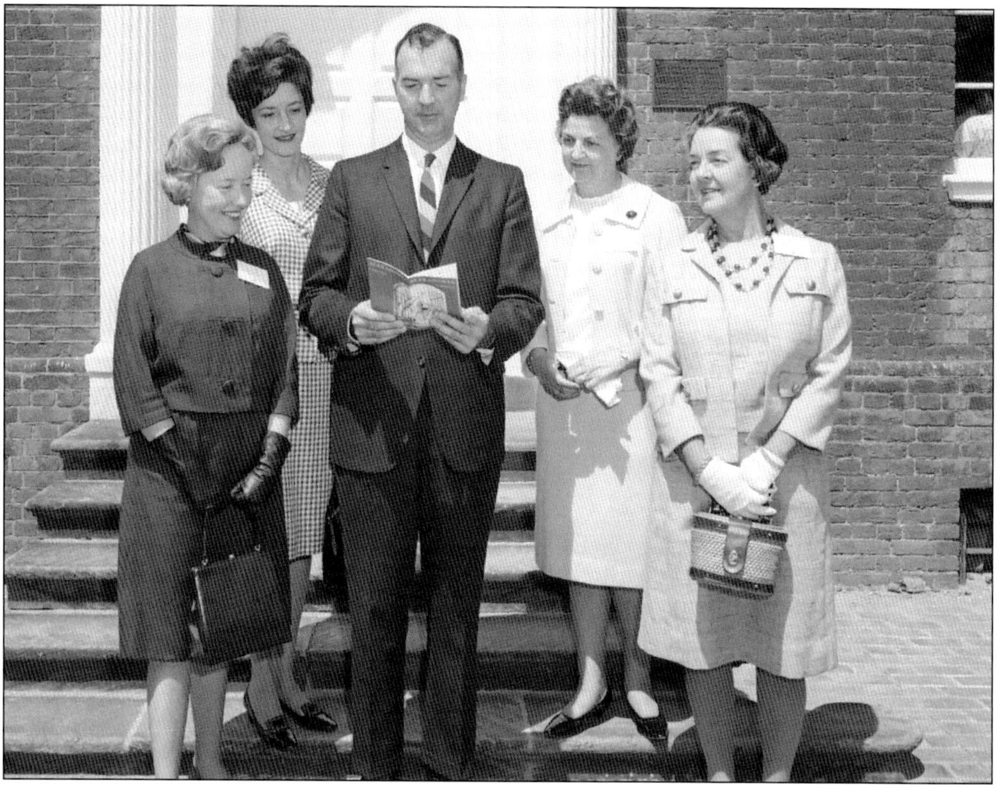

The front door and steps of Gadsby's Tavern provided a great backdrop for photographs. This May 19, 1967, photograph from the *Alexandria Gazette* archives is labeled "Bankers Wives." William Francis Smith (center) represented the Alexandria National. (ALSC.)

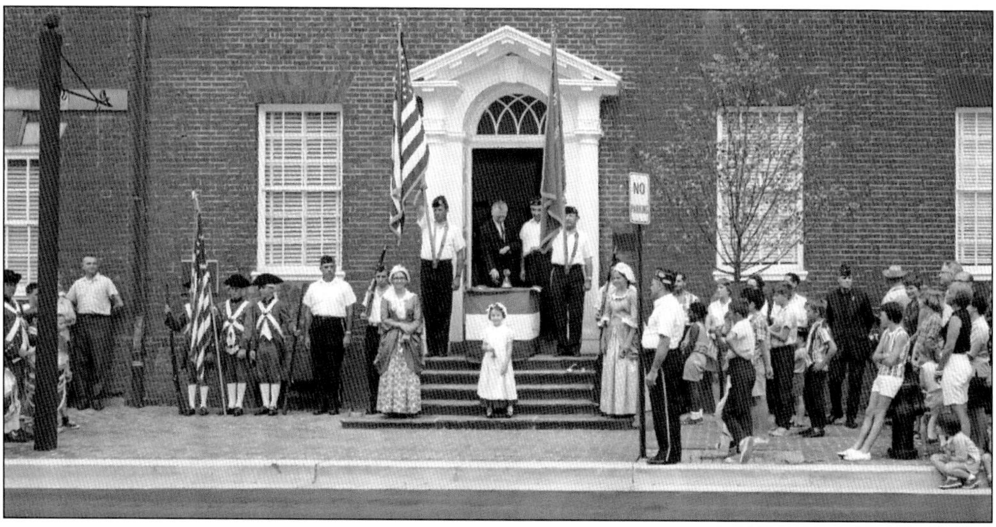

The American Legion had an annual Fourth of July tradition in the 1960s. At 2:00 p.m., a bell-ringing-for-freedom ceremony was held. The American Legion bell, placed at the entranceway of the historic door, was tolled for four minutes to duplicate the ringing of the Liberty Bell in Philadelphia. The Mount Vernon Guard's Fife and Drum Corps joined the American Legion Post 24 Color Guard in leading the Fourth of July ceremony. (ALSC.)

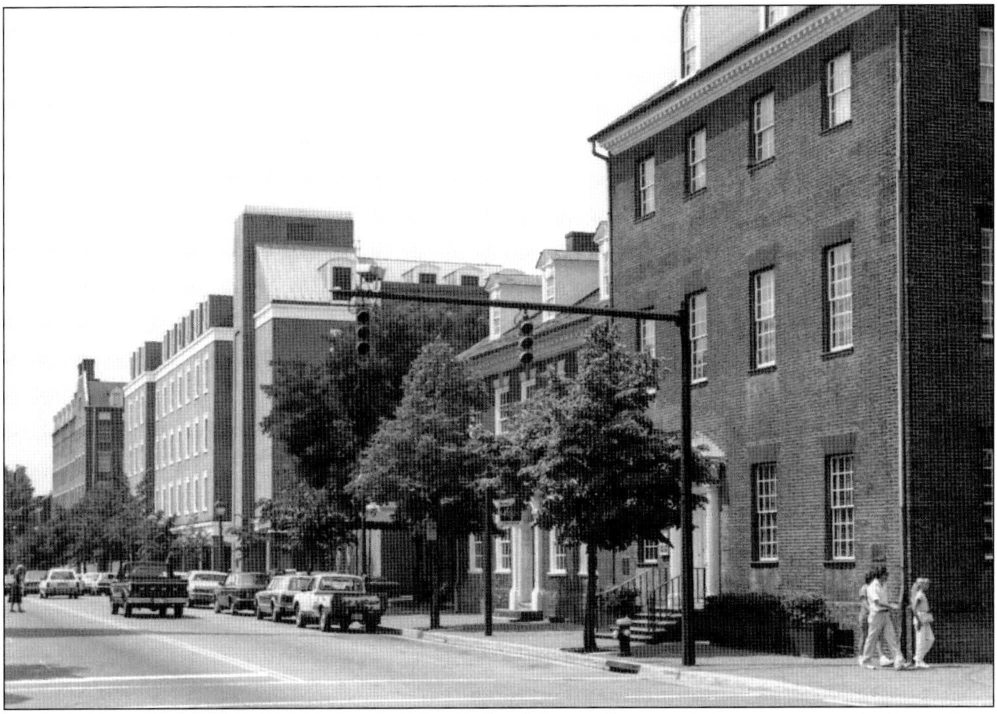

The newly constructed Tavern Square office buildings along Royal Street were dedicated on June 2, 1967. These structures were named after Gadsby's Tavern and designed with architectural elements from the historic buildings. Note the planned compatibility of the windows, dormers, and chimneys. (ALSC.)

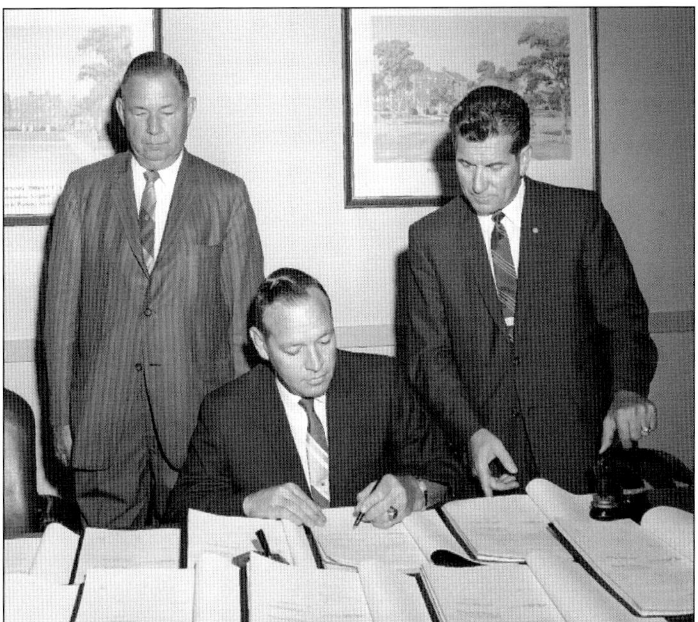

With the first phase of urban renewal complete, phase II was ready to begin. Contracts were formally signed on July 17, 1968. Donald F. Simpson, president of the developers, signs at the table. Looking on are David S. Haddock, chairman of the housing authority (left), and Harland K. Heumann, assistant redevelopment and house administrator (right). (ALSC.)

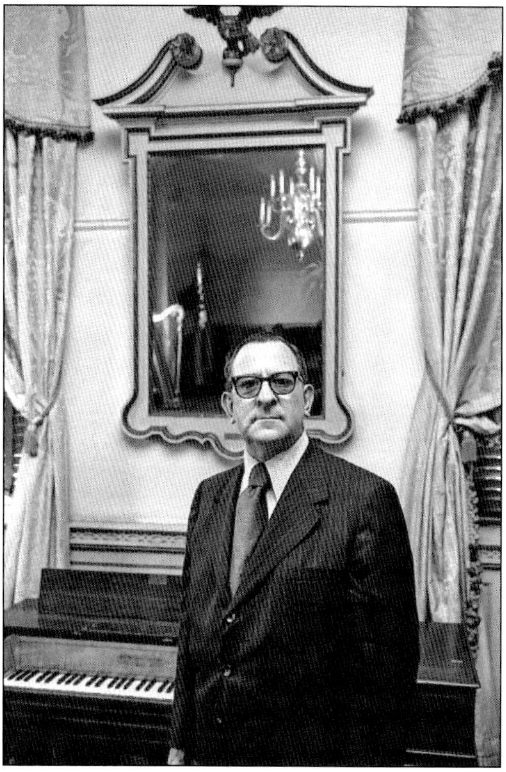

The museum's first curator, William Robert Adam, was hired by the American Legion in 1970. Adam, a native Alexandrian, had been associated with the tavern for 40 years. Recently retired as a public information officer for the Pentagon, he had worked with 10 successive secretaries of defense. Looking ahead to an increase in tourism with the nation's bicentennial, the legion knew that Adam's press skills would be invaluable. (ALSC.)

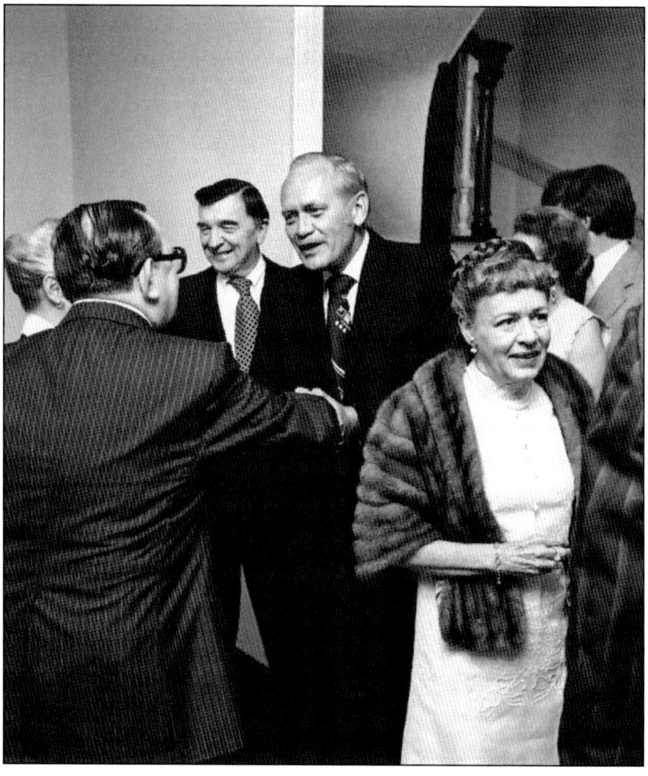

Curator William Robert Adam (back to camera) welcomes museum supporters Howard W. Smith Jr. (rear left), Don Slough (center), and Mrs. Howard Joynt (right) to an event in the museum's Assembly Room. A museum advocacy group, the Friends of Gadsby's Tavern, was established to assist the curator with fundraising, object acquisition, and museum operations. (ALSC.)

Three

A NEW ERA FOR THE MUSEUM

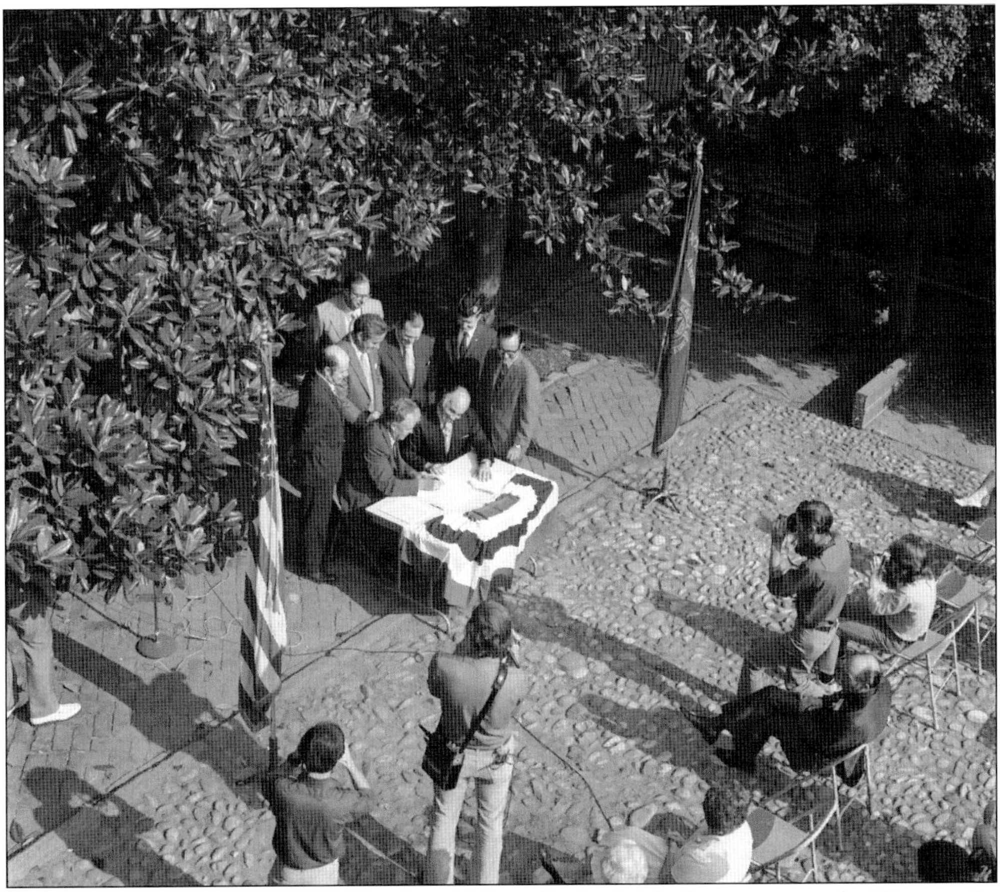

On August 11, 1972, American Legion Post 24 formally deeded the historic tavern buildings to the City of Alexandria in a public ceremony in the tavern's courtyard. This gift was made with the understanding that the city would restore the buildings in time for the nation's 1976 bicentennial commemoration and operate them as a museum. The 1878 hotel wing was retained by American Legion Post 24 as its post home.

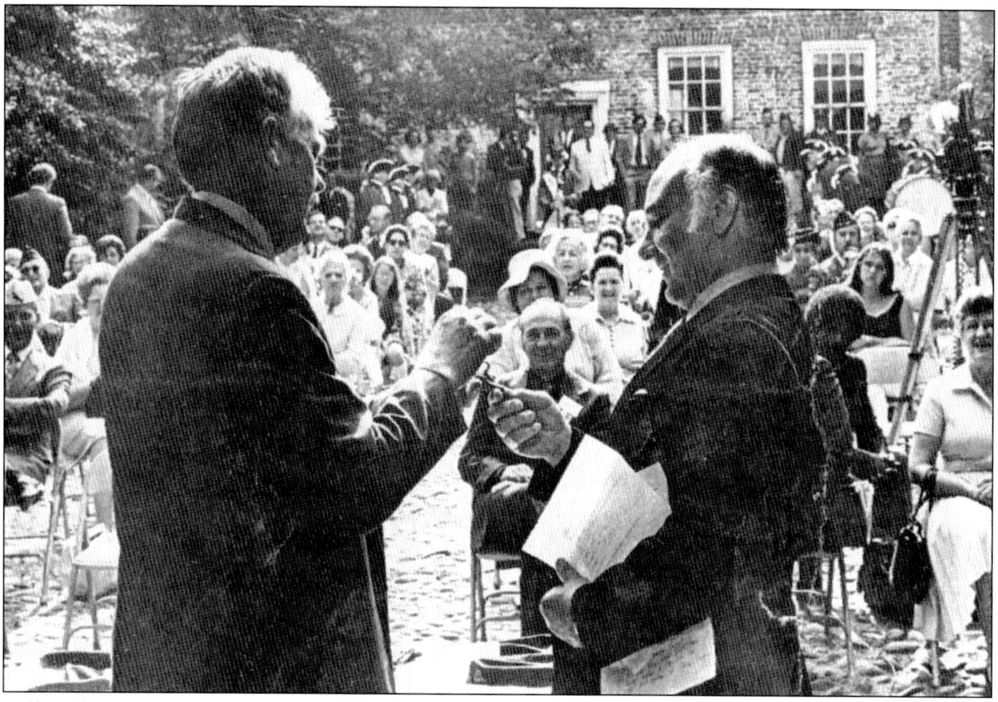

Officially transferring the historic tavern buildings, William G. McNamara (right) of American Legion Post 24, president of the Gadsby's Tavern and City Hotel, Inc., gives the keys to Gadsby's Tavern to Mayor Charles E. Beatley (left). The two historic tavern buildings were now referred to as Gadsby's Tavern Museum.

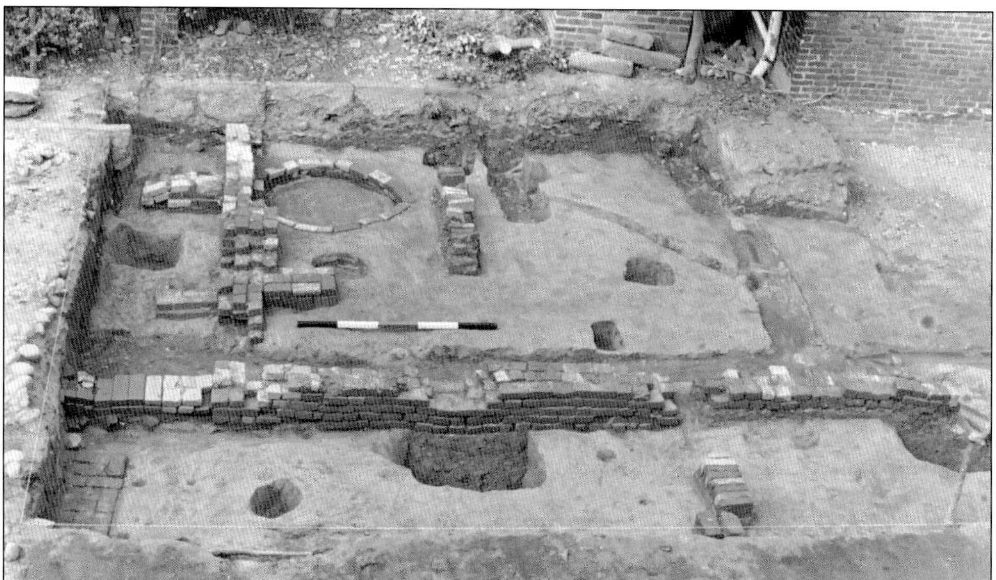

The restoration of the tavern buildings began with an archaeological excavation of the courtyard. This excavation identified structural features, such as wells, privies, and outbuilding foundations, and brought to light fragments of ceramics, glassware, and other artifacts that spoke to the daily life of the early taverns.

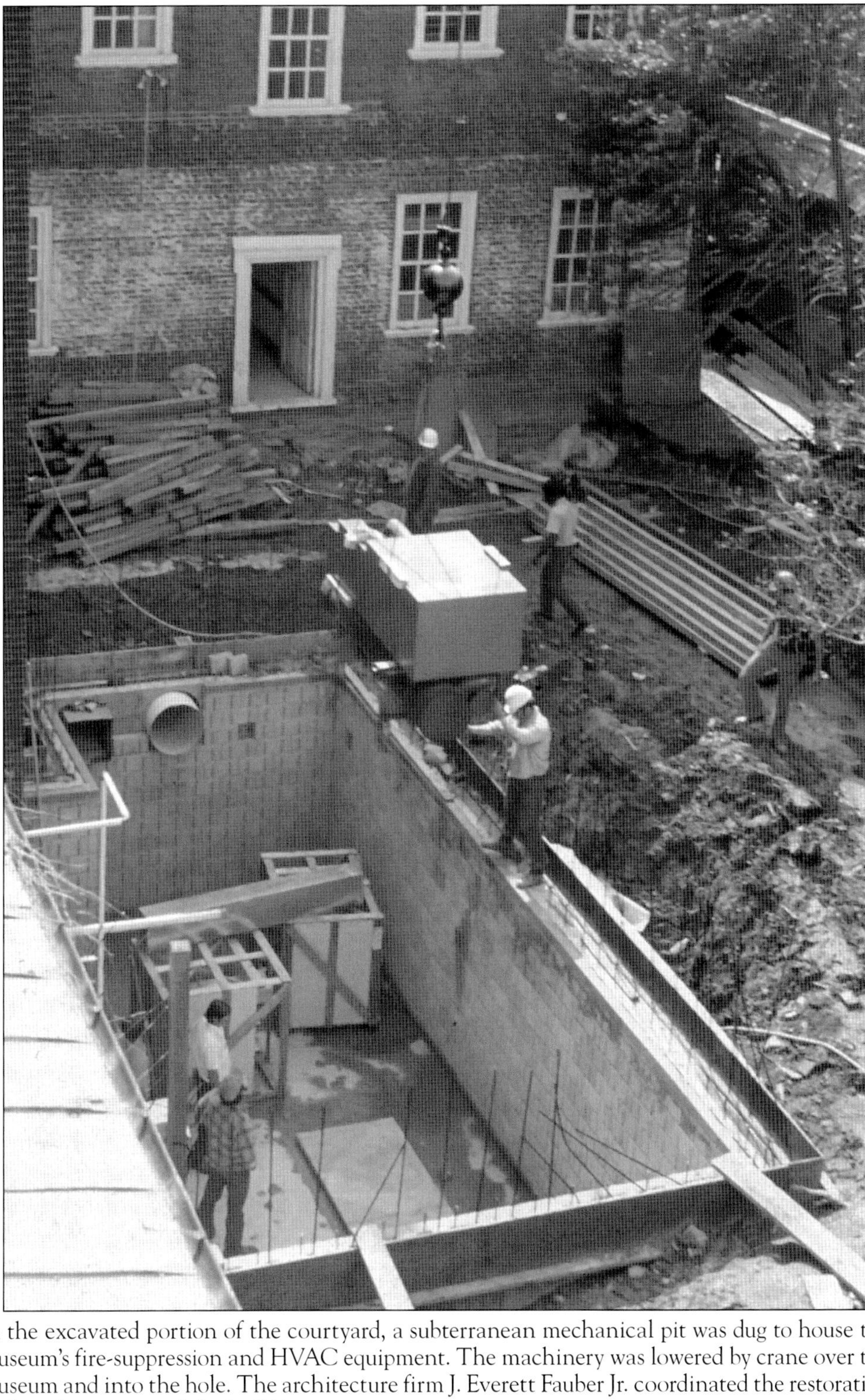

In the excavated portion of the courtyard, a subterranean mechanical pit was dug to house the museum's fire-suppression and HVAC equipment. The machinery was lowered by crane over the museum and into the hole. The architecture firm J. Everett Fauber Jr. coordinated the restoration and modernization of the buildings.

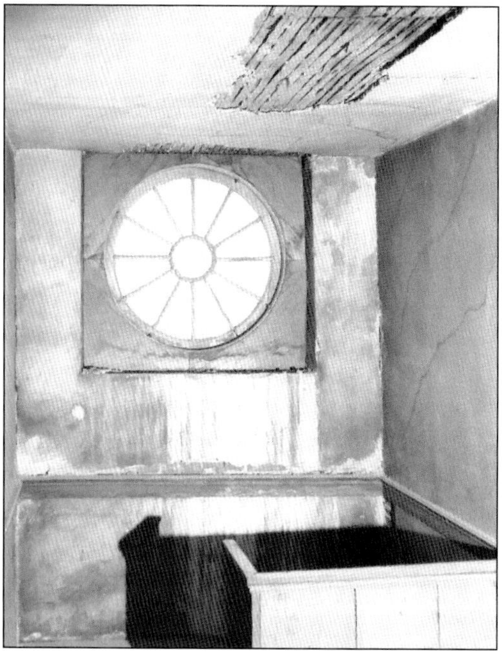

This original circular window at the head of the stairs to the fourth floor and attic of the City Hotel is an iconic detail that distinguishes Gadsby's from other Alexandria buildings. Unrestored by the American Legion, the fourth floor had four large rooms with a central hall. Each room, according to period inventories, contained three to five bedsteads. Even in fine establishments, early travelers were accustomed to sharing sleeping rooms.

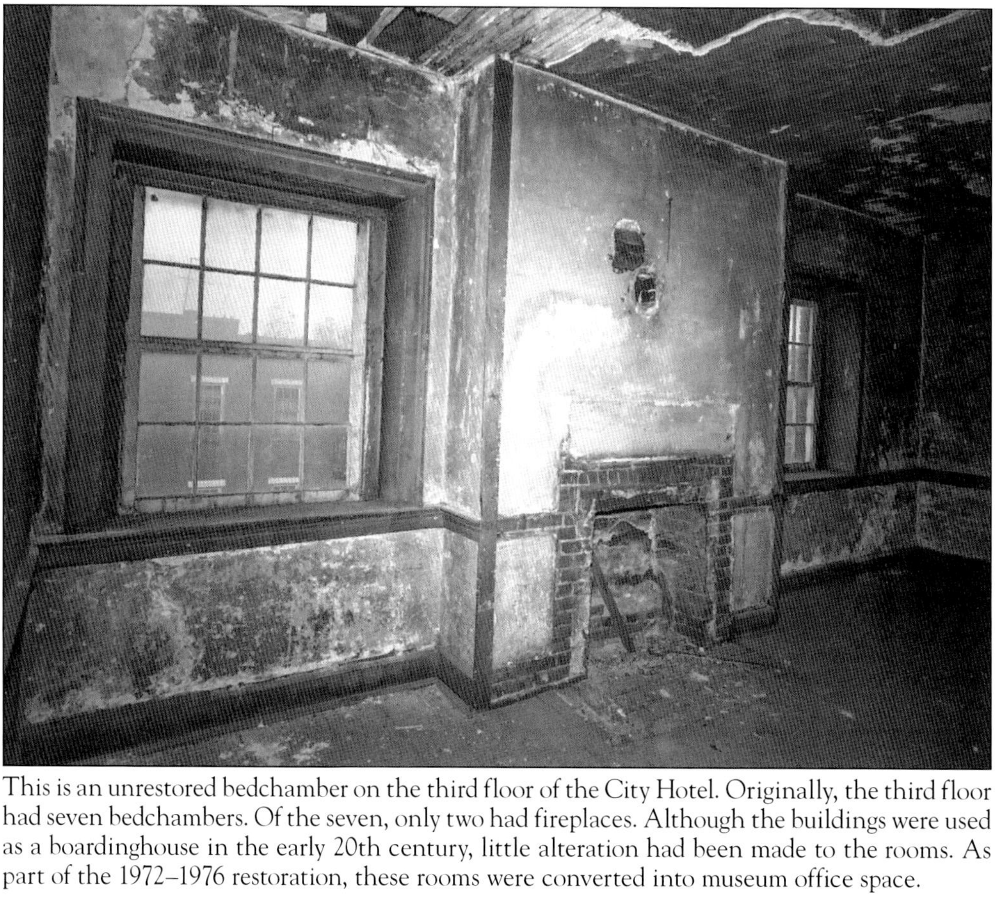

This is an unrestored bedchamber on the third floor of the City Hotel. Originally, the third floor had seven bedchambers. Of the seven, only two had fireplaces. Although the buildings were used as a boardinghouse in the early 20th century, little alteration had been made to the rooms. As part of the 1972–1976 restoration, these rooms were converted into museum office space.

The Assembly Room in the smaller tavern was the largest room in Alexandria until the 1792 ballroom was constructed. Visible in this 1974 photograph are test patches on either side of the mantel from architectural investigation. A door was cut through the wall to create a passage between the two buildings to facilitate tours. This is the last known photograph of the original Assembly Room configuration.

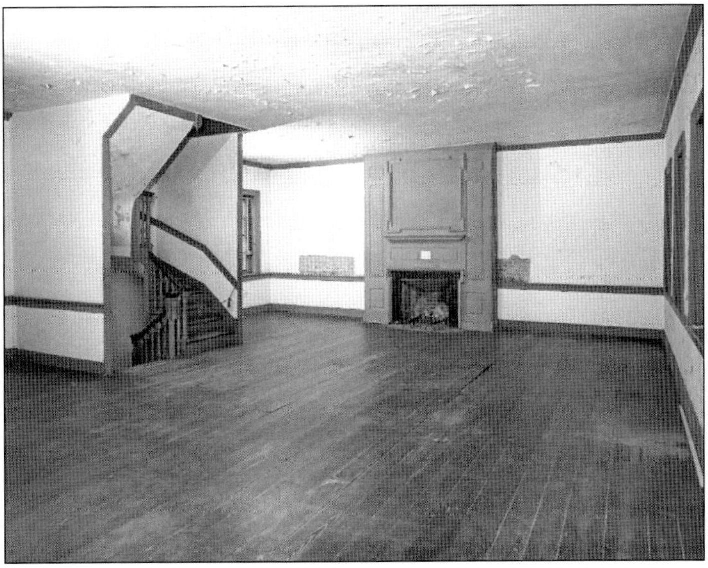

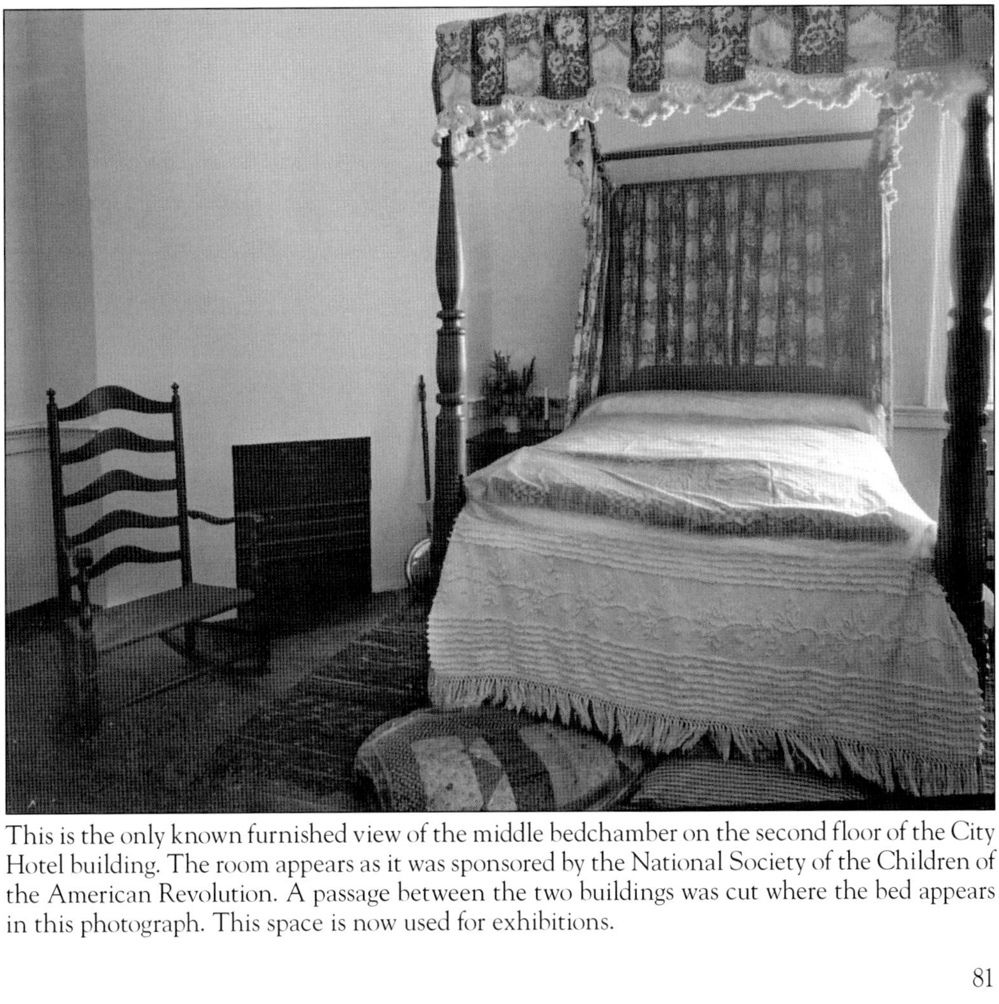

This is the only known furnished view of the middle bedchamber on the second floor of the City Hotel building. The room appears as it was sponsored by the National Society of the Children of the American Revolution. A passage between the two buildings was cut where the bed appears in this photograph. This space is now used for exhibitions.

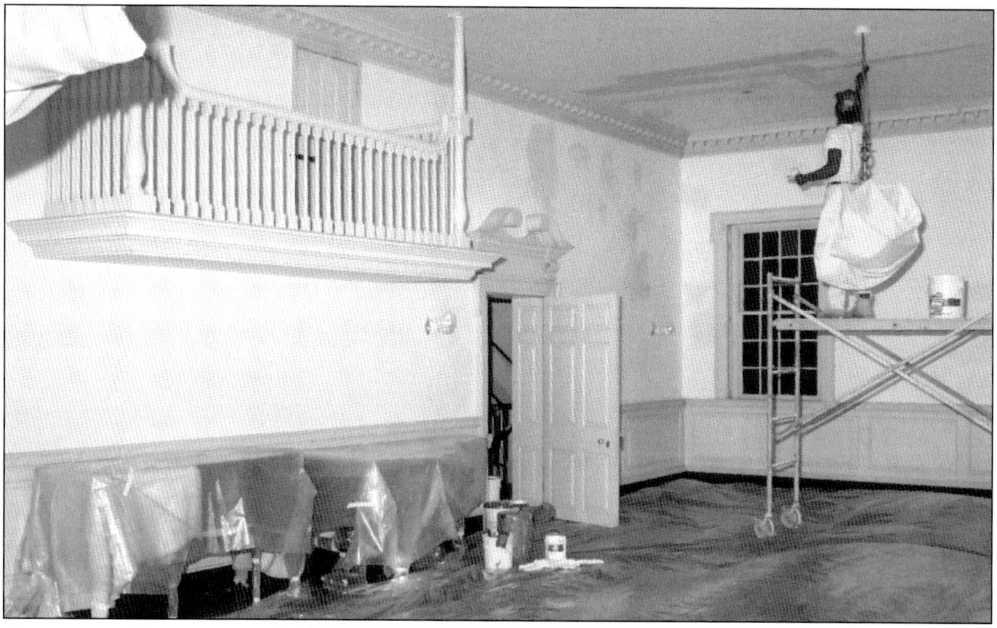

An amazing discovery was made during the architectural exploration of the ballroom. An original window, covered during the 1878 wing addition, was found. When the Metropolitan Museum of Art purchased the woodwork in 1917, this window was not visible. From the original window sash, hidden for 95 years, historic finishes consultant Matthew Mosca determined that the woodwork was painted Prussian blue during the John Gadsby era.

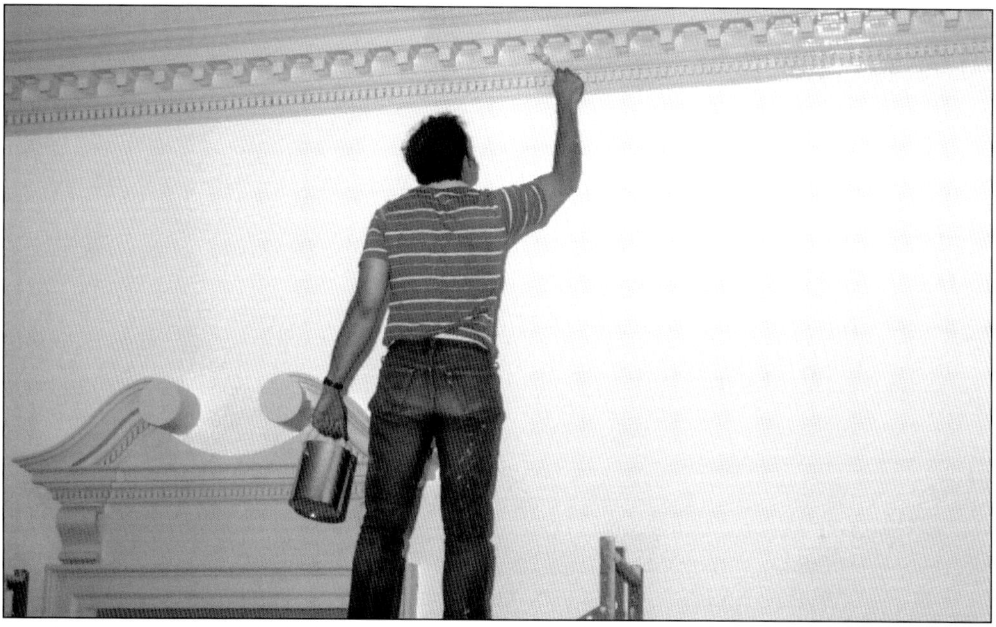

Matthew Mosca painted the ballroom woodwork Prussian blue, using paint made from hand-ground pigments. When the original woodwork was removed in 1917 and taken to the Metropolitan Museum of Art, it was completely cleaned of its paint and repainted to match its pre-stripped gray-green color, making the previously concealed window the only surviving evidence of the woodwork's original color.

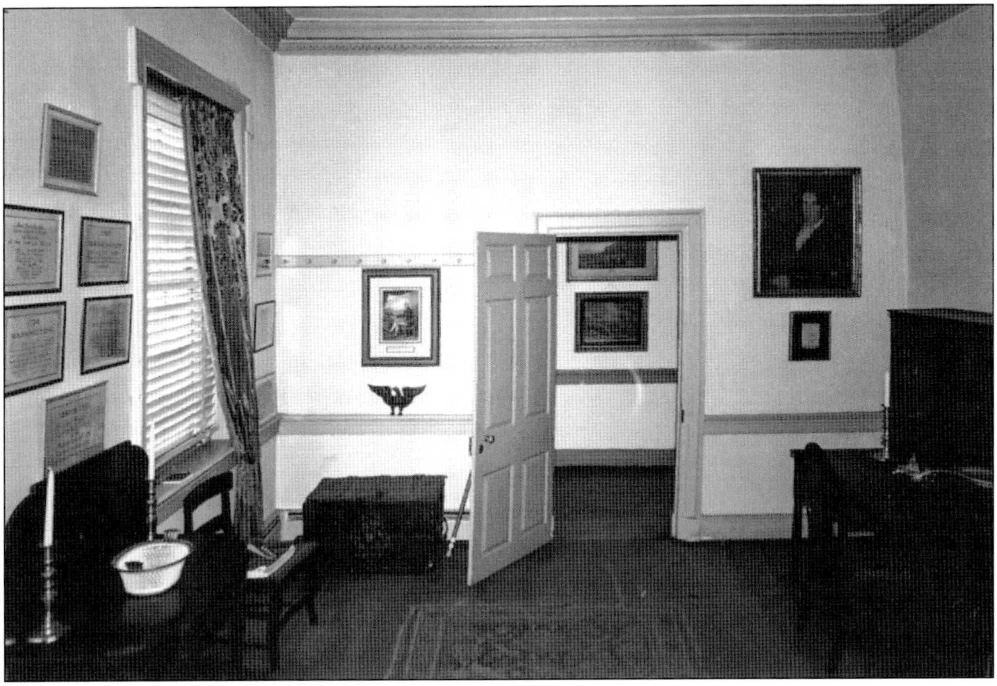

This is a view of what is now the museum's reception room and museum shop, as it was furnished by the American Legion in 1972. It was one of two original private dining rooms in the smaller tavern. Note the coat hooks behind the door. These are obscured today by the museum shop shelves.

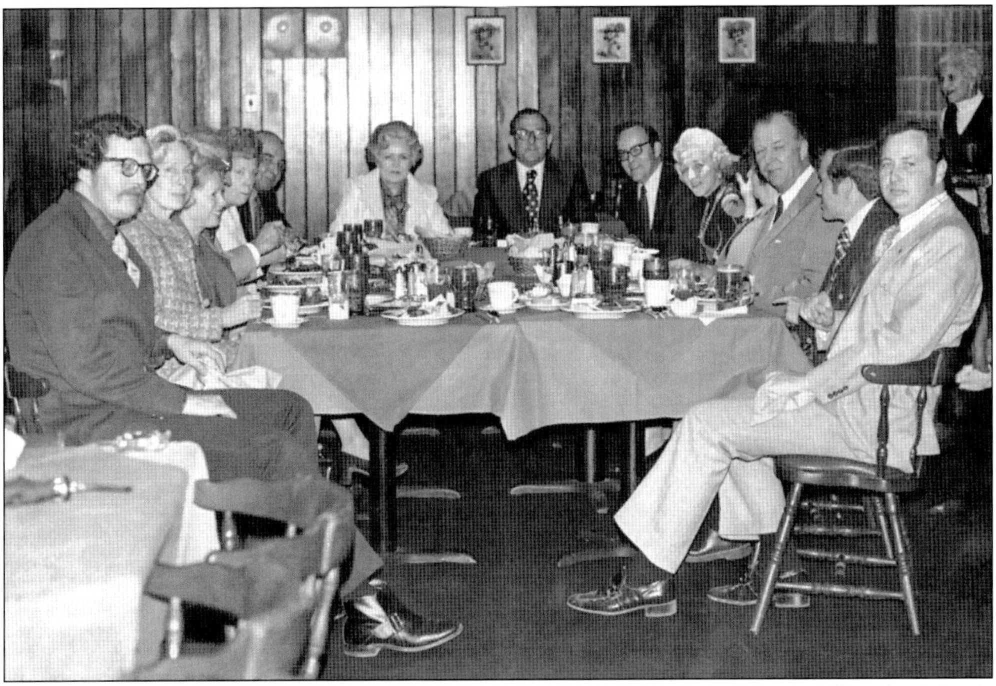

Progress on the restoration and modernization of Gadsby's Tavern was discussed at this May 8, 1975, luncheon attended by city officials, project architects, American Legion post members, museum staff, and members of the Friends of Gadsby's Tavern. (ALSC.)

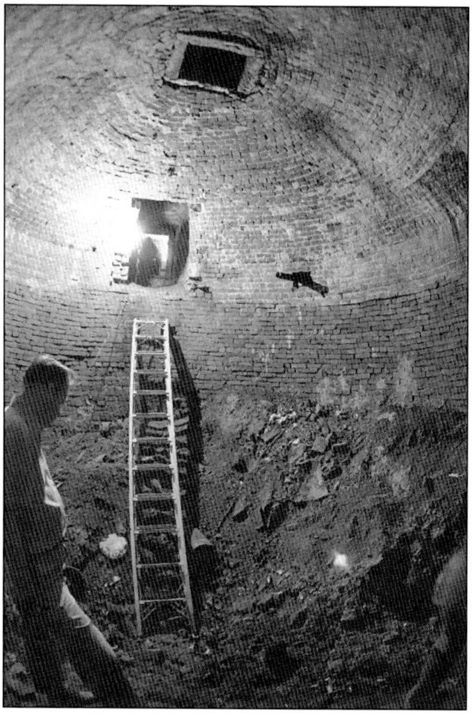

An important part of the 1970s restoration was the excavation and opening of the tavern's 18th-century ice well to public view. Before being rediscovered by the American Legion in 1950, the ice well had been used for trash. It was then forgotten with the advent of refrigeration. The ice well was excavated of the modern fill by Dr. William Kelso, assisted by Alain Outlaw and Robert Foss.

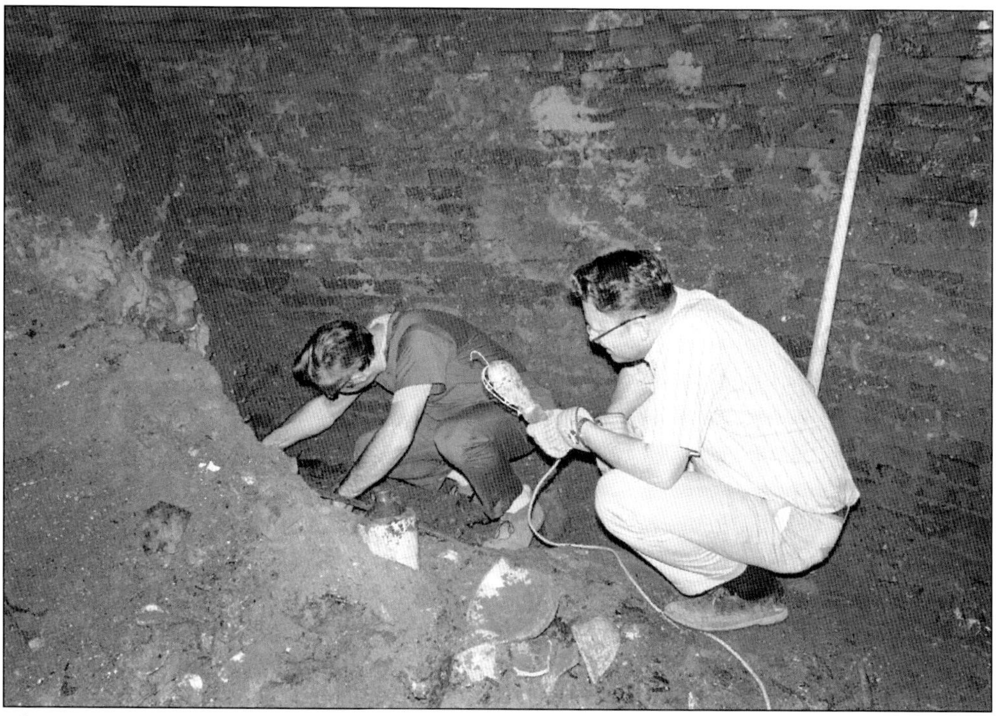

This commercial-size ice well is the only known extant American example surviving from an 18th-century urban setting. Excavation unearthed late-18th-century wine bottle fragments, an early-19th-century iron kettle, and late-19th-century china. A test trench made six feet below the present floor level revealed a thick layer of sand.

The ice well was unearthed at the street level, and a visitor viewing area was planned. To protect the structural integrity of the ice well, it was capped with concrete. Bricks were removed from one section to create a window into the ice well. Since its construction by John Wise, the ice well had been under Cameron Street. In 1793, Wise retroactively asked permission from the Alexandria Common Council to build the ice well in the public right-of-way. As part of the restoration, the sidewalk was expanded to cover and protect the ice well.

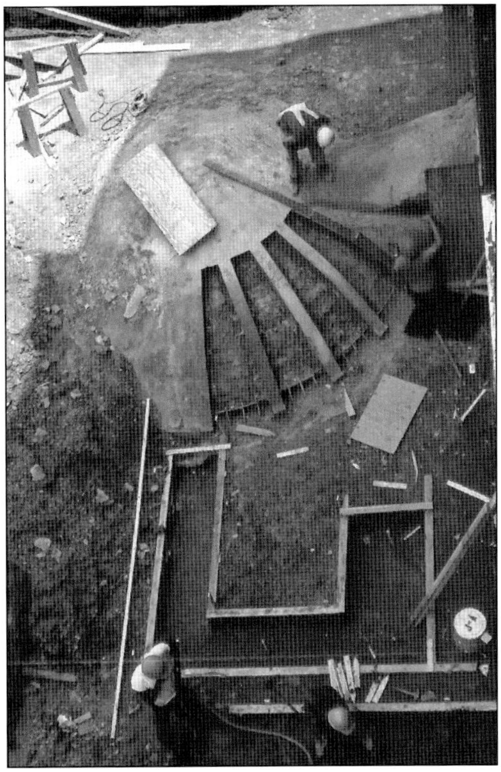

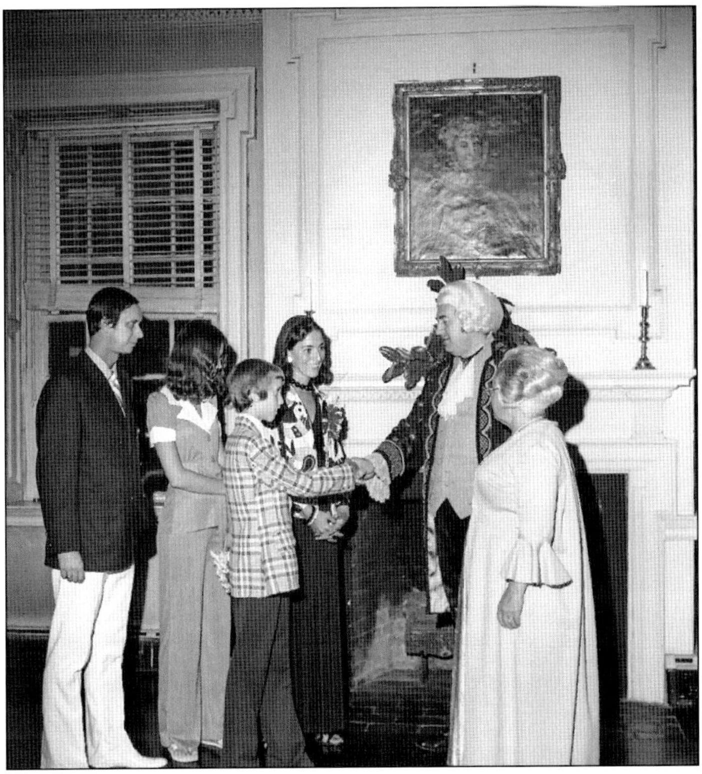

Robert E. Bellavance, the new executive vice president of the Alexandria Chamber of Commerce, and his family were welcomed at a reception at Gadsby's Tavern on June 21, 1974. They were greeted by George and Martha Washington, played by Frank Wright and Mrs. Walter Brennan. The *Alexandria Gazette* noted, "The reception evolved into a parade of city government and business leaders and citizens." (ALSC.)

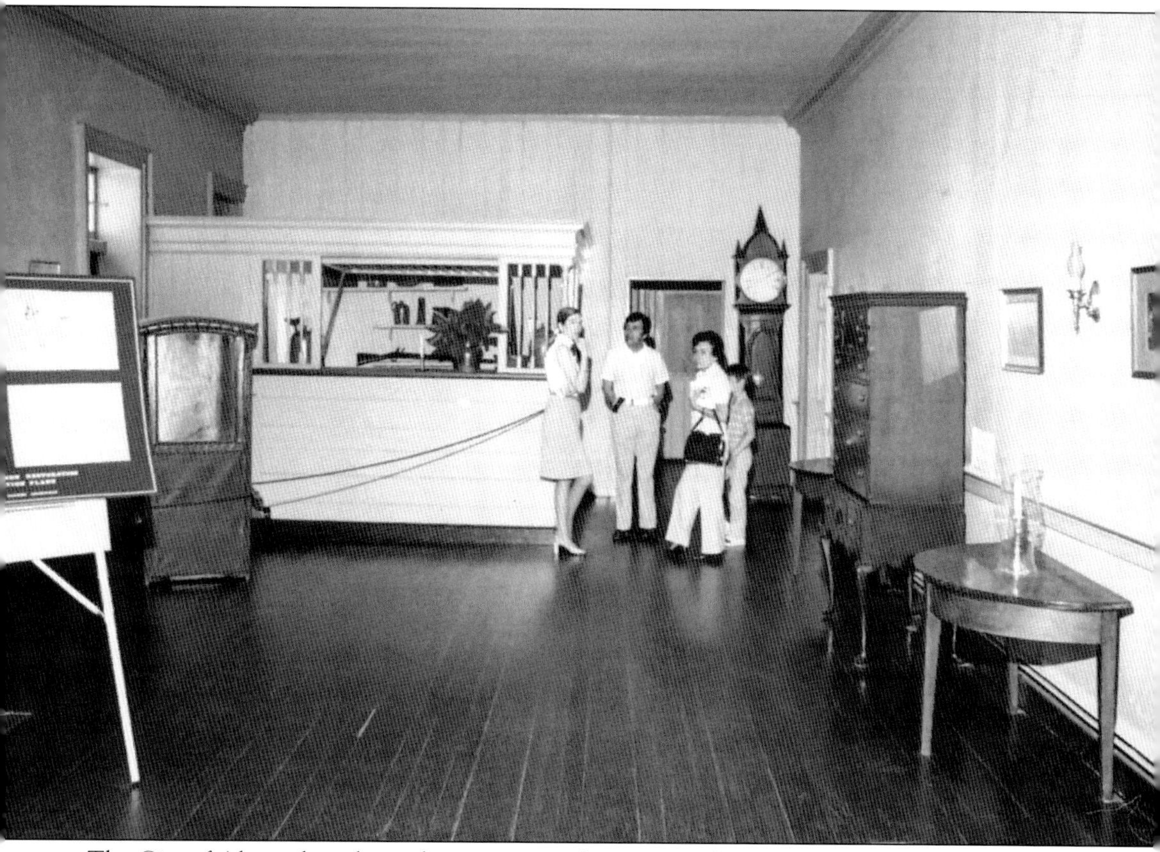

The City of Alexandria planned an operational restaurant for the first floor of the City Hotel building to enhance visitors' 18th-century tavern experience. The Taproom is seen here just before the restaurant was established. Special tours were conducted in June 1974 to show the planned changes for the building. Architectural drawings for the restoration were on display for public viewing. (ALSC.)

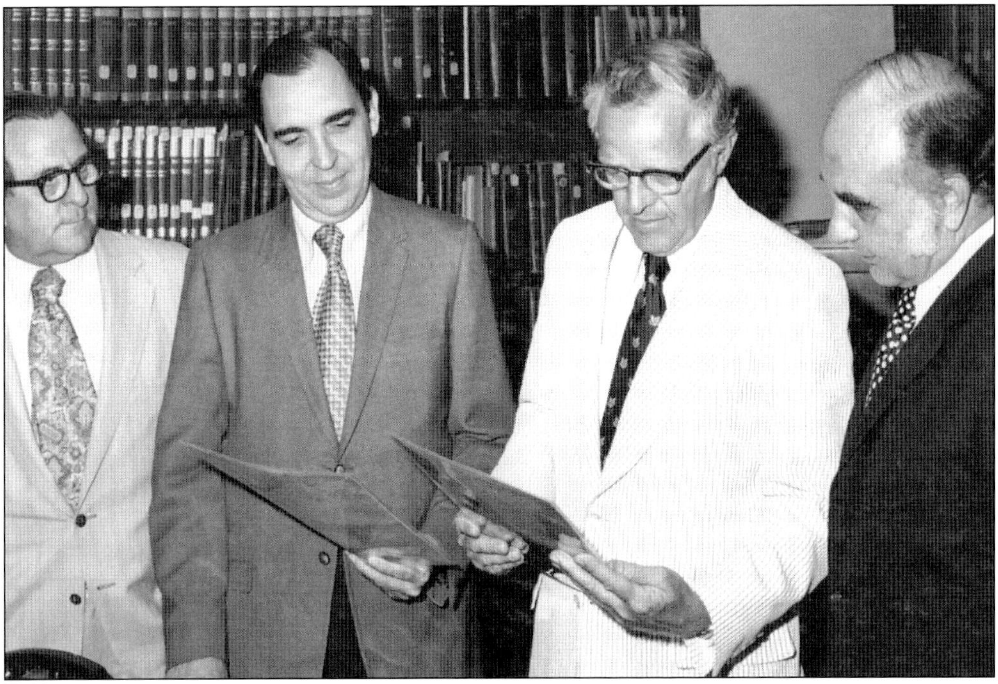

John Broderick (second from left) of the Library of Congress and Congressman Stan Parris (second from right) look at the original copy of the Fairfax Resolves. This document protested Britain's response to the Boston Tea Party. The original document, signed in Alexandria, was loaned to Gadsby's Tavern for a reenactment of this event. Robert Adam (far left) and William G. McNamara (far right) cochaired the Fairfax Resolves Re-Enactment Committee.

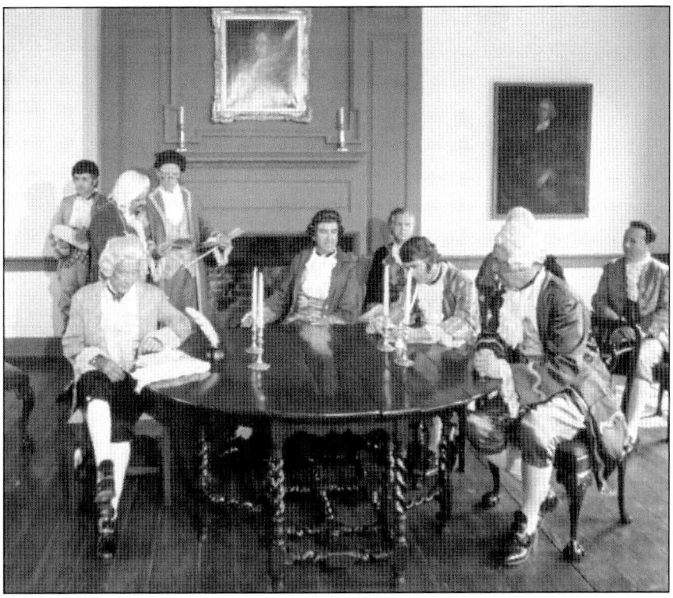

On July 18, 1774, George Washington presided over a meeting in Alexandria at which the Fairfax Resolves were adopted. The document called for a trade boycott and affirmed colonists' rights as British citizens. Actors from the Little Theatre of Alexandria re-created the signing at two performances, one in the Taproom of Gadsby's (pictured) and the other in front of city hall. Thousands attended the performances and viewed the document in the museum.

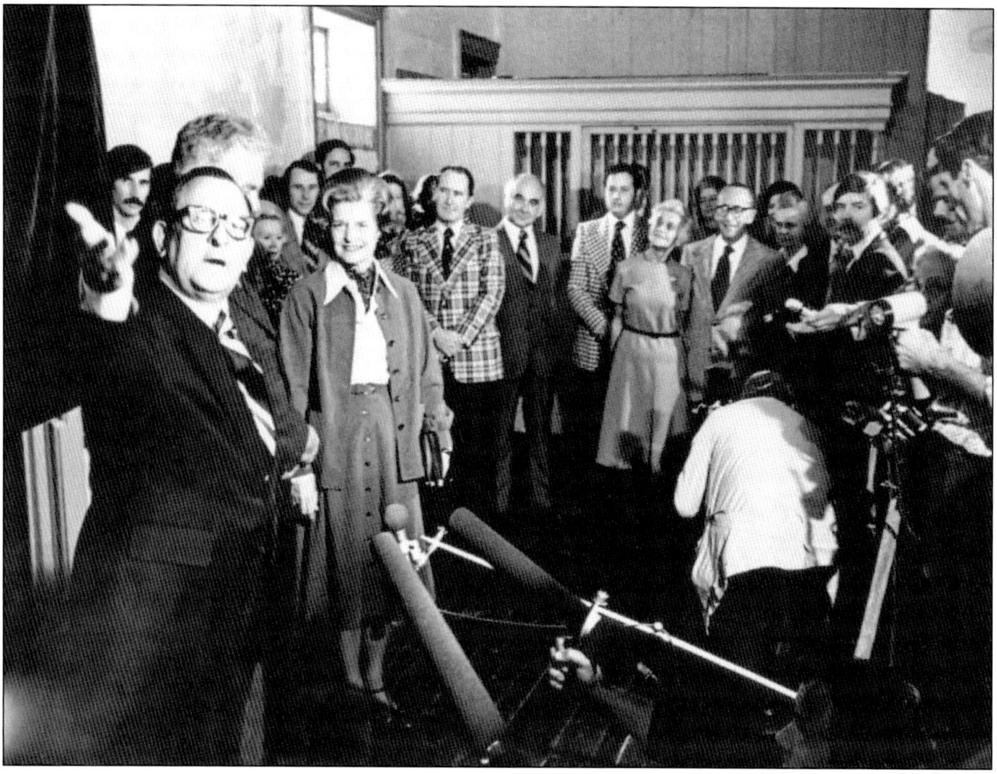

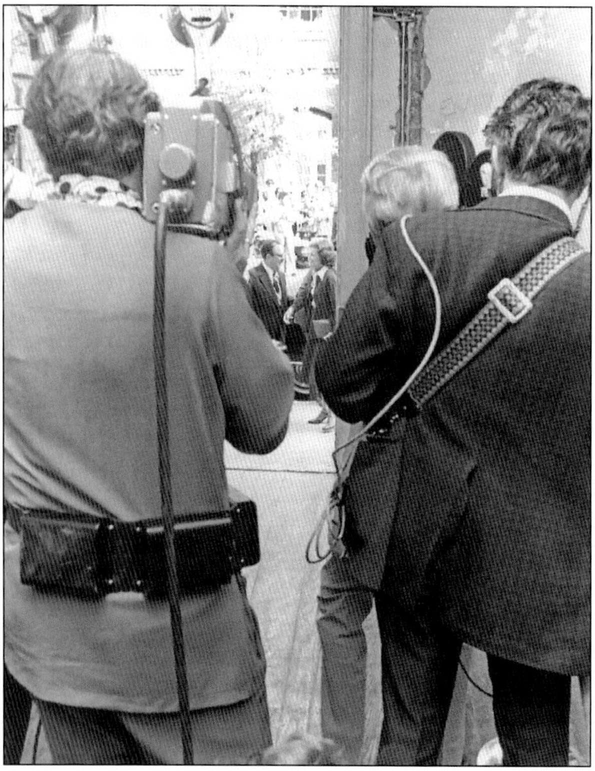

One of the original mantels purchased in 1917 by the Metropolitan Museum of Art was returned on loan to the museum in 1975. It was reinstalled in the Taproom of the City Hotel building. Special guest First Lady Betty Ford visited the museum as part of the rededication ceremony on October 16, 1975. This mantel remains on loan from the Metropolitan Museum of Art to this day.

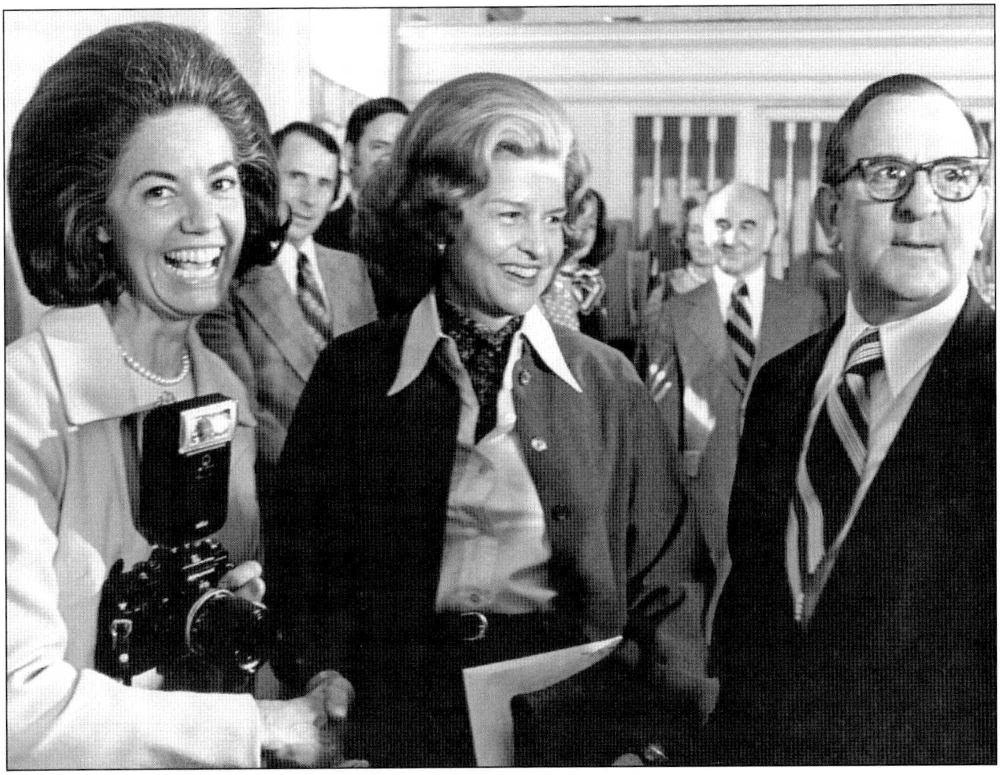

First Lady Betty Ford (center) graciously agreed to be the honorary chairman of the newly formed Friends of Gadsby's Tavern. Pictured with the first lady are June Hennage and William Robert Adam.

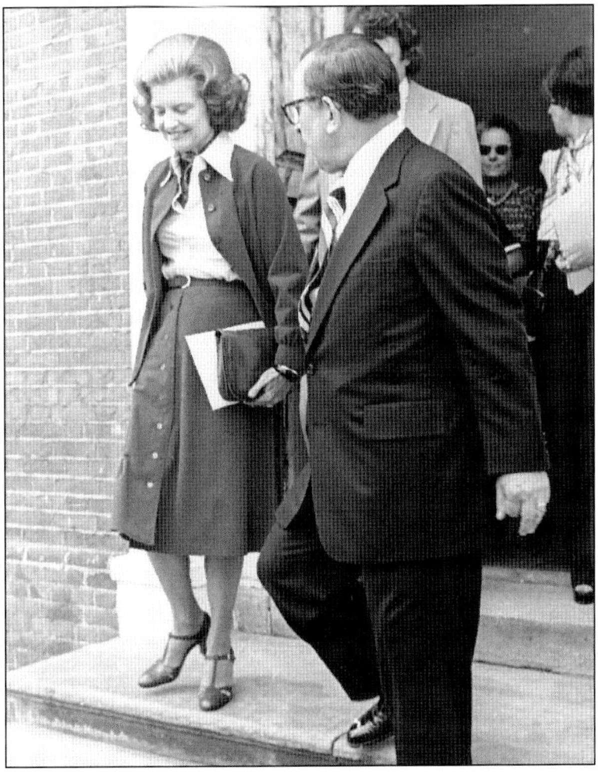

Hundreds of people gathered to see Betty Ford participate in the October 16, 1975, dedication ceremony. With the ballroom woodwork reproduced in 1940 and the original doorway returned in 1949, the return of the mantel was the final action in "reclaiming" the original woodwork removed to the Metropolitan Museum of Art in 1917.

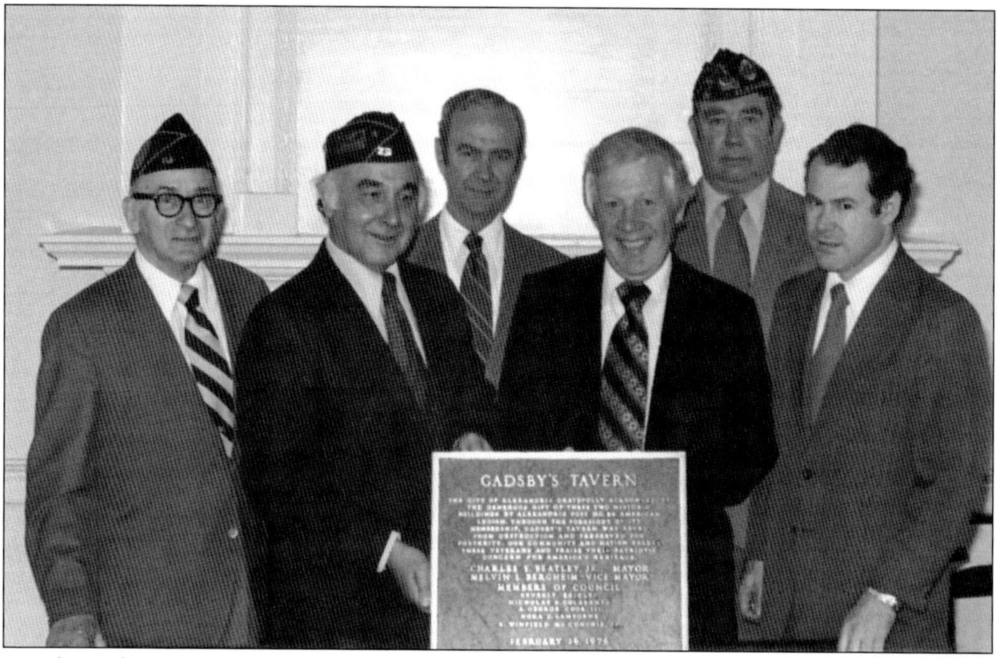

Members of American Legion Post 24 and the Alexandria City Council posed with Mayor Frank Mann (third from right) at the presentation of the official plaque commemorating the gift of Gadsby's Tavern from American Legion Post 24 to the City of Alexandria. This plaque was hung in the entrance of the museum and can be seen in the same location today.

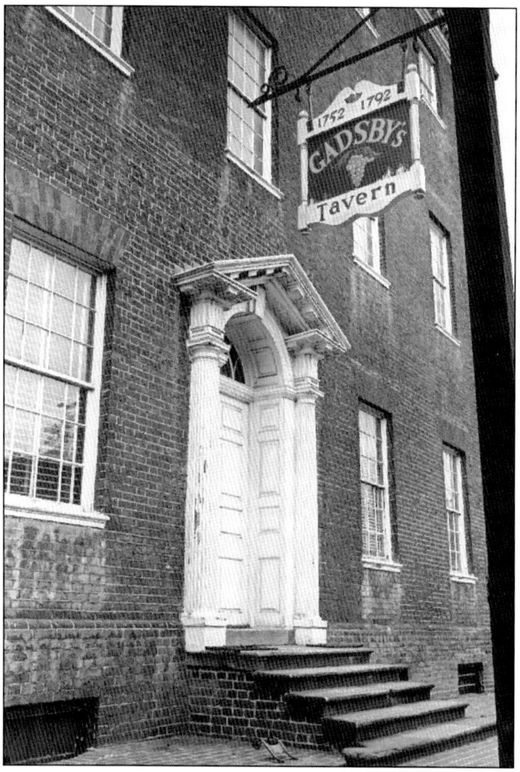

The restoration began in 1972 with comprehensive documentation of the buildings, architectural analysis, and archaeological investigations. From there, the modernization process began, including HVAC equipment, fire suppression, plumbing, upgraded wiring, and lighting to meet modern code requirements. A kitchen facility was added to the basement, and food service equipment, including two dumbwaiters, was installed on the first floor of the City Hotel building to establish an operating tavern restaurant.

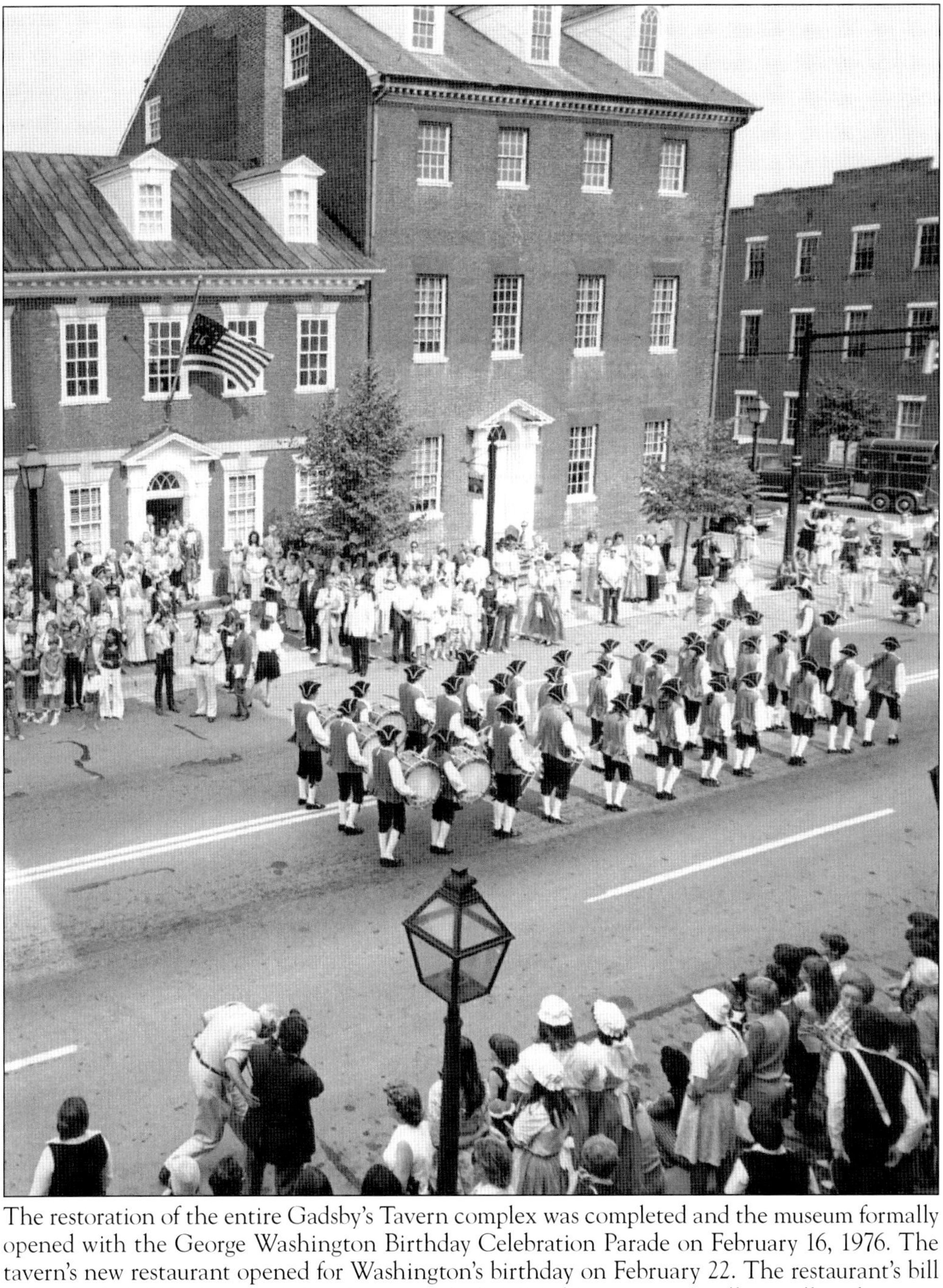

The restoration of the entire Gadsby's Tavern complex was completed and the museum formally opened with the George Washington Birthday Celebration Parade on February 16, 1976. The tavern's new restaurant opened for Washington's birthday on February 22. The restaurant's bill of fare included Washington's favorite, roast duck in Madeira sauce, as well as scalloped oysters, English "rabbit," pecan pie with whipped cream, and English trifle.

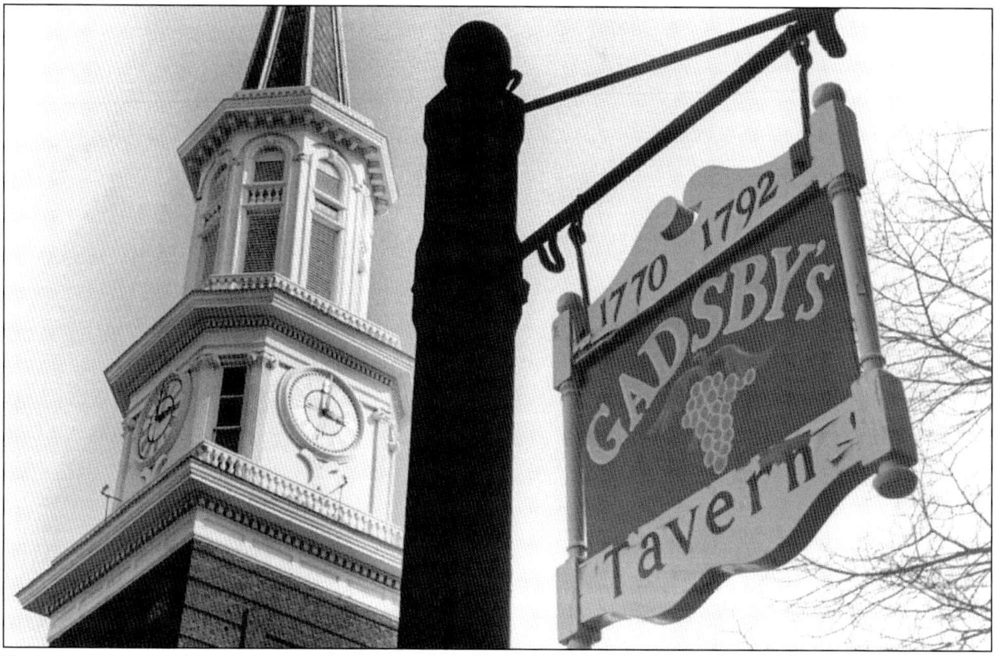

Reexamining the historic record, museum staff confirmed that Mason's Ordinary had been torn down as part of the urban renewal process. Research now suggested that the smaller building was constructed c. 1770 and operated by the widowed female tavern keeper Mary Hawkins. The tavern sign was changed from 1752 to reflect this new date, 1770.

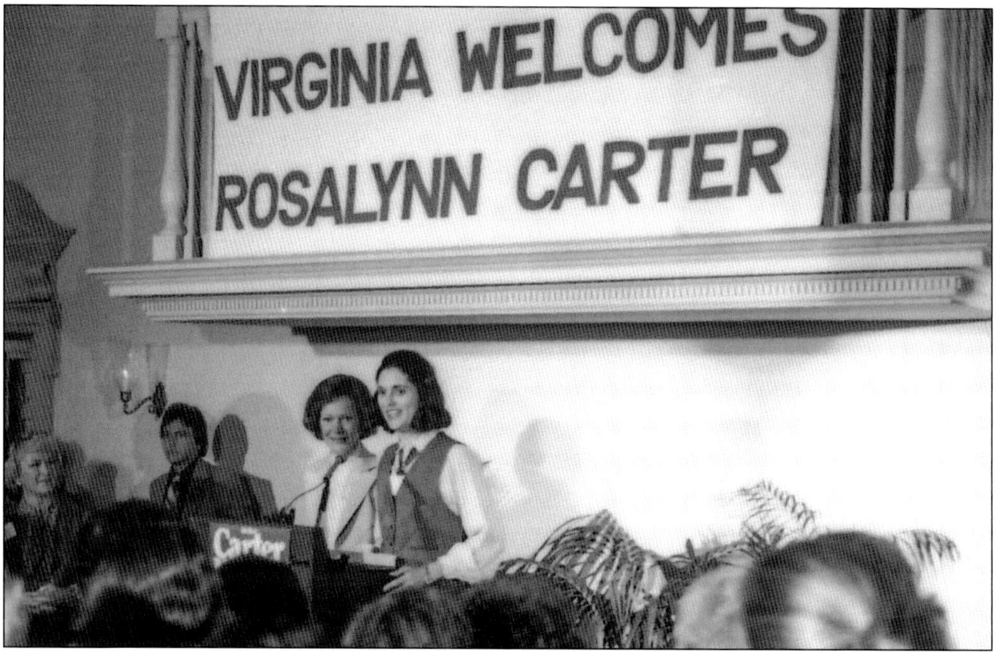

Continuing the 18th-century tradition of the tavern as a venue for political debate, First Lady Rosalynn Carter gave a campaign speech at Gadsby's Tavern Museum on October 10, 1980, as part of her husband's reelection campaign. She was introduced by Lynda Bird Johnson Robb, whose husband, Chuck Robb, was lieutenant governor of Virginia at the time.

The Scottish Country Dance Society performed in the Gadsby's Tavern Museum Ballroom on December 5, 1981, as part of the annual Scottish Christmas Walk. The Scottish Walk was established in 1970 to support the Campagna Center, an Alexandria nonprofit that helps families. This festive event continues to kick off the holiday season in Alexandria each year.

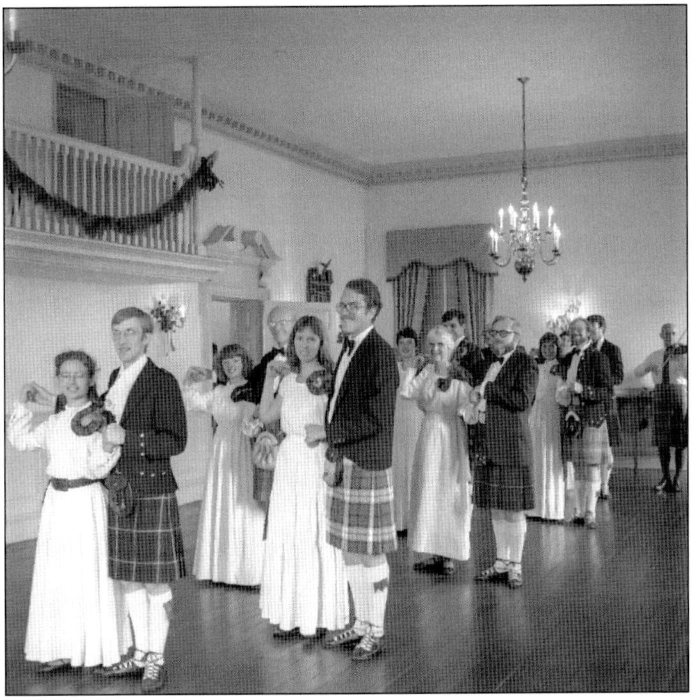

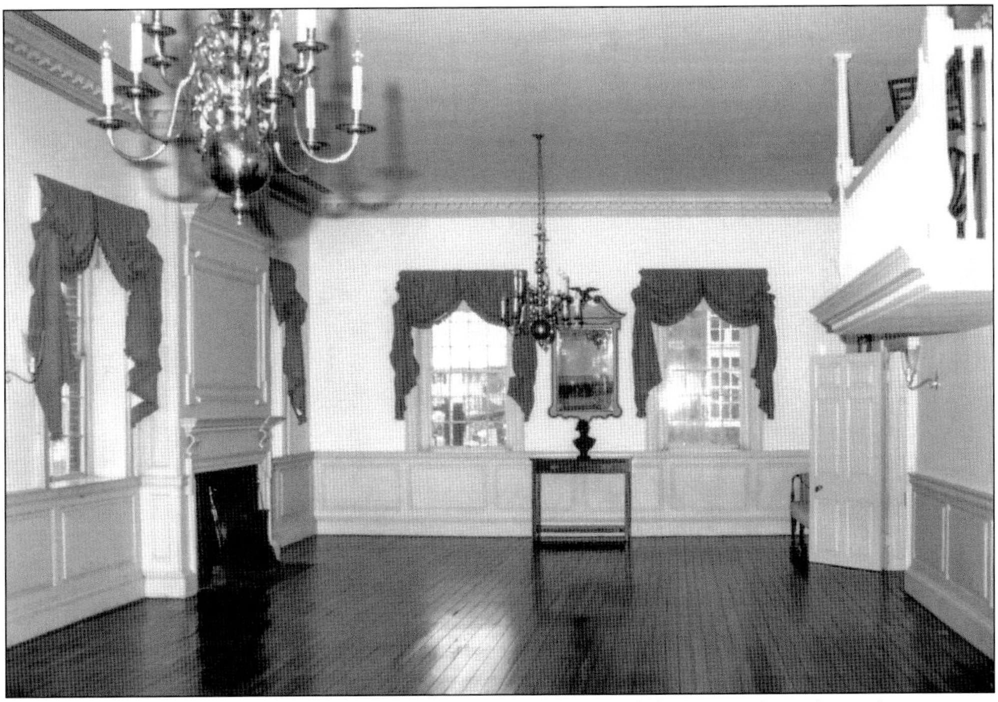

With an emerging field of trained museum professionals, work began on furnishing the museum to reflect Mary Hawkins's c. 1770s tavern and John Gadsby's City Tavern and Hotel. A grant from the Institute of Museum Services funded the development of a Historic Furnishing Plan, based on the 1777 probate inventory of Mary Hawkins and the 1802 lease negotiation between John Wise and John Gadsby.

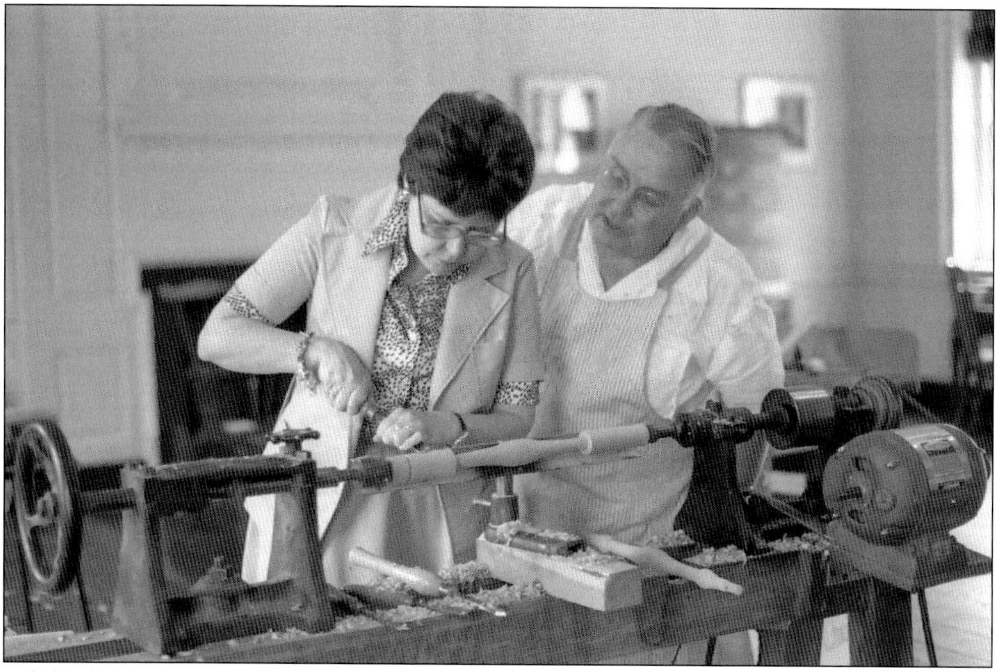

While the museum staff worked to acquire furnishings reflecting the planned interpretation of Mary Hawkins's 1770s tavern, a series of exhibits strengthened the museum's interpretive programs. In 1982, the Assembly Room was the location for a special Windsor chair–making demonstration. Visitors were given the opportunity to use a lathe. Several examples of Windsor chairs from local collections were on exhibit to illustrate the evolution of this chair style over time. Later, the Assembly Room served as a canvas for a large quilt exhibition.

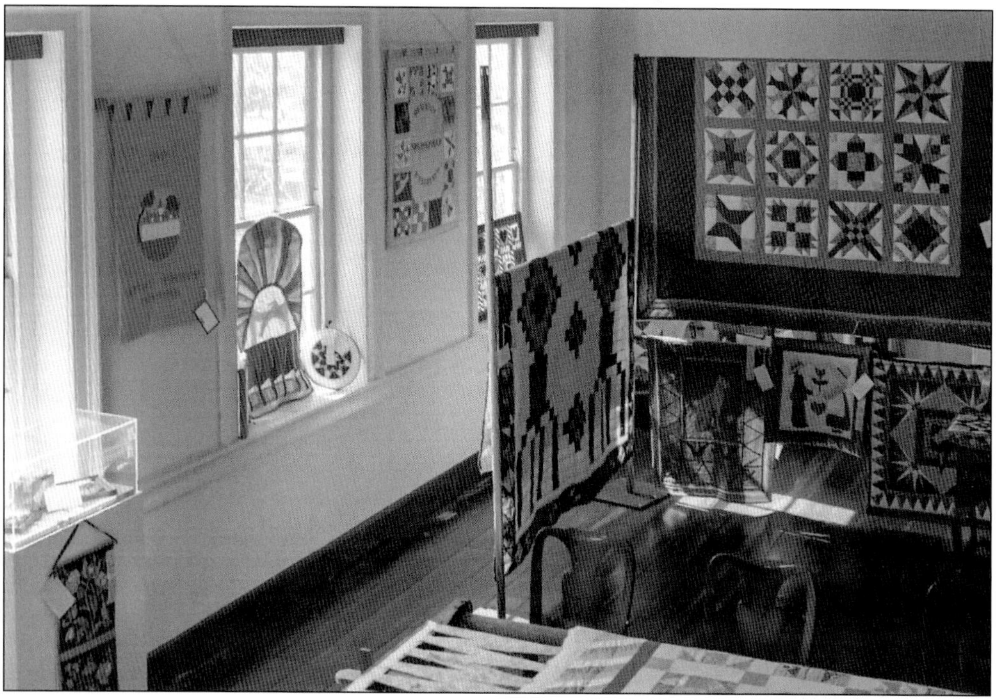

Museum director Carl Nold shares the latest scholarship on the museum. The 1976 *Restoration Report* by J. Everette Fauber Jr. had reexamined the history of the site and restoration of the buildings. The 1980 *Furnishings Plan* by Gretchen Sorin (museum director) and Ellen Donald (consultant) provided the blueprint for furnishing the tavern. The next step was an interpretive plan to help bring the tavern to life for museum visitors.

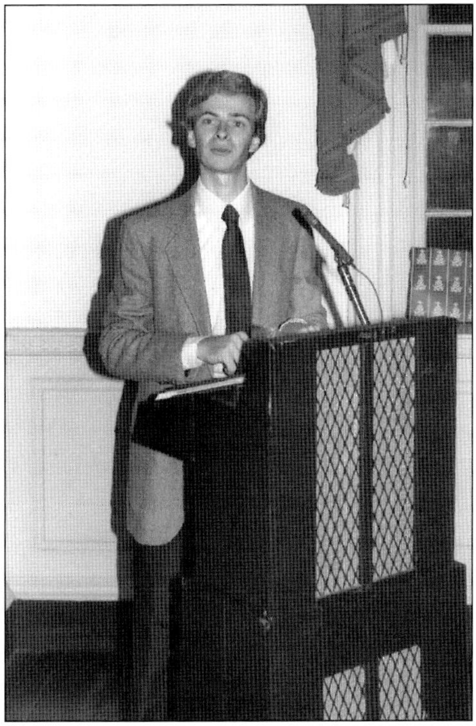

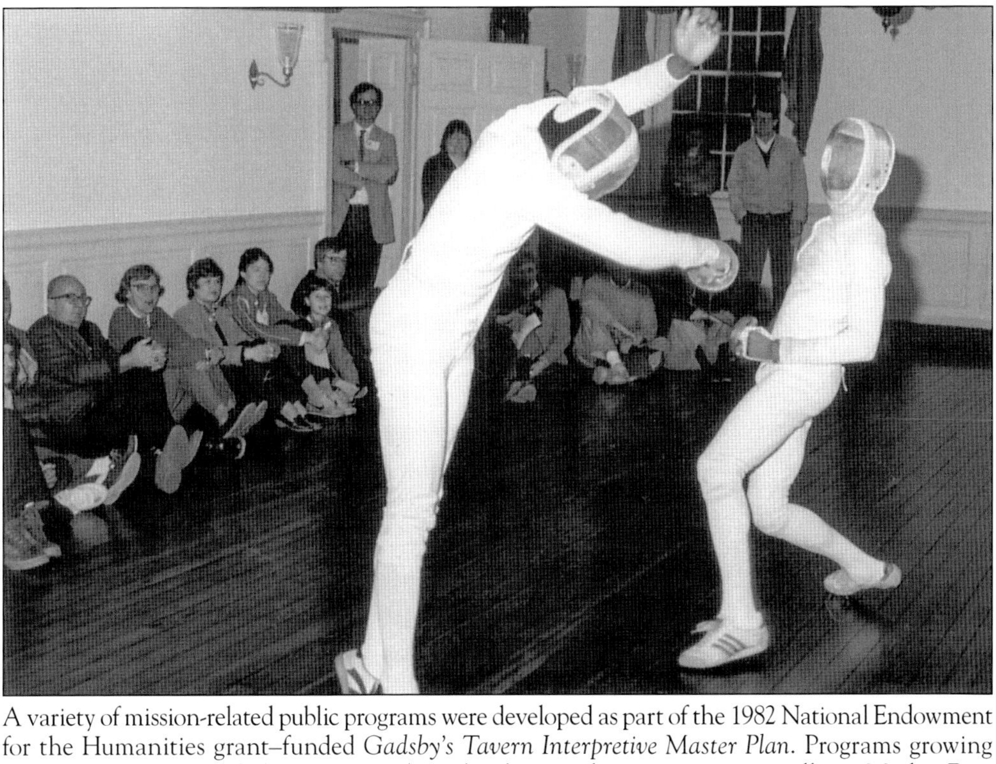

A variety of mission-related public programs were developed as part of the 1982 National Endowment for the Humanities grant–funded *Gadsby's Tavern Interpretive Master Plan*. Programs growing out of this effort included activities such as this fencing demonstration, as well as a Market Day, Tavern Days, and 18th-century balls.

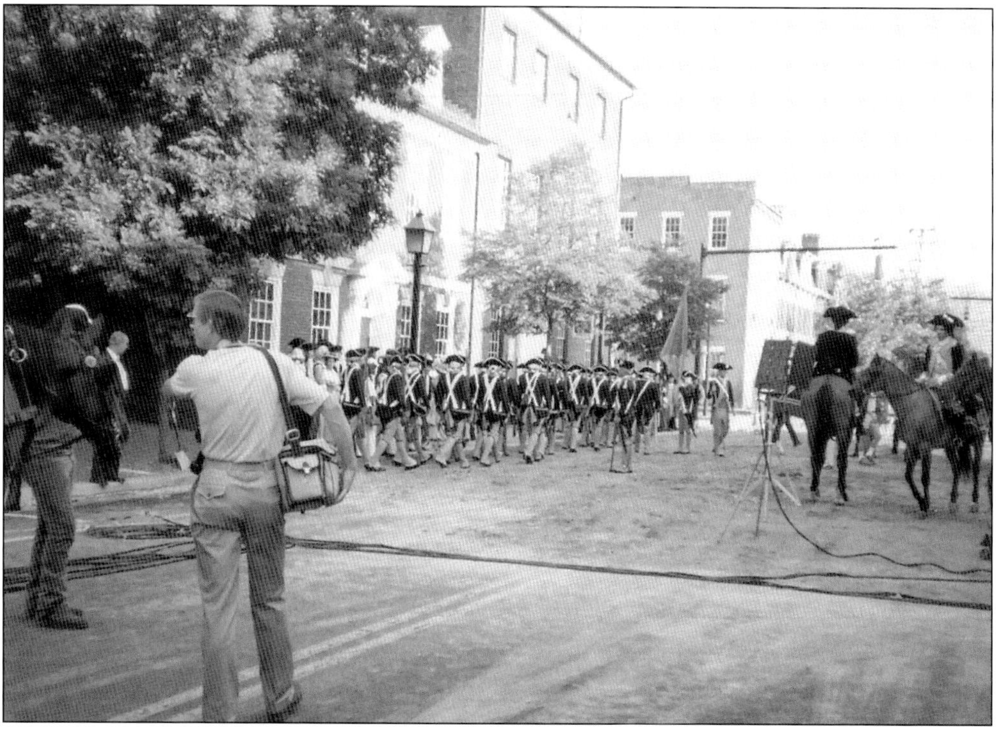

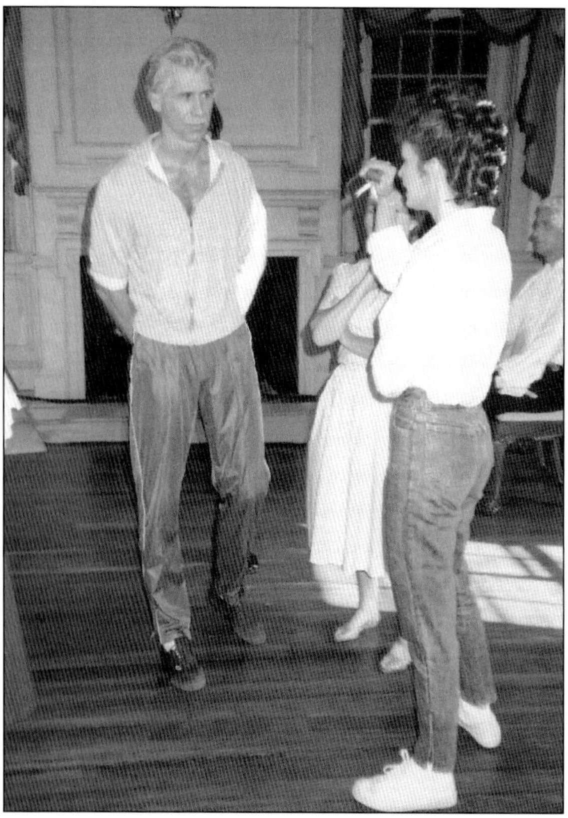

Scenes for the *George Washington* television miniseries were filmed at Gadsby's Tavern in September 1983. Gadsby's stood in for scenes intended to represent both Colonial New York and Williamsburg. To make the exterior scenes more realistic, two truckloads of dirt covered Royal Street in front of the tavern, parking meters were removed, and the tavern sign was changed to identify New York's Fraunces Tavern.

The series was based on the life and career of Washington through the Revolutionary War. It was directed by Buzz Kulik. The cast of the miniseries included Barry Bostwick as George Washington and Jaclyn Smith as Sally Fairfax. Here, the actors rehearse their lines in the ballroom.

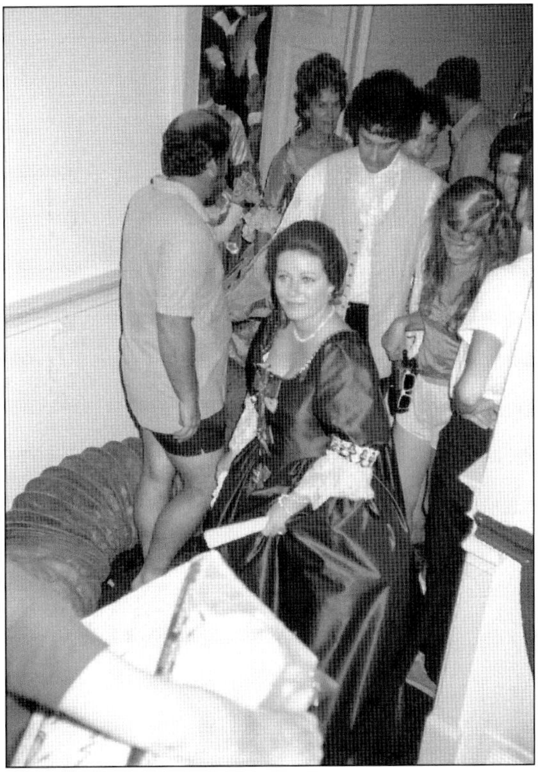

Actresses Patty Duke as Martha Washington (right) and Jaclyn Smith as Sally Fairfax (below) wait in the museum hallway to enter the ballroom for filming. The scene portrayed a 1766 ball in Williamsburg. Smith is talking to museum volunteer and costume assistant Edith Cornwell.

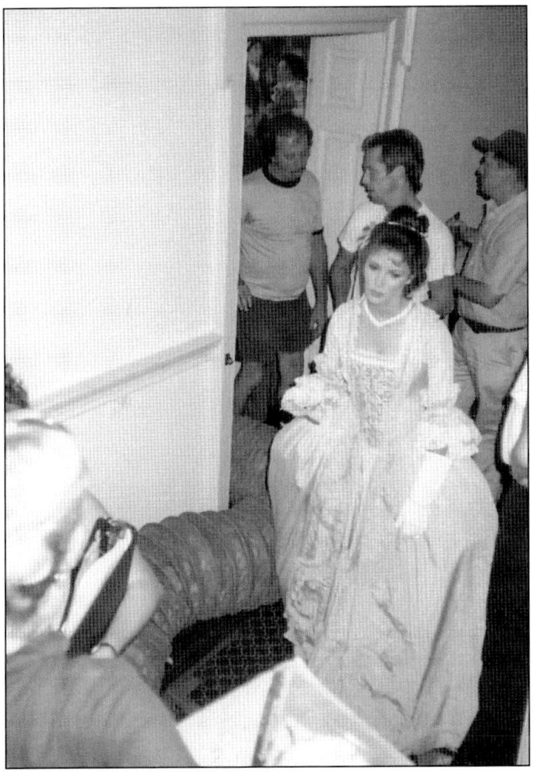

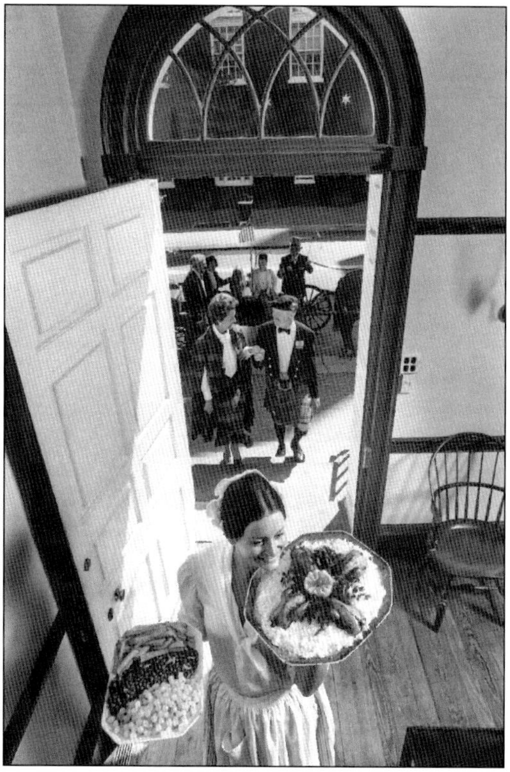

Gadsby's Tavern Restaurant featured a Colonial dining experience, with an 18th-century-inspired menu, costumed servers, and period table wares. The restaurant seated 85 patrons, and its candlelit ambience quickly made it a popular dining choice for tour bus groups, group luncheons, wedding receptions, and family celebrations.

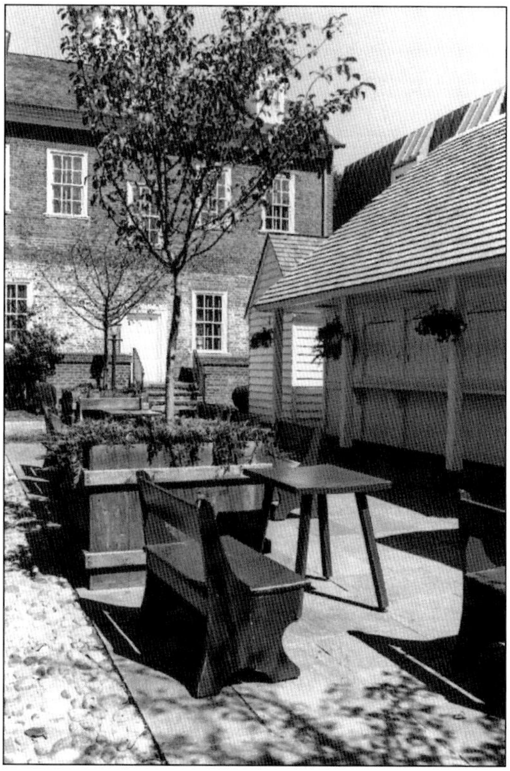

As part of the restoration of the tavern site, outbuildings based on the 1796 Mutual Assurance Map were reconstructed in the courtyard. The map recorded the location, size, and materials of the buildings on the lot that were insured by property owner John Wise in the event of fire. These new buildings served as a restaurant office, outdoor bar, and restroom.

A popular part of the restaurant's tavern experience was live entertainment. John Douglas Hall, who initially portrayed a "balladeer" and later an 18th-century gentleman, began performing on August 25, 1978. He offered music and commentary about life 200 years ago to the day. Hall continues to entertain guests with conversation and songs today. (ALSC.)

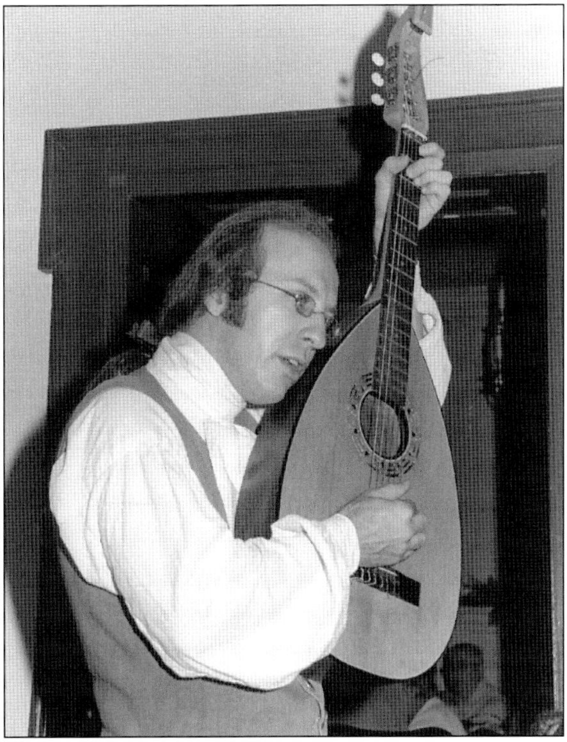

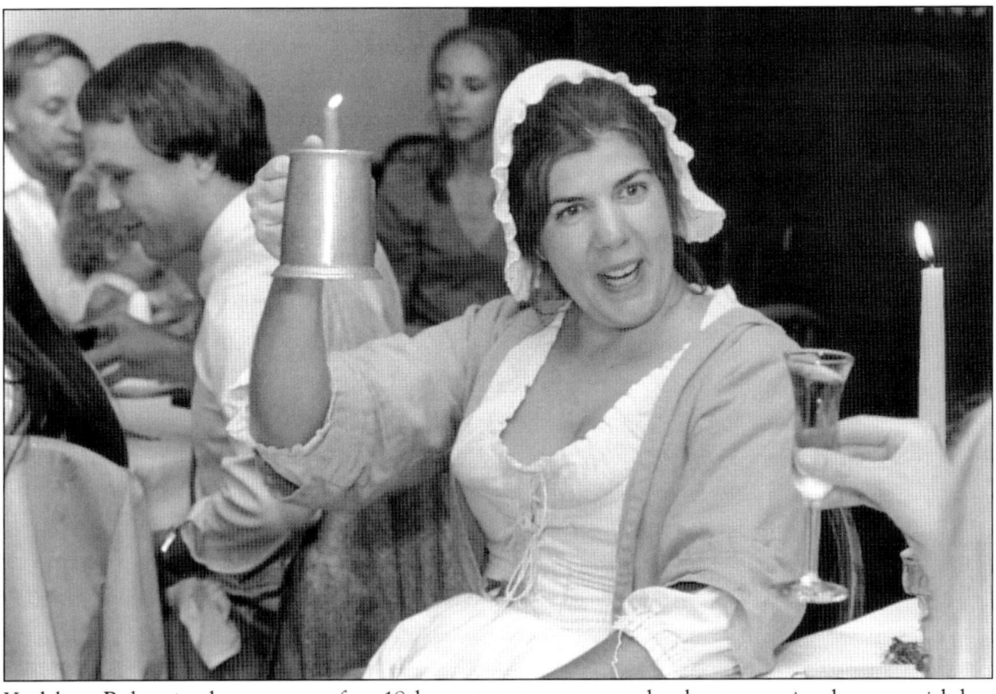

Kathleen Baker, in the persona of an 18th-century tavern wench, also entertained guests with her singing. She was known for her Publick Table performances and lively interactions with restaurant patrons. According to a promotional advertisement, she "served up" toasts, songs, news of the day, and humorous commentary as well as a bountiful feast from the tavern's kitchen. (ALSC.)

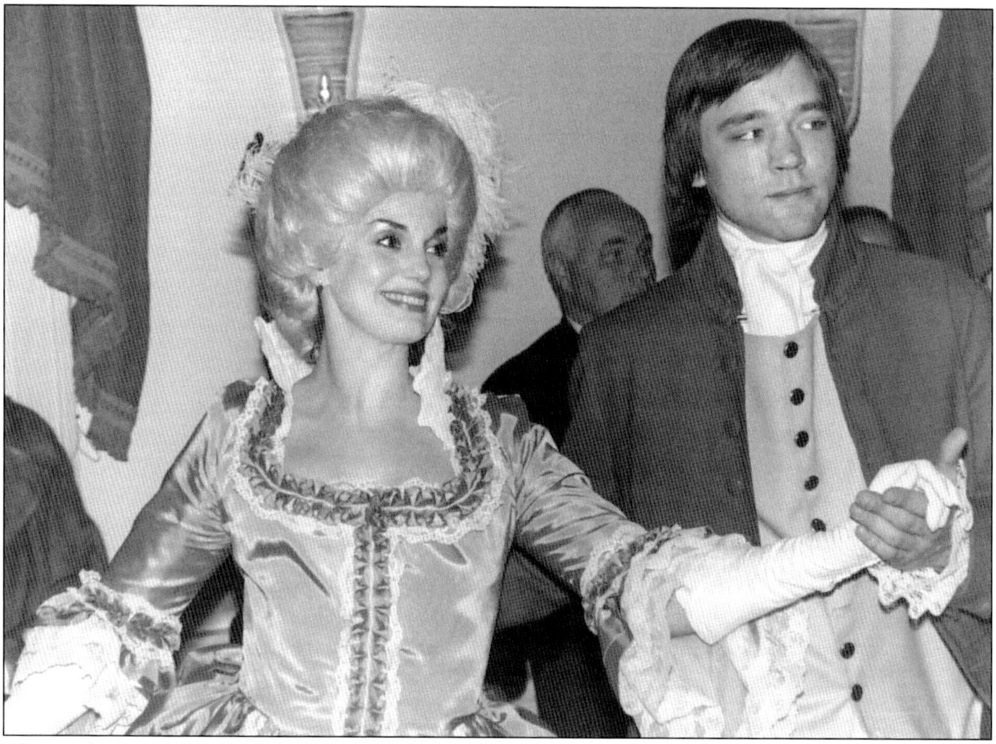

The tradition of the Birthnight Ball at Gadsby's Tavern, begun by John Wise and made famous by John Gadsby, was revived for the 1976 bicentennial. The format was expanded to include a formal banquet at a nearby hotel. After dinner, guests progressed to Gadsby's Tavern for the ball. In 1985, a member of the Colonial Cotillion performance dance group, Kerry DeHaven, was escorted to the floor for a dance.

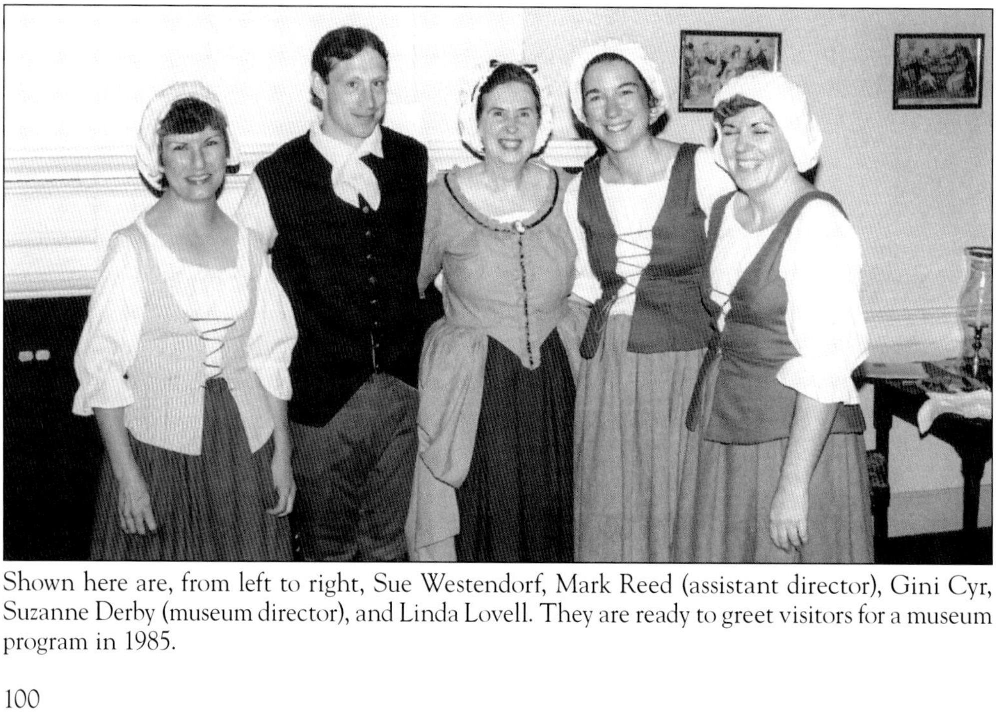

Shown here are, from left to right, Sue Westendorf, Mark Reed (assistant director), Gini Cyr, Suzanne Derby (museum director), and Linda Lovell. They are ready to greet visitors for a museum program in 1985.

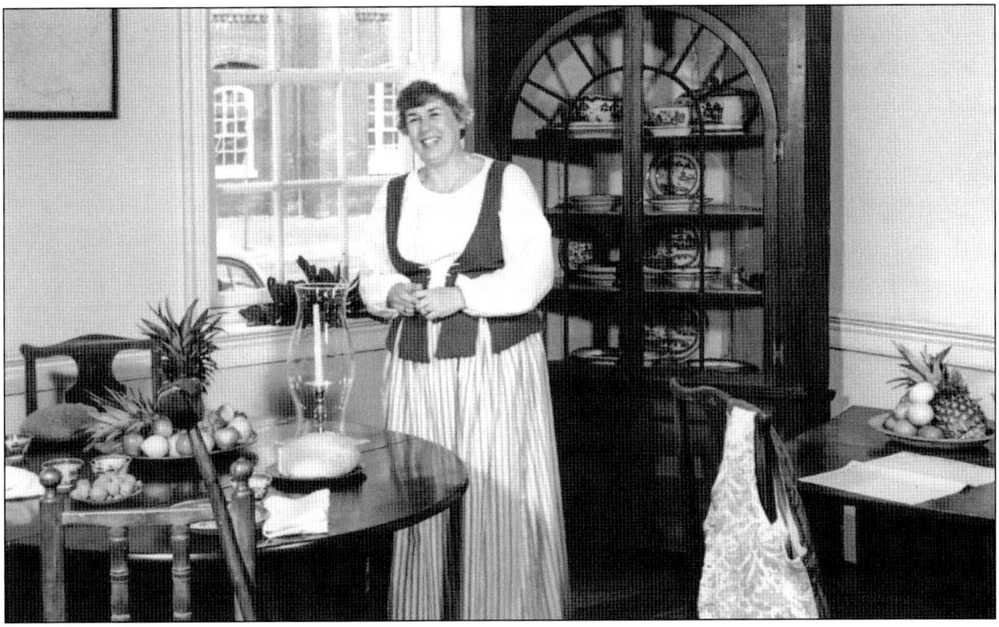

Connie Nelson, museum volunteer, gave a tour to the public as part of the annual Historic Alexandria Candlelight Tour program. The Taproom was decorated for the holidays with fresh greens and Colonial Revival fruit displays, inspired by the decorations of early-20th-century Colonial Williamsburg.

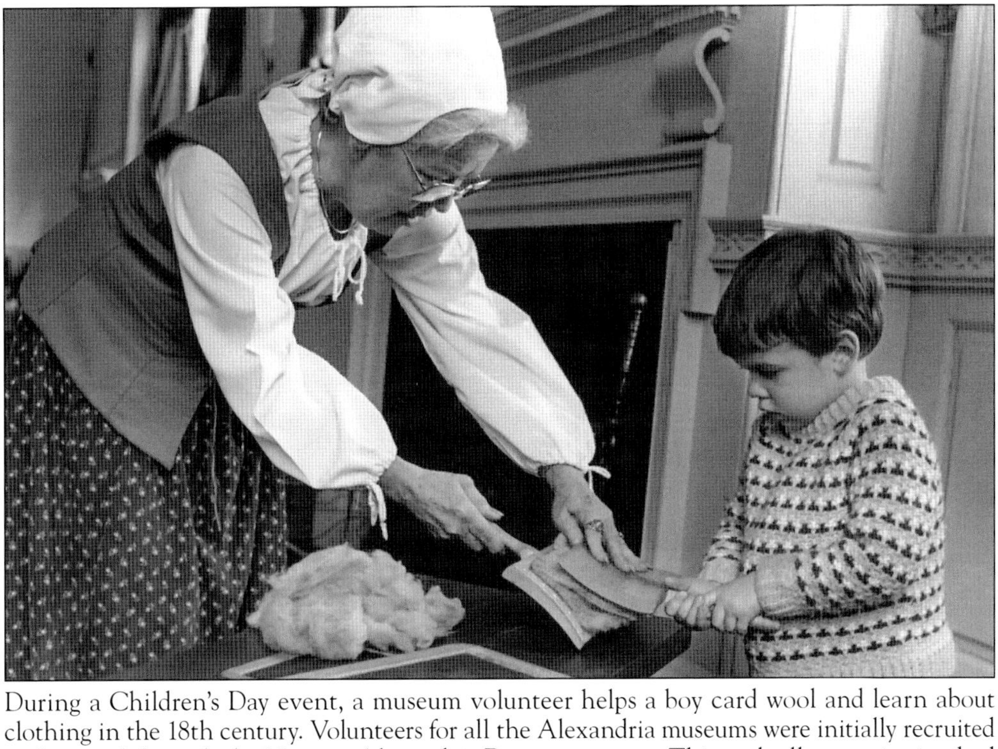

During a Children's Day event, a museum volunteer helps a boy card wool and learn about clothing in the 18th century. Volunteers for all the Alexandria museums were initially recruited and trained through the Historic Alexandria Docent program. This umbrella organization had a separate board and offered volunteers various social and educational opportunities.

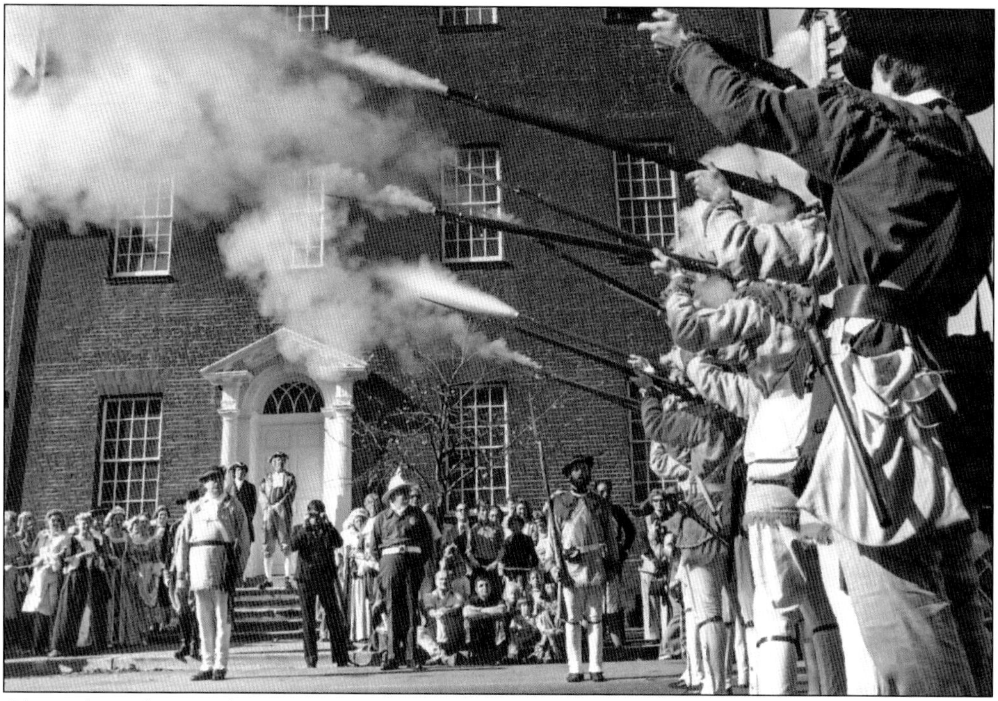

Alexandria is host to three parades each year, and Gadsby's Tavern Museum is often the backdrop for the reviewing stand and mini-reenactments. Residents and visitors to Alexandria enjoy the annual George Washington Birthday Celebration Parade in February, the St. Patrick's Day Parade in March, and the Scottish Christmas Walk in December.

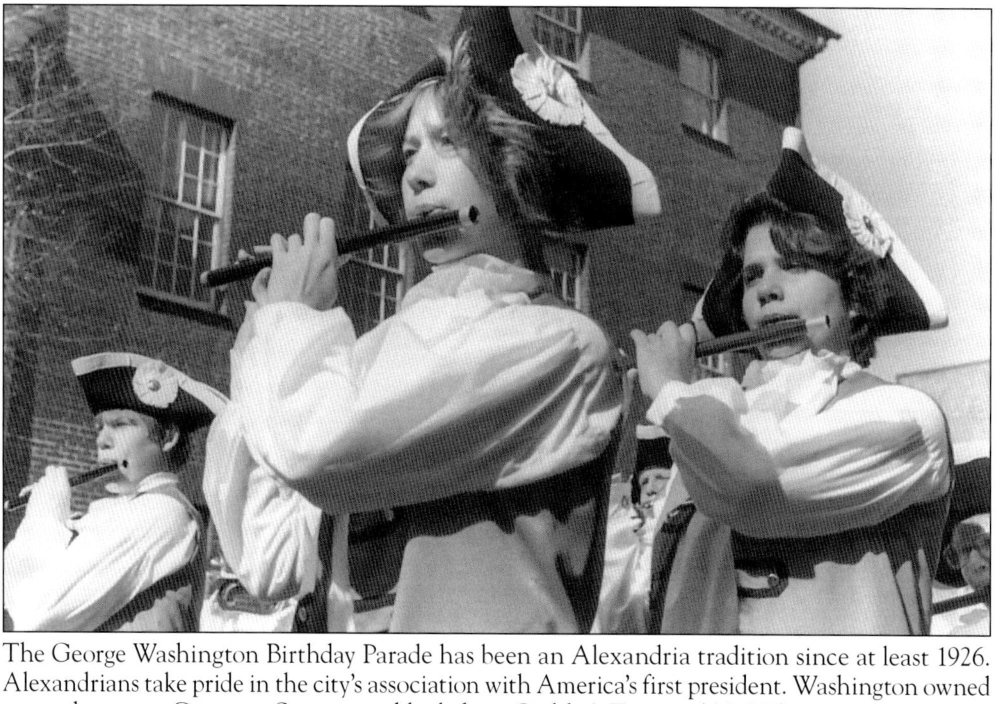

The George Washington Birthday Parade has been an Alexandria tradition since at least 1926. Alexandrians take pride in the city's association with America's first president. Washington owned a townhouse on Cameron Street, one block from Gadsby's Tavern. (ALSC.)

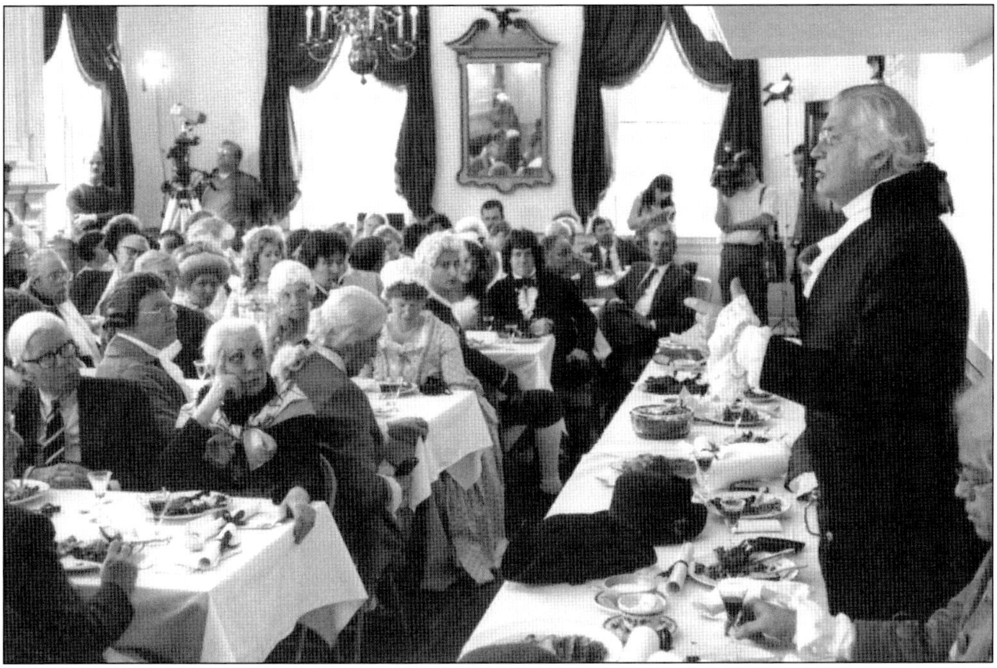

On April 16, 1789, newly elected president George Washington addressed a group of Alexandria citizens before leaving Virginia for New York to be sworn in as America's first president. This event was commemorated with a special banquet in the ballroom of Gadsby's Tavern Museum in 1989. The American Legion had re-created this event in 1939, on the 150th anniversary. Here, William Somerfield portrays Washington.

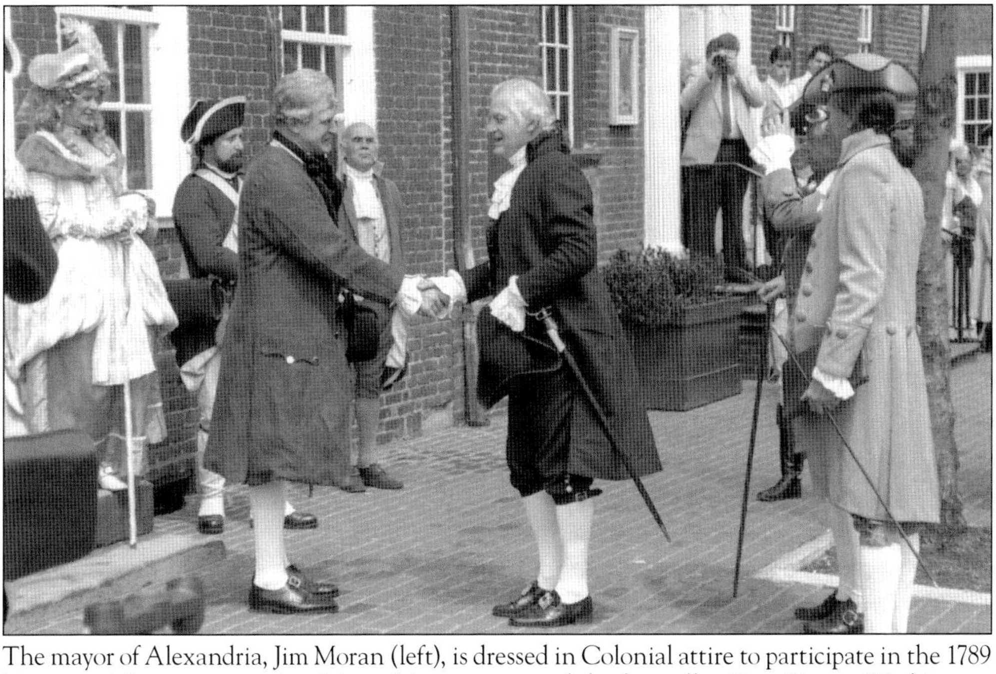

The mayor of Alexandria, Jim Moran (left), is dressed in Colonial attire to participate in the 1789 bicentennial commemoration. Mayor Moran reenacted the farewell to Pres. George Washington outside of Gadsby's Tavern as part of the historic send-off to New York.

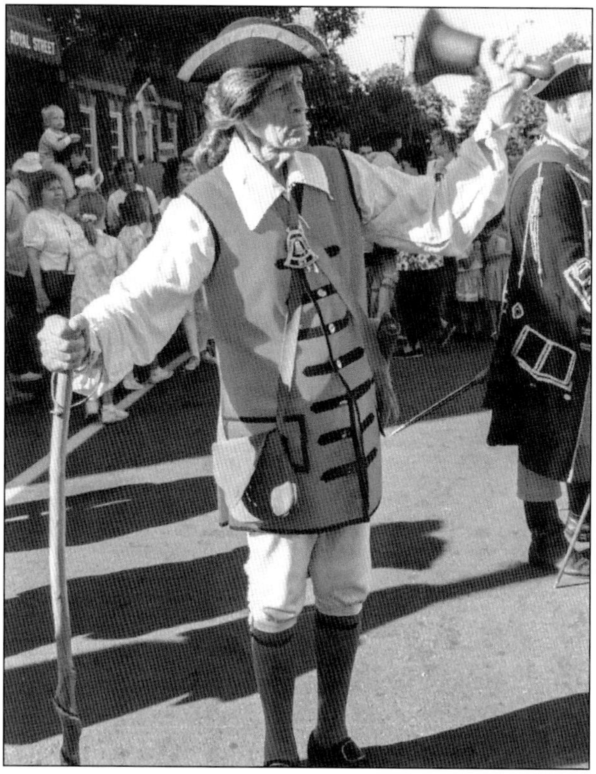

Frank Slate was Alexandria's first modern town crier. He marched in parades, made public announcements for a variety of events and organizations, and competed in both national and international "crying" competitions.

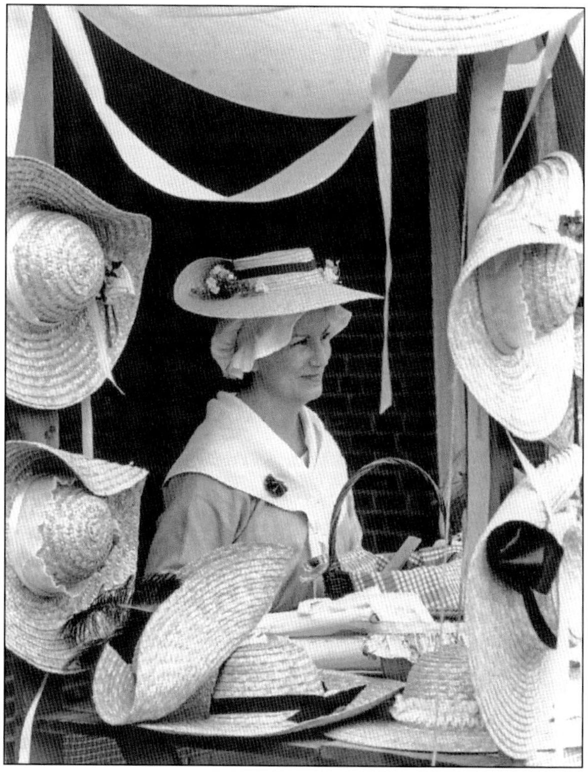

The museum staff re-created an 18th-century street fair in front of the taverns and on Market Square for 10 years. As part of the fair, visitors enjoyed a variety of period vendors and activities. Museum volunteer Sue Westendorf, portraying a milliner, demonstrates fashionable trimmings for hats.

As part of the 18th-century street fair, townspeople were called to "muster." Steve Diatz (left), Tad Miller (right), and other volunteers demonstrate the process of loading a musket for the public.

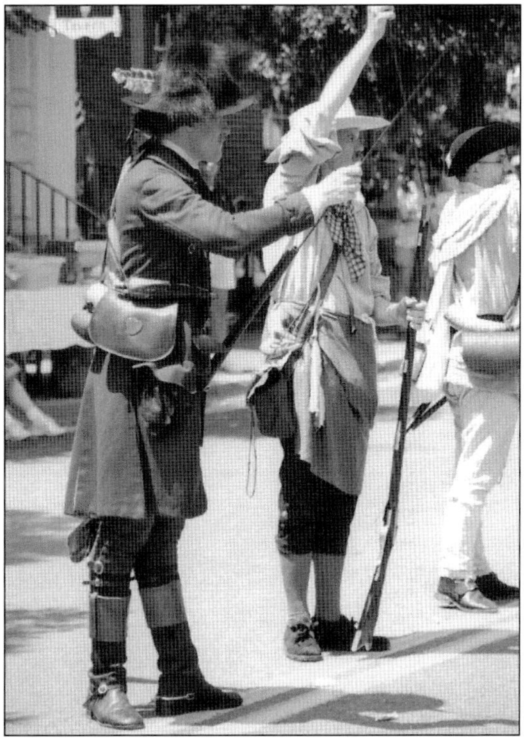

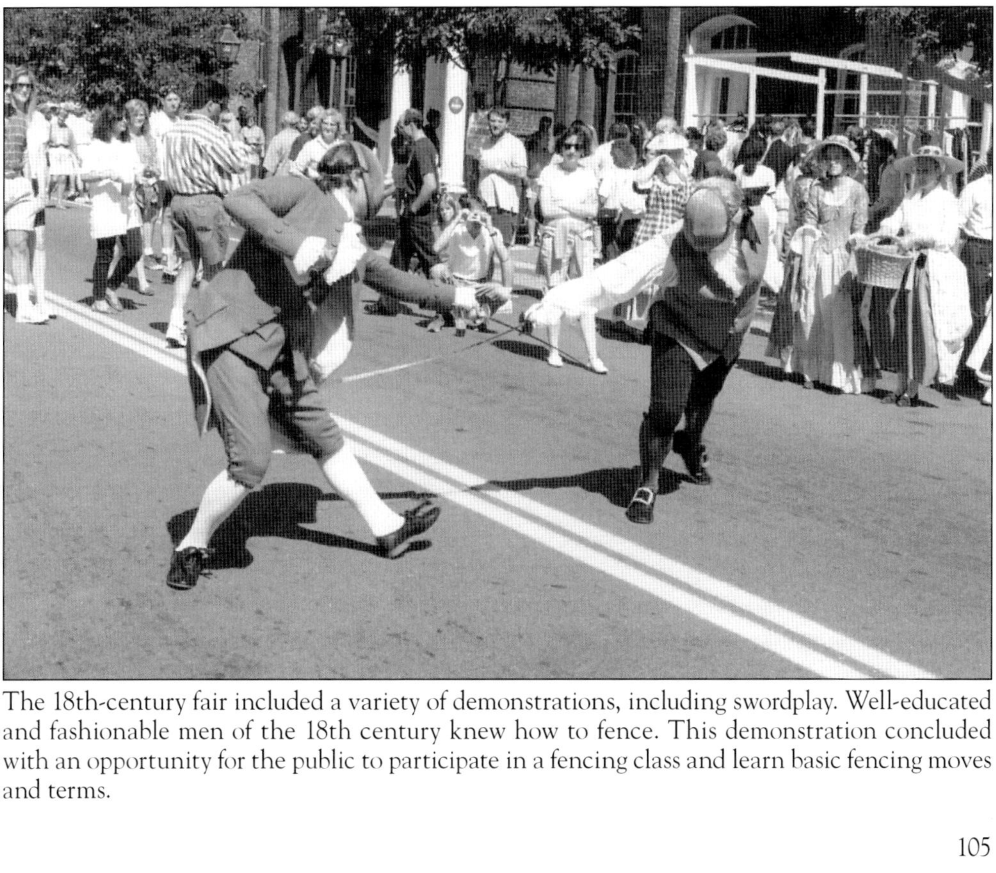

The 18th-century fair included a variety of demonstrations, including swordplay. Well-educated and fashionable men of the 18th century knew how to fence. This demonstration concluded with an opportunity for the public to participate in a fencing class and learn basic fencing moves and terms.

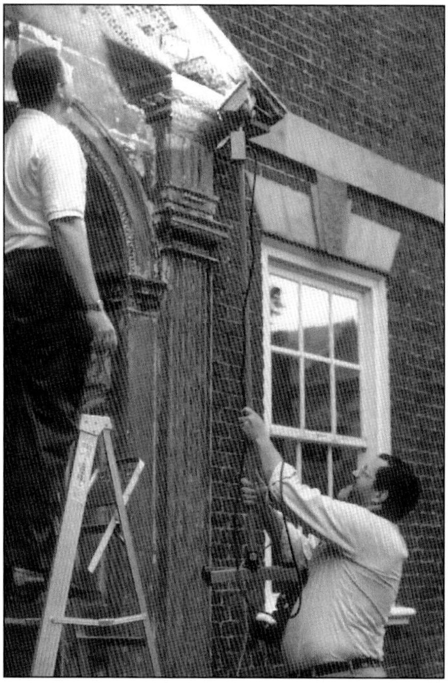

Restoration and research about the building's history and construction continued. In 1994, assistant director Jim Mackay (left) and preservation architect C. Richard Bierce (right) investigated the construction and stability of the 1770 tavern doorway. Layers of paint were carefully removed to reveal original details that had been obscured over time by repainting.

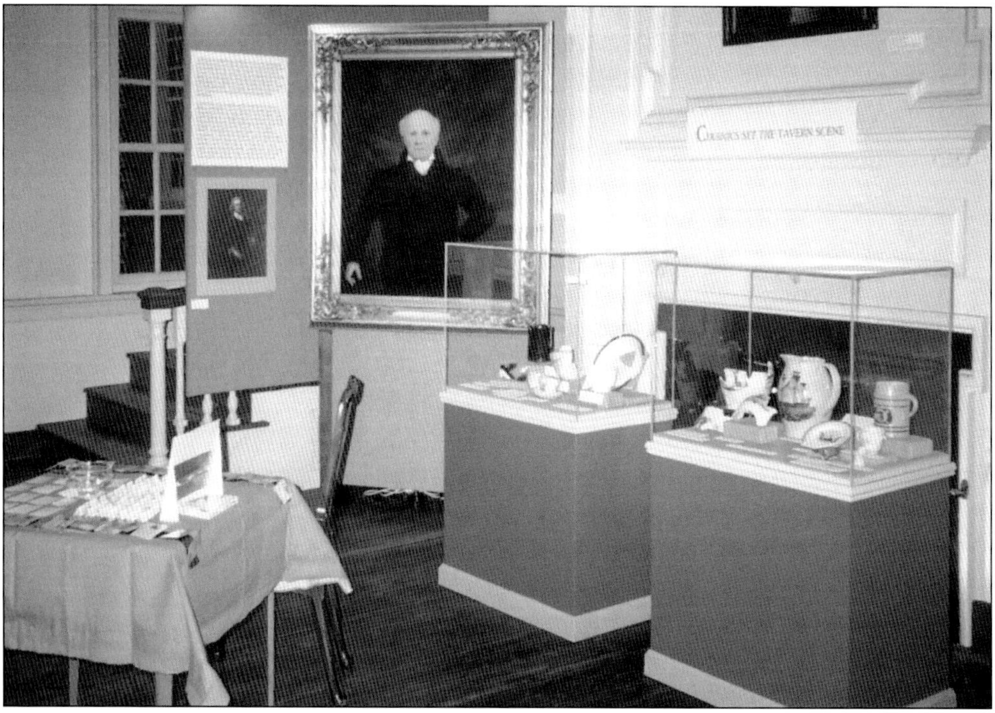

The museum staff, with the assistance of dedicated volunteers, created the Tavern Ceramics Research Project. This project involved researching ceramic fragments excavated from the tavern courtyard and other nearby Alexandria tavern sites that were uncovered as part of the urban renewal effort. Their work in cataloging the types of tavern ceramic wares culminated in the exhibition Archaeology Sets the Tavern Table as well as a publication.

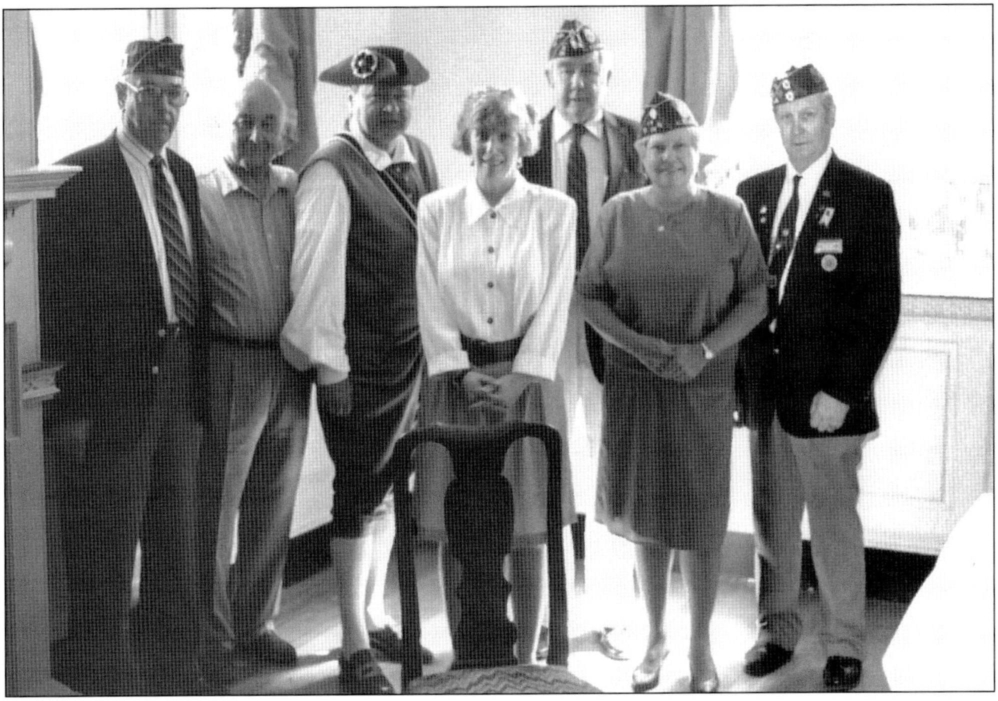

Continuing their support of Gadsby's Tavern Museum, members of American Legion Post 24 donated a c. 1775 side chair to the museum in 1994. Pictured here are, from left to right, H. Warden Foley, William G. McNamara, Edward Michaels, Monta Lee Dakin (museum director), W. Calvin Reid, Eleanor Osborne, and Jim Stevenson.

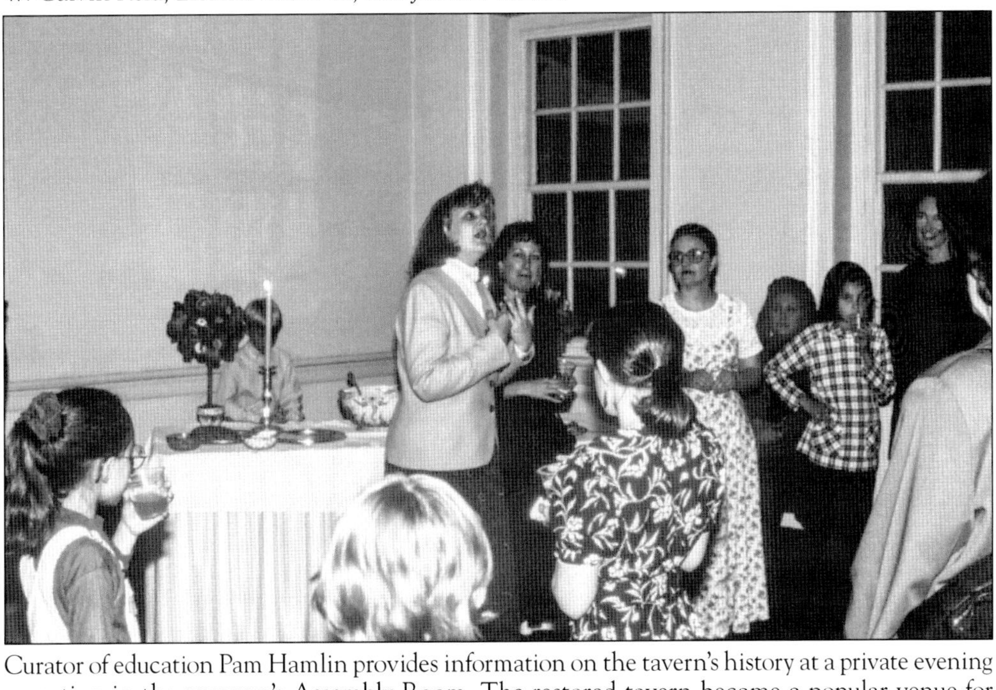

Curator of education Pam Hamlin provides information on the tavern's history at a private evening reception in the museum's Assembly Room. The restored tavern became a popular venue for wedding receptions, corporate events, and private parties.

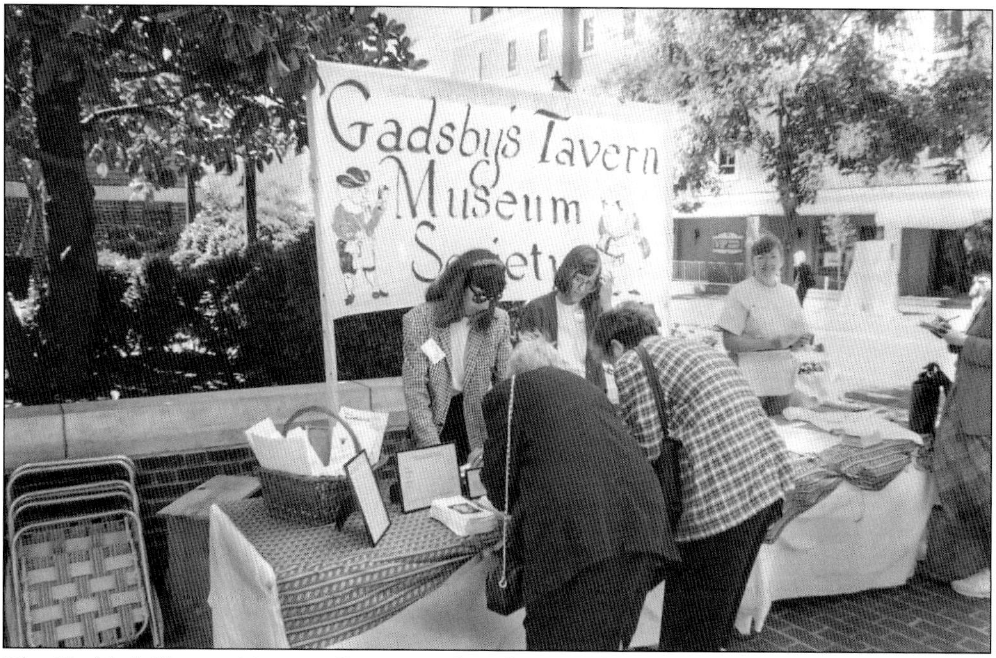

The Gadsby's Tavern Museum Society, referred to as "the Society," was founded in 1992 to support the museum through advocacy and fundraising. Here, board members Janet Hawkins (left), Sue Walker (center), and Kim Sheridan (right) sign up new members at an outreach event on Market Square.

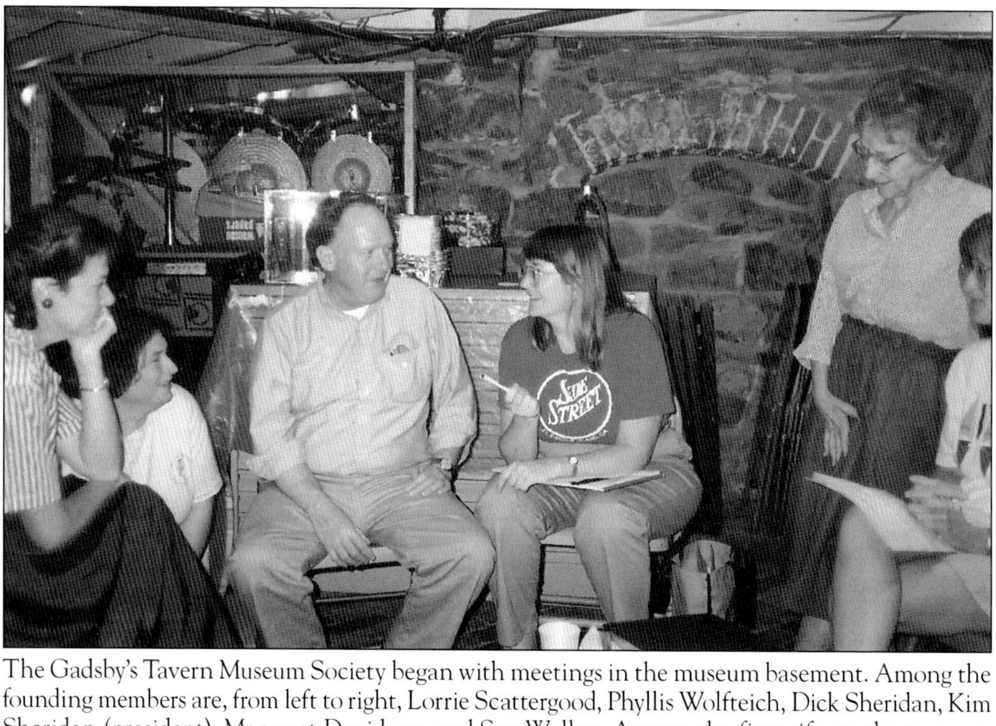

The Gadsby's Tavern Museum Society began with meetings in the museum basement. Among the founding members are, from left to right, Lorrie Scattergood, Phyllis Wolfteich, Dick Sheridan, Kim Sheridan (president), Margaret Davidson, and Sue Walker. Among the first gifts to the museum were a reproduction blanket for the dormer bedchamber and an iron trivet for the Taproom.

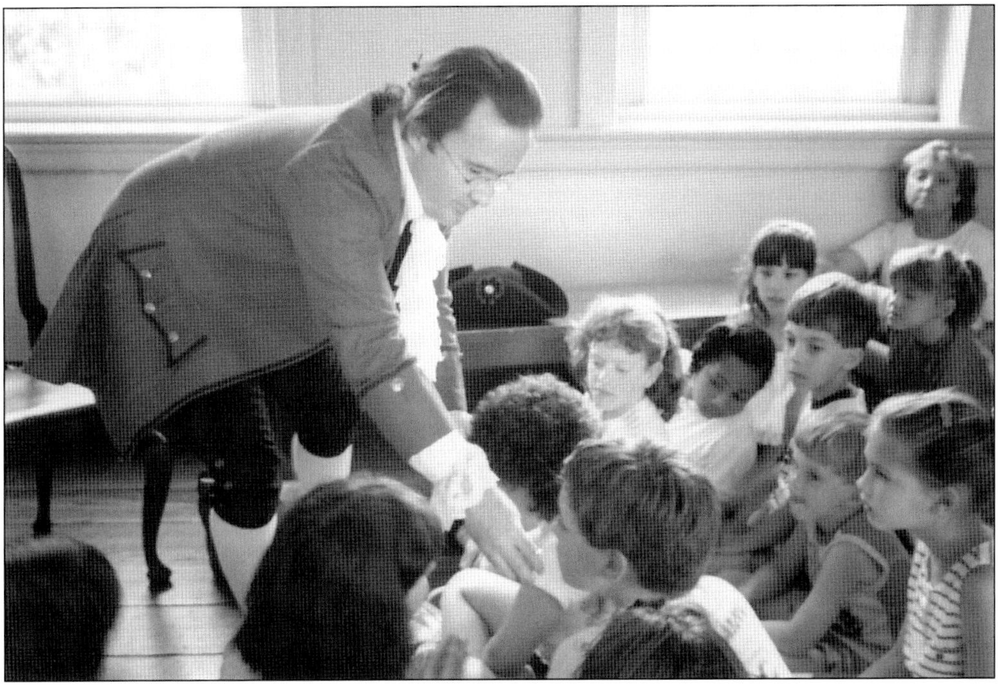

Volunteer Don McAndrews portrays Alexandria physician Dr. James Craik at the museum's Children's Day event. In the 18th century, itinerant merchants, entertainers, and dentists advertised their services and set up shop in the tavern's Assembly Room.

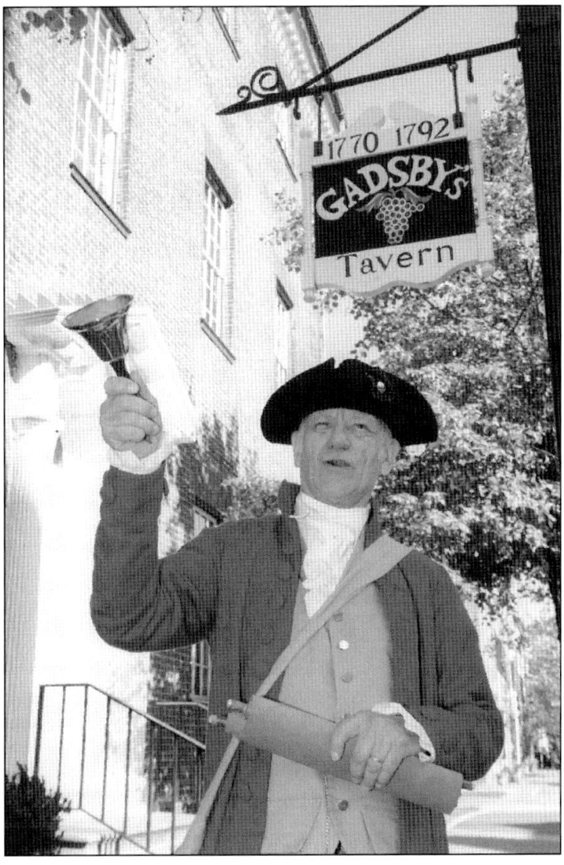

John Yagerline was selected as Alexandria's town crier in October 1998. The application process asked, "Can you shout but still be understood clearly? Do you have a sense of humor that can stand up to the extremes of cold and heat? Are you available for most city-wide commemorative events?" Yagerline added his own historical touch to his "cries" at public events.

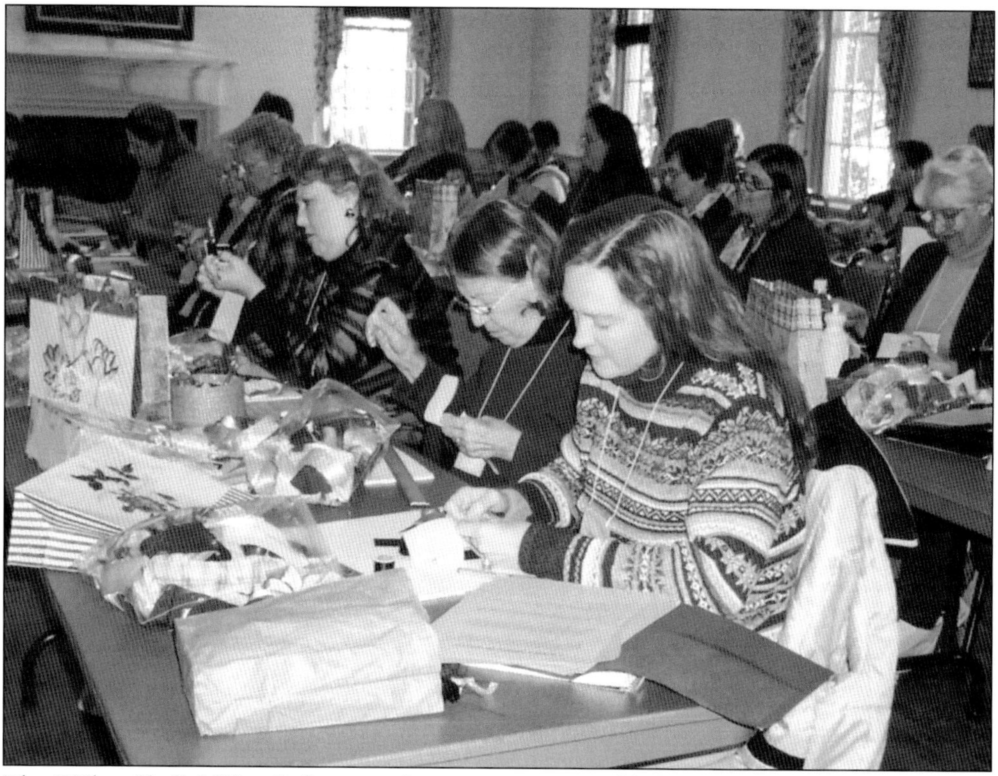

The "What Shall I Wear?" Costume Symposium was established in collaboration with Sally Queen and Associates to help the museum staff and event participants learn more about late-18th- and early-19th-century clothing. The annual symposium topics ranged from "Dressing the First Presidents" to "Dressing for a Ball." A variety of hands-on workshops, examination of original clothing items, and lectures from the top costume scholars were offered.

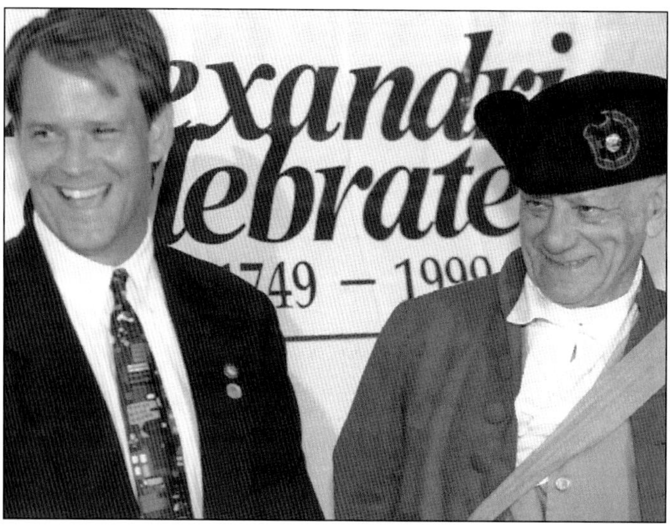

Mayor Kerry Donley (left) and town crier John Yagerline (right) ring in the 250th anniversary of the founding of Alexandria at a press conference at Gadsby's Tavern Museum. The City of Alexandria established an official 250th Anniversary Commission to create public events to commemorate the city's founding in 1749. Events ranged from outdoor concerts to an 18th-century fair to a fishing contest.

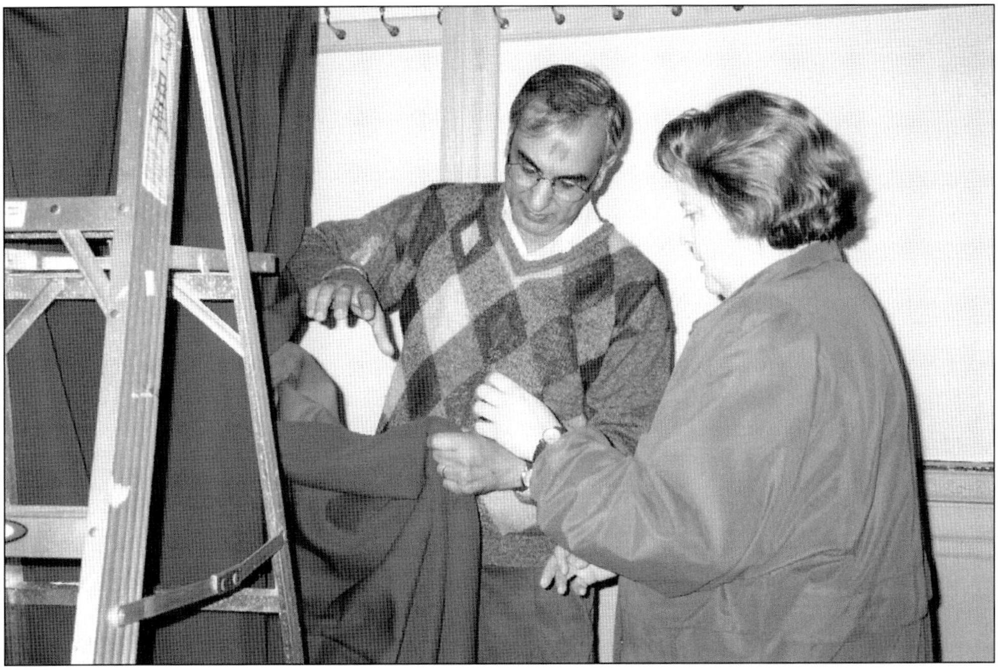

New, historically accurate curtains were designed by Gretchen Bulova, museum director, and Ellen Donald, decorative arts consultant. The wool fabric was woven on 18th-century looms by Context Weavers in England. Leroy Graves hand-crafted 21 tassels. The curtains were constructed by Market Place Interiors, under the direction of Aku Merali. Here, Merali (left) works with Donald (right) on the final construction details.

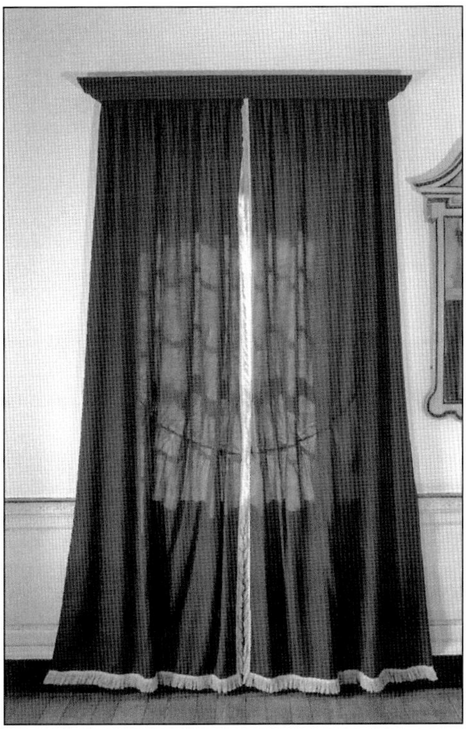

The new curtains for the Ballroom were thoroughly researched, designed, and constructed with the generous financial support of the Gadsby's Tavern Museum Society. The Society spent three years raising funds for this project with the campaign "It's Curtains for Gadsby's!" This drive included collecting loose change in the Ballroom, in a container labeled "coppers for curtains," as well as events such as a golf tournament and an evening boat cruise.

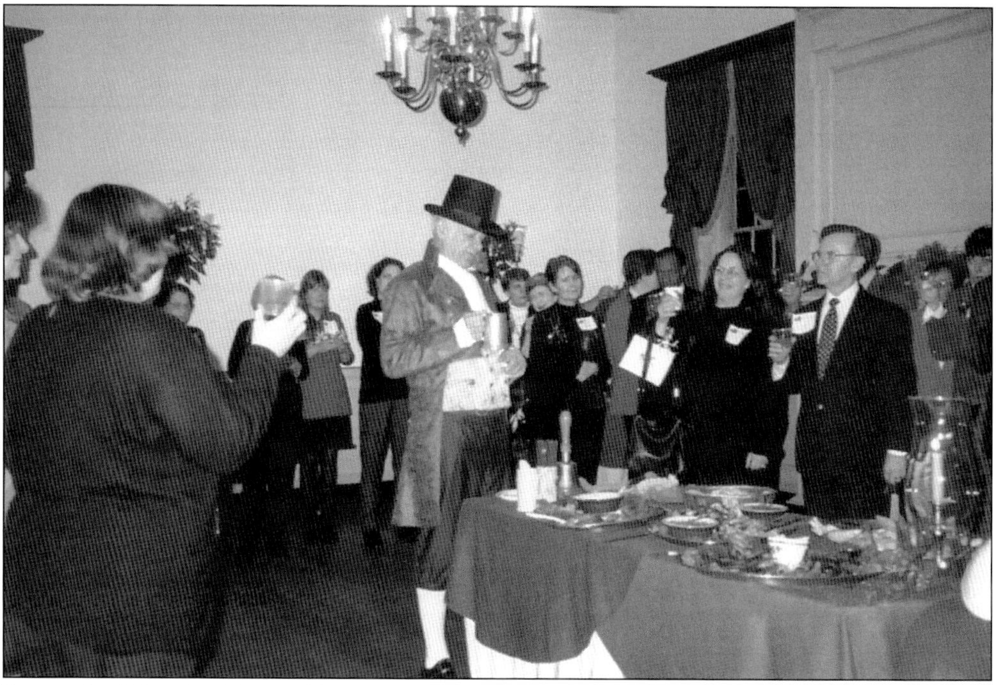

The staff of Gadsby's Tavern Museum continues to interpret the tavern and re-create historical events and activities into the 21st century, with the invaluable assistance of more than 150 dedicated volunteers. Here, town crier John Yagerline offers a toast to the museum's generous and talented volunteers at the 1999 holiday party.

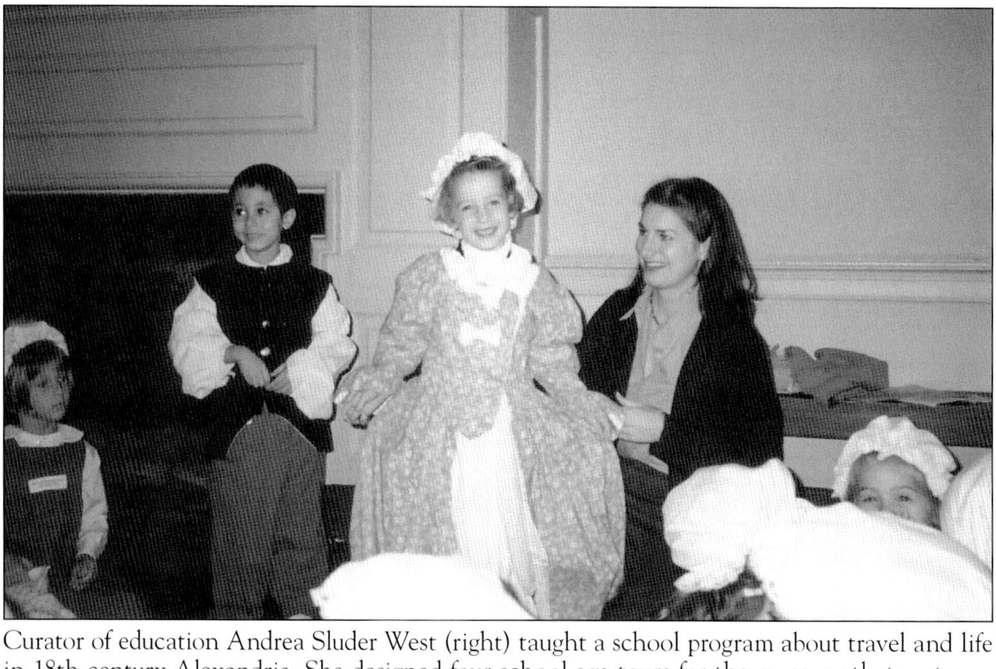

Curator of education Andrea Sluder West (right) taught a school program about travel and life in 18th-century Alexandria. She designed four school-age tours for the museum that met new state and local school curriculum requirements and created an outreach kit, Tavern in a Trunk, that can be rented and shipped to any school in the United States.

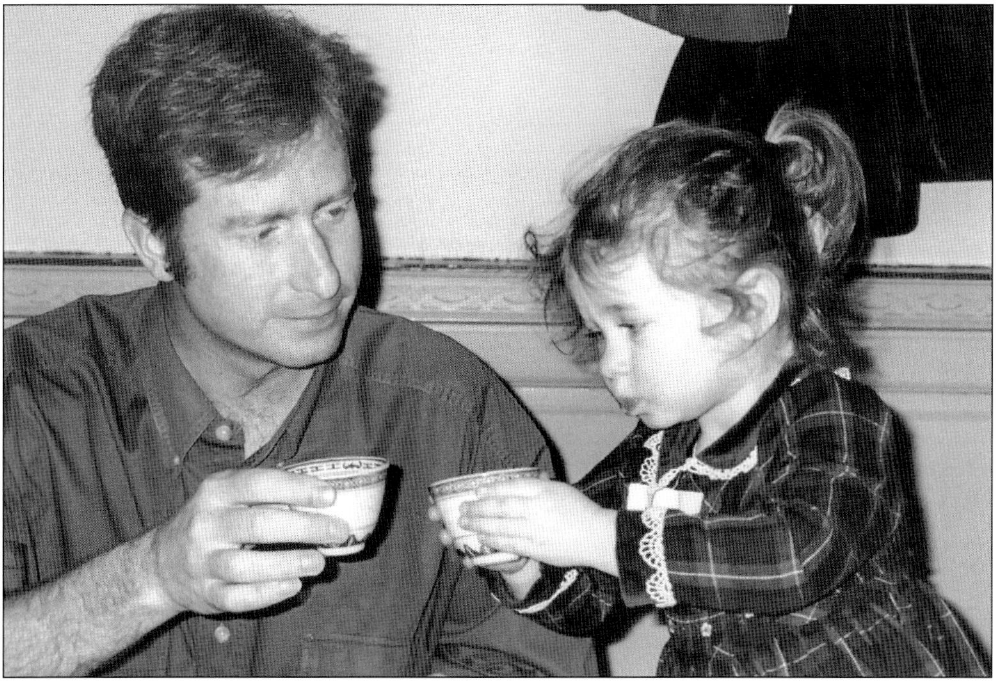

Father and daughter David and Josette Bulova enjoy taking tea as part of the annual February "Tea with Martha Washington" program. As part of the special event, participants were taught the etiquette and customs of tea drinking by Mrs. Washington while enjoying 18th-century-inspired foods.

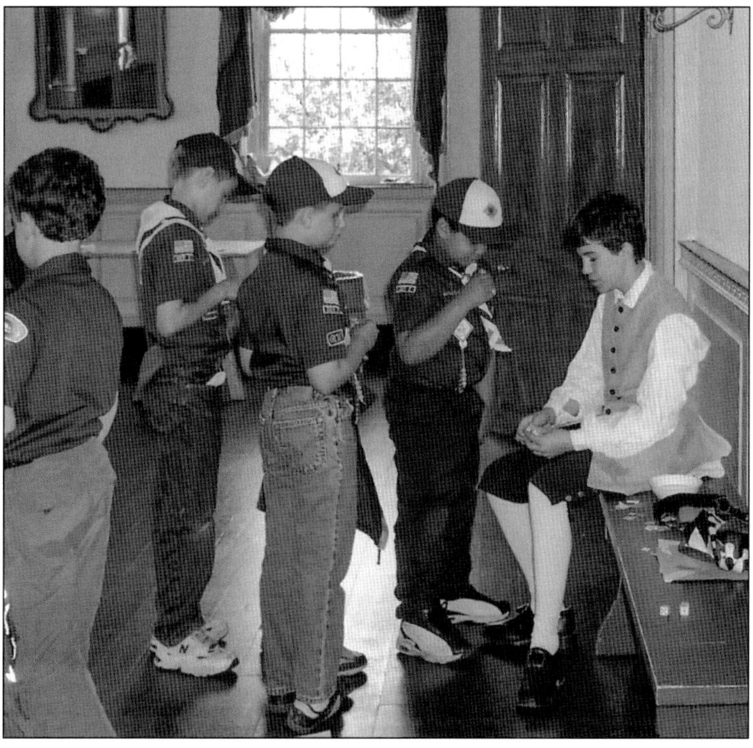

Boy Scouts and Cub Scouts can earn badges and special museum patches through a variety of educational museum programs, including fencing demonstrations, knot-tying, and 18th-century games. Here, museum volunteer Philippe Halbert assists a Bear Den with seafaring activities.

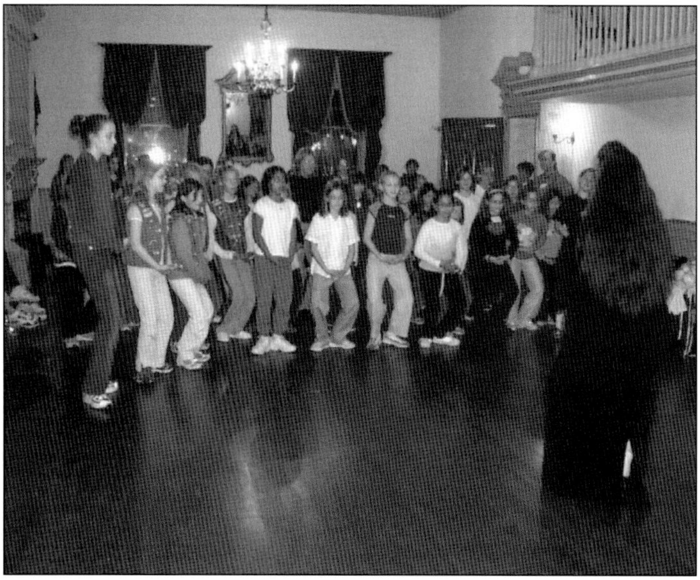

A Girl Scout Overnight program created in 1999 offers the opportunity for young girls to participate in a variety of educational activities and to spend the night at the museum. As part of the Girl Scout Overnight, scouts learn 18th-century dancing and deportment. Here, Girl Scouts are taught "courtesies" by dance mistress Pat Sowers. At the conclusion of the evening, the girls slept on the Ballroom floor.

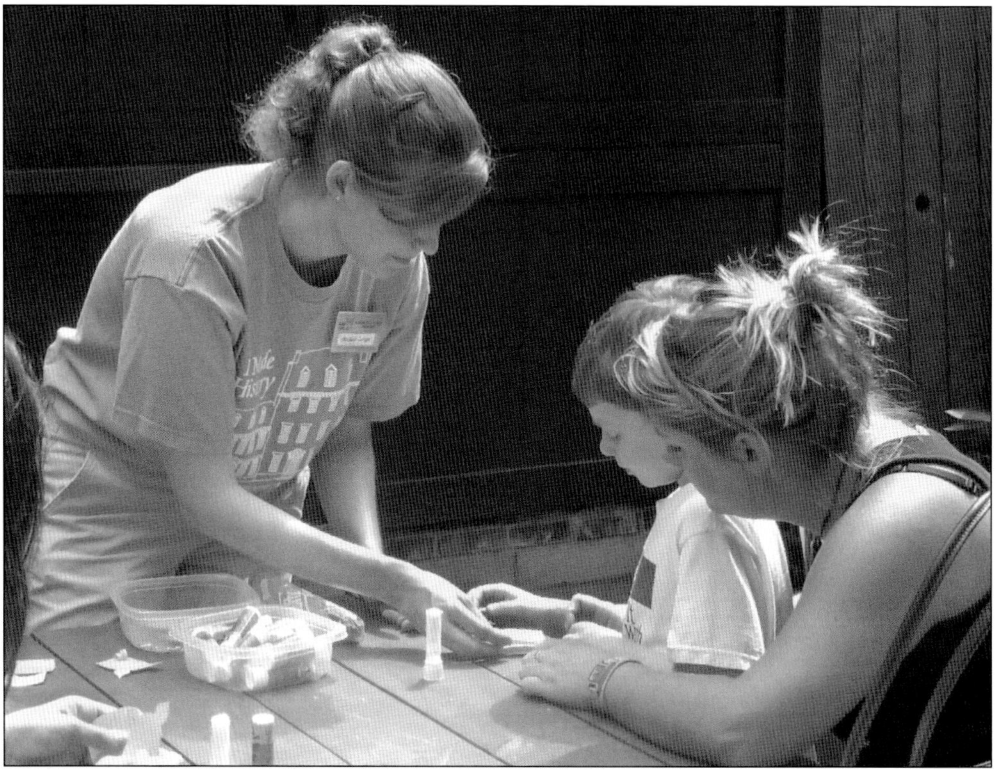

Michele Longo (left), curator of education, demonstrates a craft activity as part of Children's Day, a special event that welcomes daycares and families to the museum in the summer. The museum offers educational activities for all ages, including special programs for toddlers, elementary school students, day camps, and home-school families. Engaging children through hands-on activities helps them connect with and understand the tavern's story.

Museum volunteer Millie Nash helps to decorate the museum Ballroom for the annual holiday program, Historic Alexandria Candlelight Tour. At this event, begun in 1982, visitors tour Gadsby's Tavern Museum, Carlyle House, and the Lee-Fendall House illuminated by candlelight to learn about holiday customs in the 18th and 19th centuries. The museums are decorated for the season, and visitors are treated to special tours, refreshments, music, and dancing.

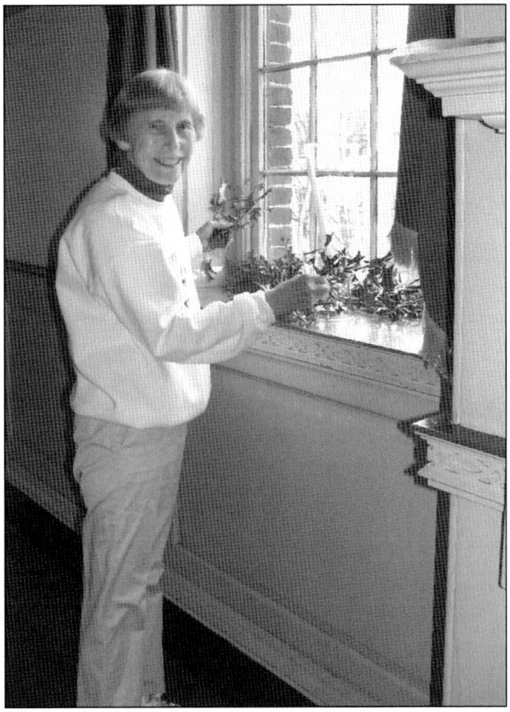

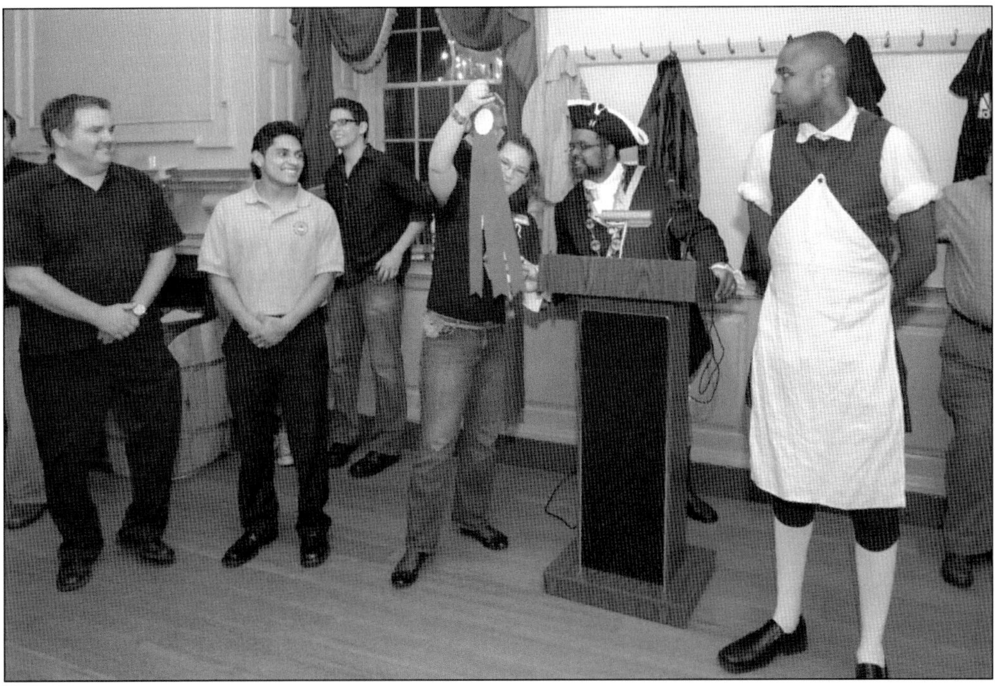

The Rum Punch Challenge is a popular annual museum fundraising event started in 2004. The event involves tasting and voting for 18th-century-style punch recipes created by participating restaurants and caterers. Here, the second-place ribbon is awarded to Alan White (right) with Gadsby's Tavern Restaurant. First place was taken by Jeffrey Allen (left) with Bittersweet Catering-Café-Bakery. Town crier Ben Fiore-Walker (second from right) announces the winners.

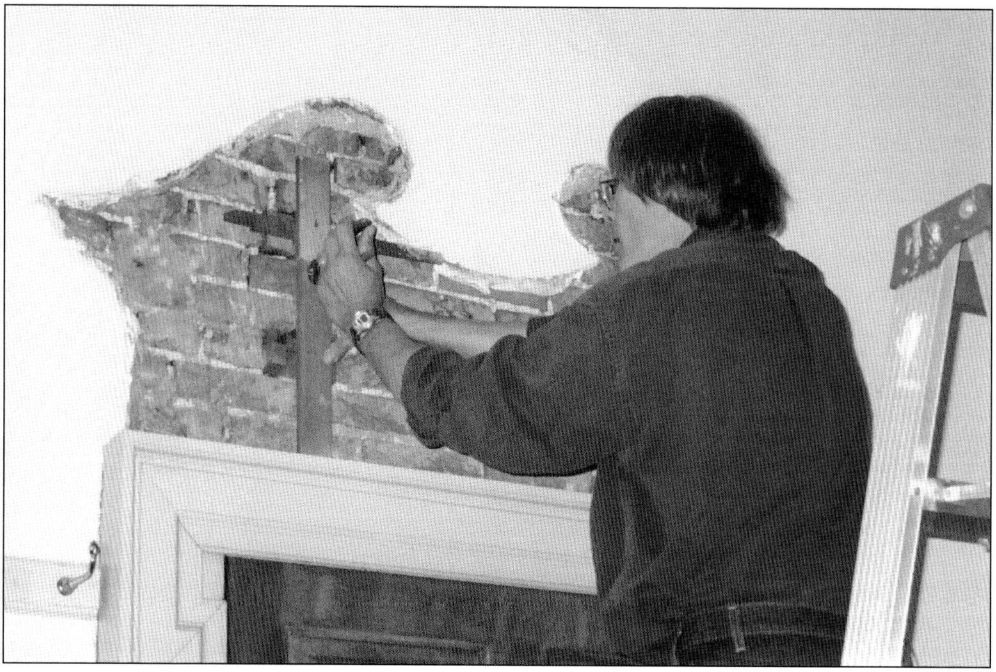

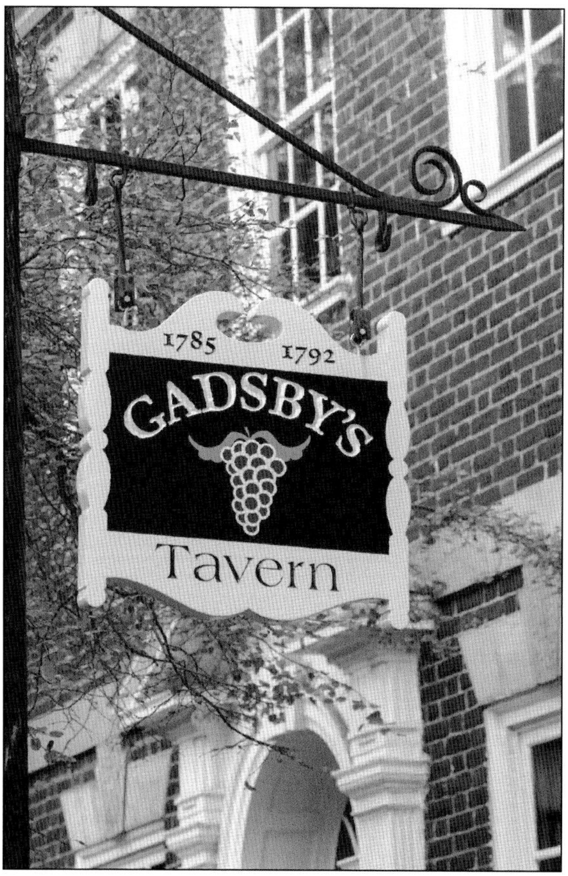

The maintenance and historic preservation of the museum is an ongoing process. Here, historic woodwork expert Christopher Owens removes the 1940s scroll pediment above the Ballroom door to replace shrunken nailing blocks. The exposed surface revealed that, originally, there was a smaller, less-ornate pediment. The woodwork for this room was reproduced from the panels purchased by the Metropolitan Museum of Art in 1917.

In 2001, the museum staff undertook a research project reviewing archival evidence, paint analysis, and structural assessments. Staff concluded that the smaller tavern, first thought to have been the 1752 Mason's Ordinary and then the c. 1770 tavern operated by Mary Hawkins, was actually constructed by John Wise in 1785. The museum staff modified the interpretation, and the iconic tavern sign was changed from 1770 to 1785.

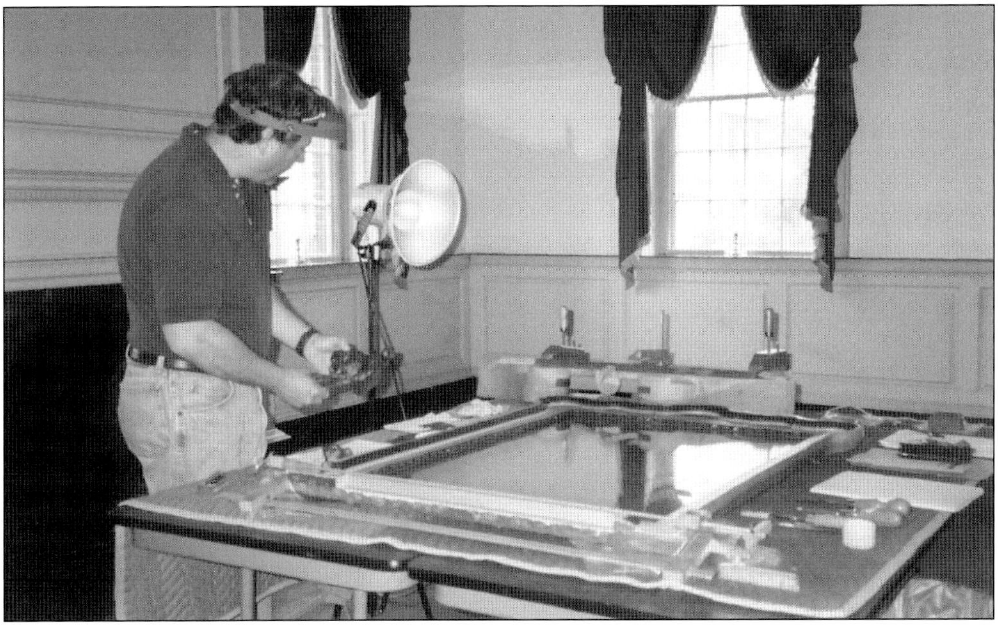

Furniture conservator Ron Blank (above) examines the mirror installed in the Ballroom in 1940. John Gadsby's 1802 inventory of the City Tavern and Hotel recorded two looking glasses valued at $60 in the Ballroom. In 2010, the museum staff commissioned master cabinetmaker Mack Headley and conservator Chris Swan, both from Colonial Williamsburg, to duplicate the existing 18th-century mirror. Today, two matching mirrors hang in the Gadsby's Tavern Ballroom.

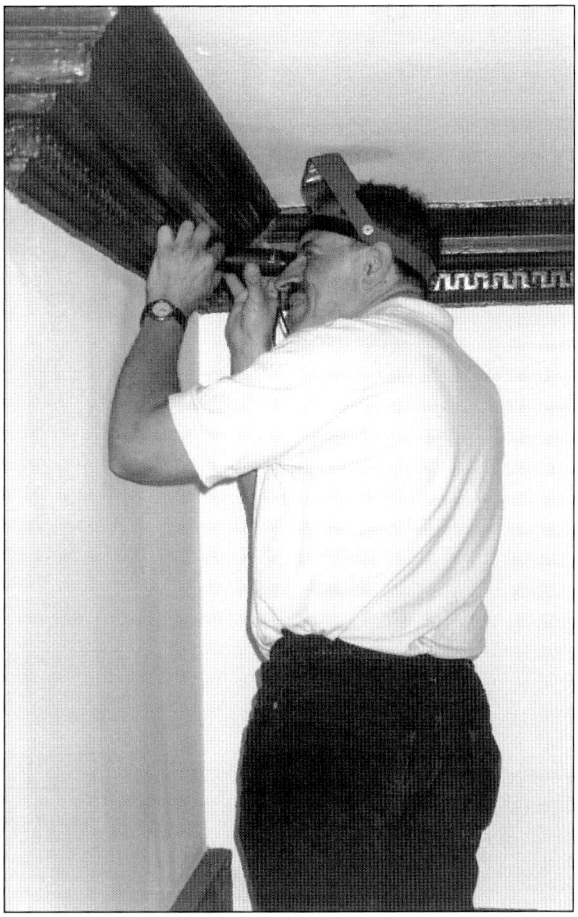

To confirm the original construction date of John Wise's City Tavern building, Matthew Mosca examines paint layers on an original section of woodwork. Along with dendrochronology of original attic beams and a thorough examination of extant archival information, staff confirmed that the building was constructed in 1792 and opened for business in 1793.

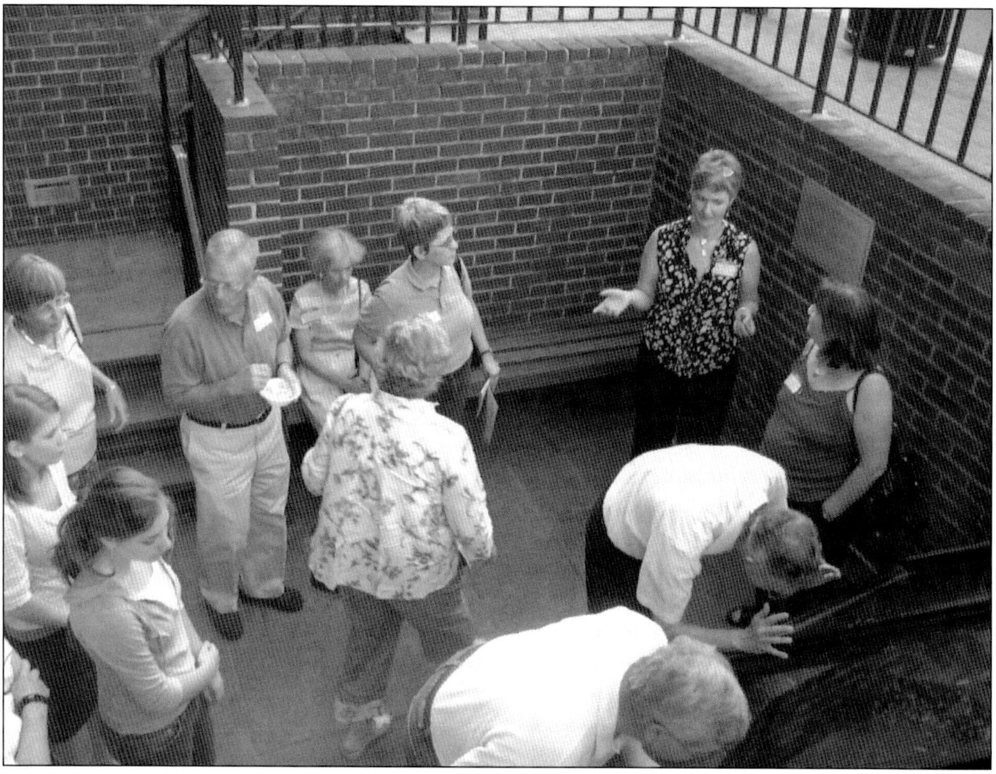

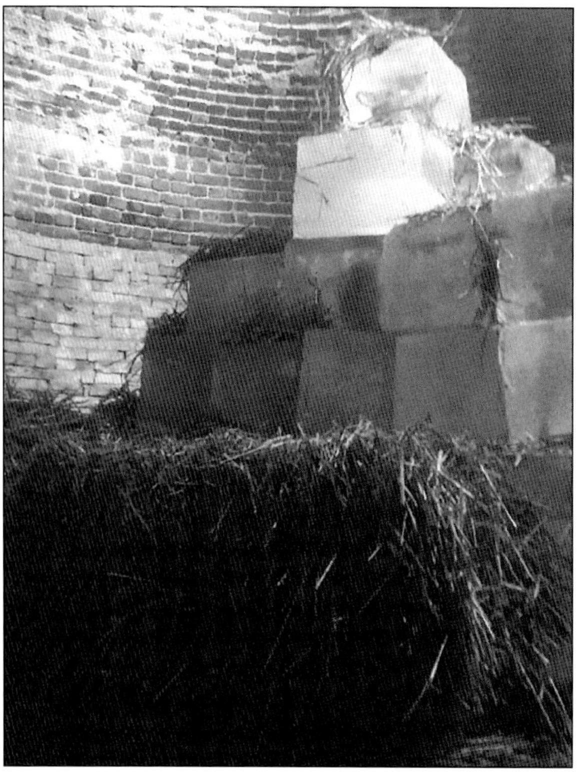

Anne Bernat (top right), the 2008 president of the Gadsby's Tavern Museum Society, shares plans to restore and renovate the historic ice well with members of the Society. Members peered through the viewing glass in an effort to see the ice well interior. The restoration plans focused on improving the visitor experience by raising the level of the viewing deck, installing nonreflective glass, and adding interpretive signage.

As part of a fundraising event, the ice well was partially filled with modern-size blocks of ice. In the 18th century, ice was cut from frozen rivers and stored in this subterranean well. Packed in a solid mass, it was then covered in straw. A steady supply of ice was an amenity that set Gadsby and the City Tavern and Hotel apart from competitors.

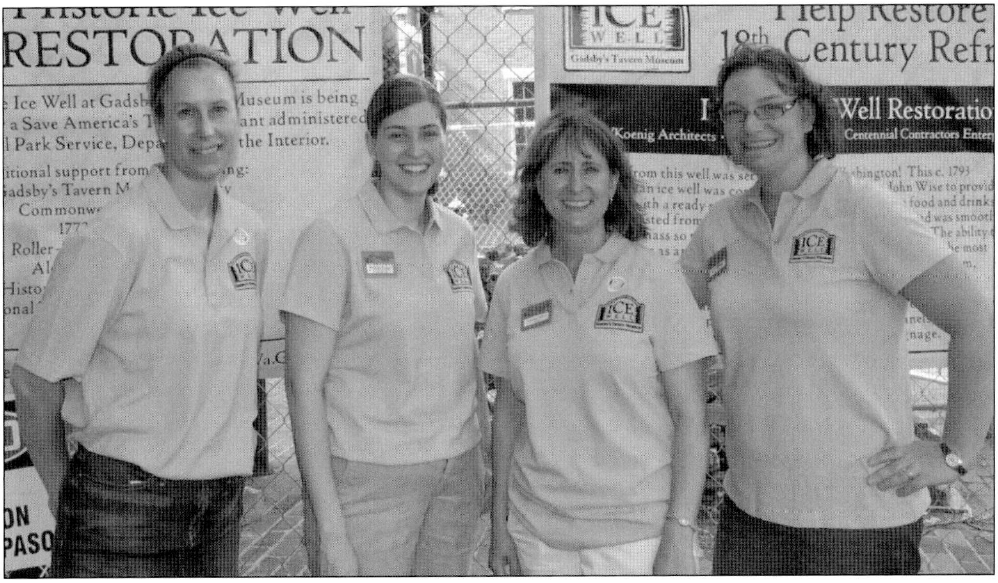

The staff of Gadsby's Tavern Museum are, from left to right, Callie Stapp (curator of collections), Michele Longo (curator of education), Gretchen Bulova (museum director), and Liz Williams (assistant director). They pose at the ground-breaking ceremony of the ice well restoration in August 2012. The demolition of the 1970s features, improvement to drainage, construction of steps and a new viewing deck, and installation of interpretive panels were planned to take one year to complete.

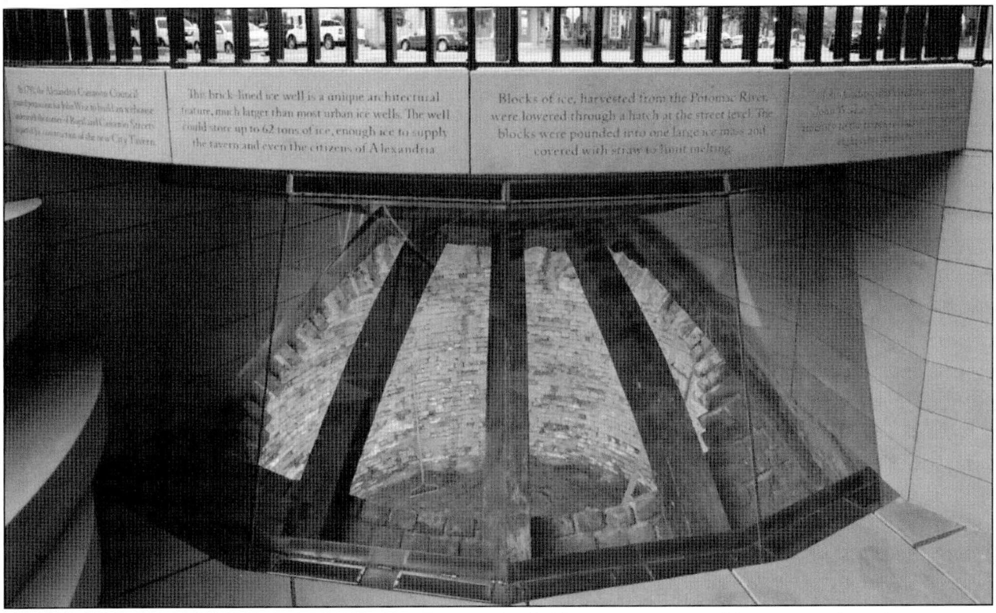

The ice well restoration was completed in August 2013. Now, visitors could see into the subterranean well and experience the unique historic feature. The new design by Bell Architects with Larson/Keonig Architects won three awards: 2013 American Institute of Architects (AIA) DC Special Citation in Historic Resources; 2014 Preservation Virginia's Outstanding Preservation Project, the Gabriella Page Preservation Award; and 2014 Virginia Society of the AIA (VSAIA) Historic Preservation Merit Award.

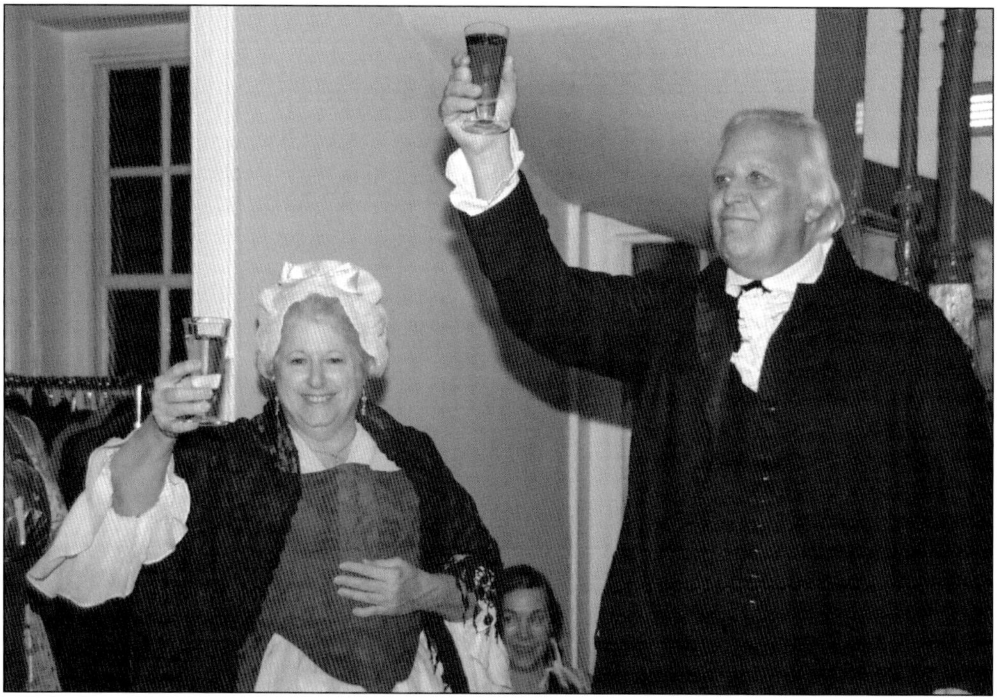

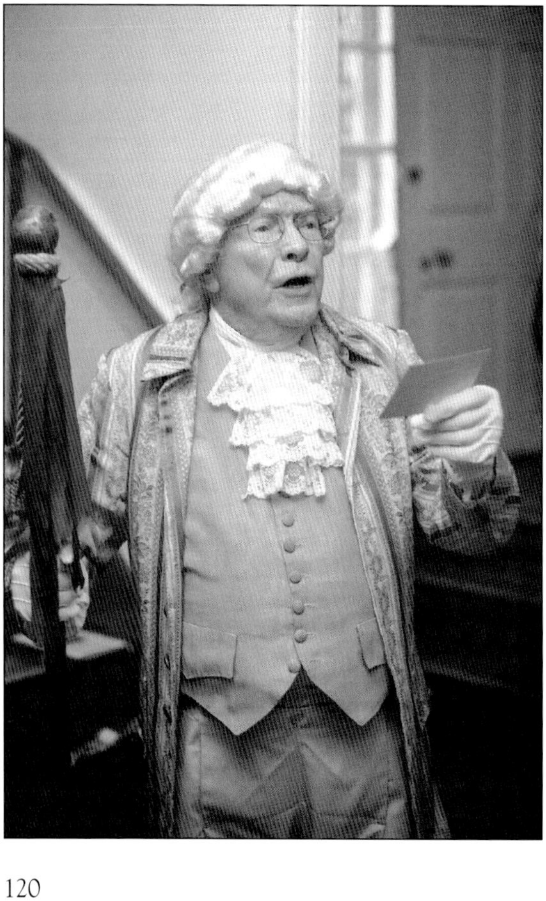

General and Mrs. Washington, portrayed by Don DeHaven and Kari LaBell Seidelman, were welcomed to the annual George Washington Birthnight Banquet and Ball with a toast in their honor. The Birthnight Ball, first held at the City Tavern by John Wise in 1793, was continued by John Gadsby, who personally hosted the Washingtons in 1798 and 1799. The museum continues to re-create the 1799 Birthnight Ball each year.

Guests were welcomed to the Birthnight Ball and formally announced to the assembled company by a major domo. Ernie Sult, the Birthnight Ball's major domo for more than 20 years, announced guests to the Little Theatre of Alexandria productions at Gadsby's Tavern in the 1950s.

Steve Diatz (left), portraying a member of the Jockey Club of Alexandria, invites Peter Ryan (right), portraying the mayor of Alexandria in 1799, John Dundas, to try a game of chance. While taking a break from dancing, Birthnight Ball guests have an opportunity to enjoy tavern libations, period-style desserts, and a variety of card and dice games.

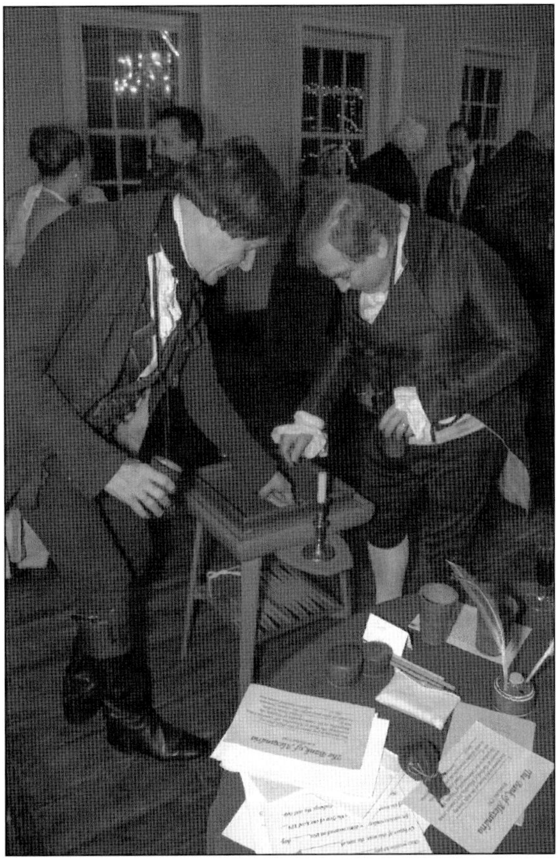

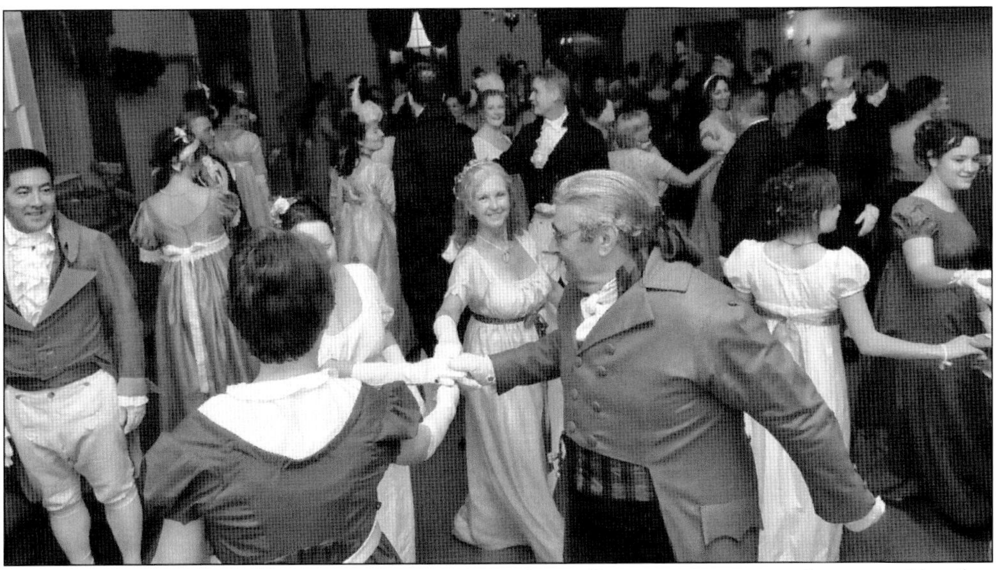

Dancing is the highlight of the annual Birthnight Ball. "Virginians are of genuine blood—they will dance or die." This quotation from Philip Vickers Fithian's journal in August 1774 illuminates the importance of dancing in the 18th century. Gen. George Washington was known to love dancing.

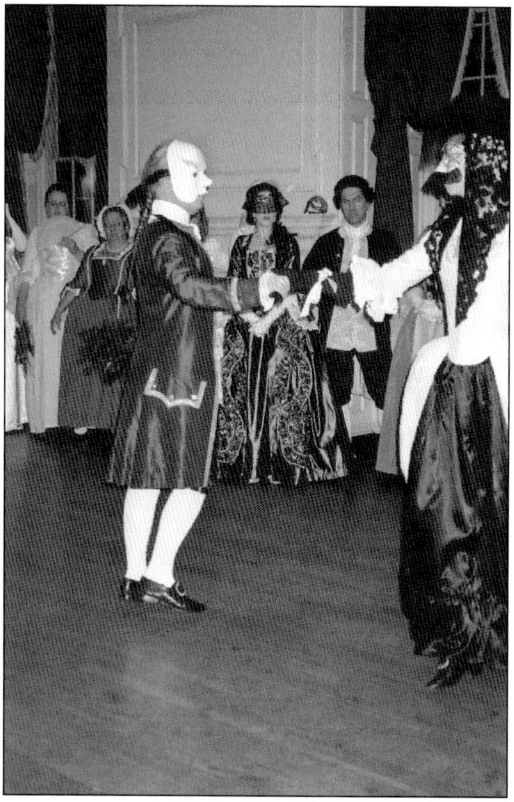

The museum is noted for its period balls, with different themes and eras of attire throughout the year. It is one of the few venues where one can dance in an 18th-century ballroom, with musicians playing in the suspended balcony. Here, Mark Hutter dances with Barbara Tyler Mullins at a Masquerade Ball. This popular October ball includes an unmasking at the end of the evening.

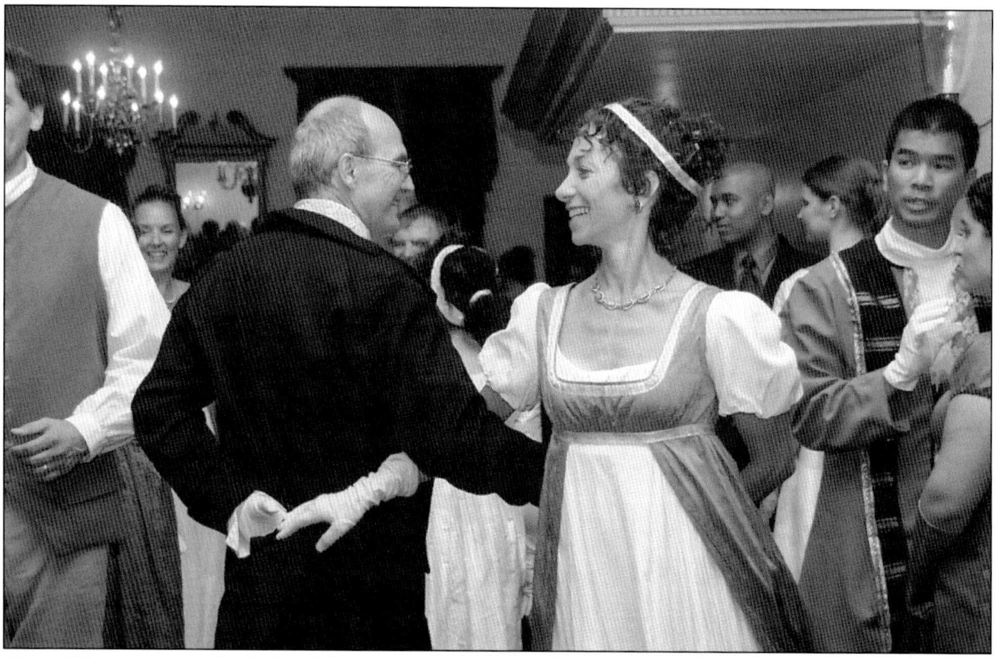

One of the most popular balls of the museum's series is the annual Jane Austen Ball. Guests dress in early-19th-century attire, reflecting what Alexandrians wore in the early Federal era. Here, George and Teresa Kitchen perform the allemande as part of the Allemande Swiss dance from 1795.

Each ball has a ball manager, who "calls" the individual dances. An 18th-century-style ball at Gadsby's Tavern Museum includes an opening minuet, English country dances, a short intermission to enjoy a dessert collation, and then more dancing. The evening concludes with three cheers to the assembled company. Seen here dancing are Janice Ryan and Ted Borek (center) and Helen Anderson (far right).

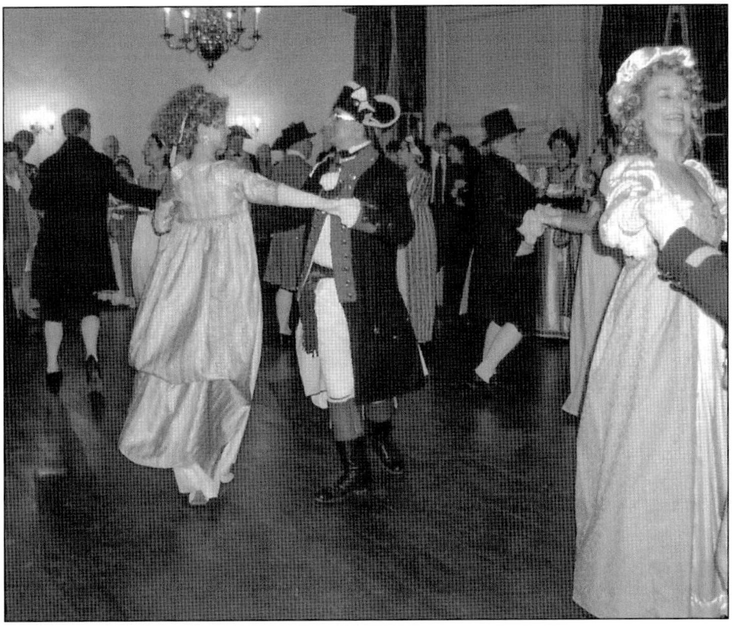

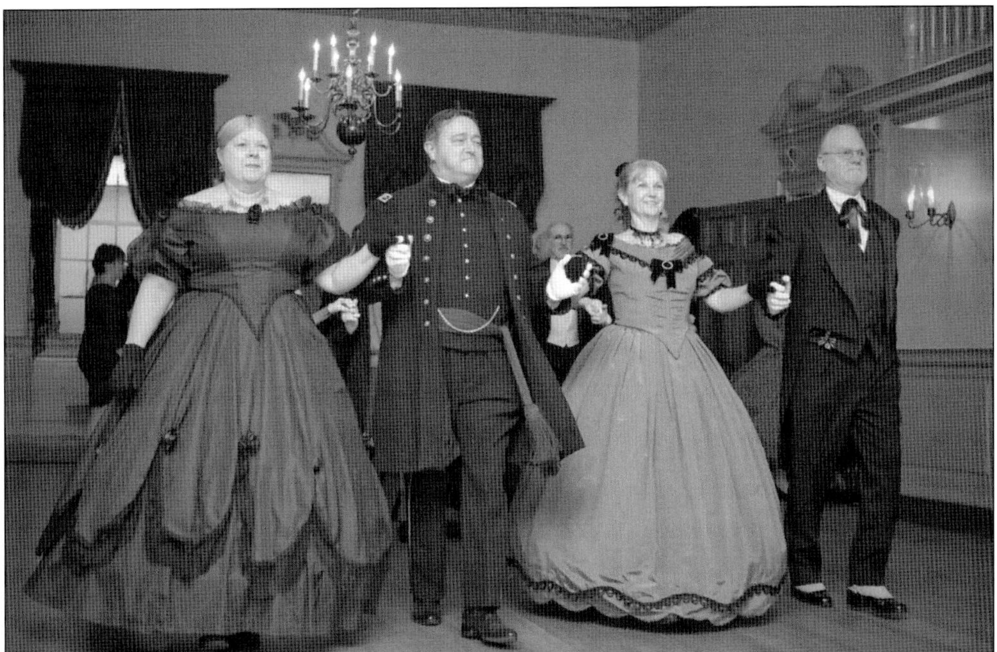

The Civil War–era ball opens with a Grand March, which invites all of the event participants to the dance floor. Other dances enjoyed throughout the evening include the waltz, Virginia reel, schottische, quadrille, and polka. Shown here are, from left to right, Marilyn and Charles Court and Cindy and Corky Palmer.

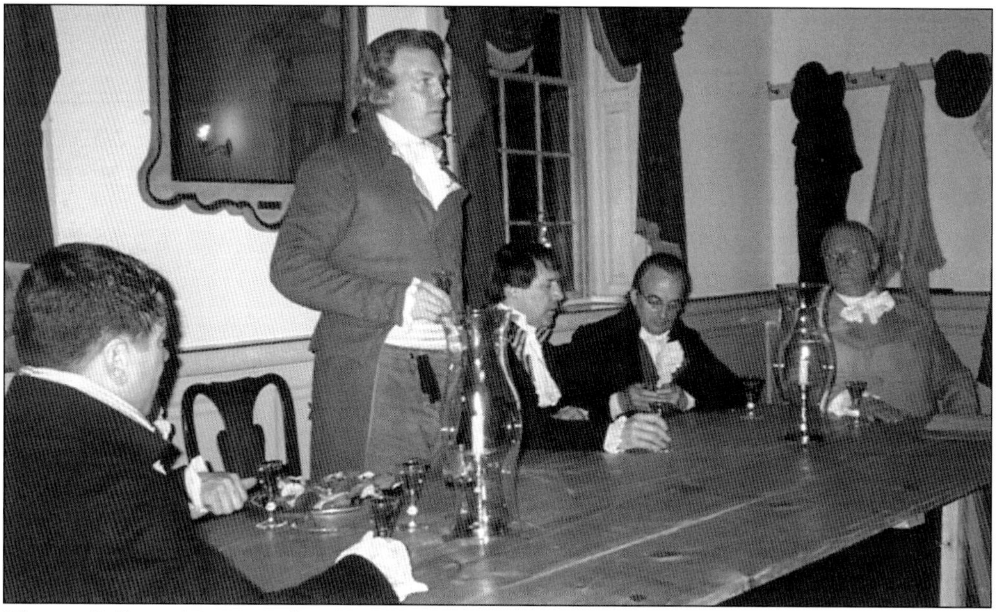

Thomas Jefferson's Inaugural Banquet was held at the tavern on March 14, 1801. The *Alexandria Gazette* reported, "The company who partook of the entertainment was the largest ever known at a public dinner prepared at any tavern in this town; and the style and elegance with which it was furnished . . . reflect the highest credit on the taste and industry of Mr. Gadsby." Bill Barker portrays President Jefferson at this 2001 event.

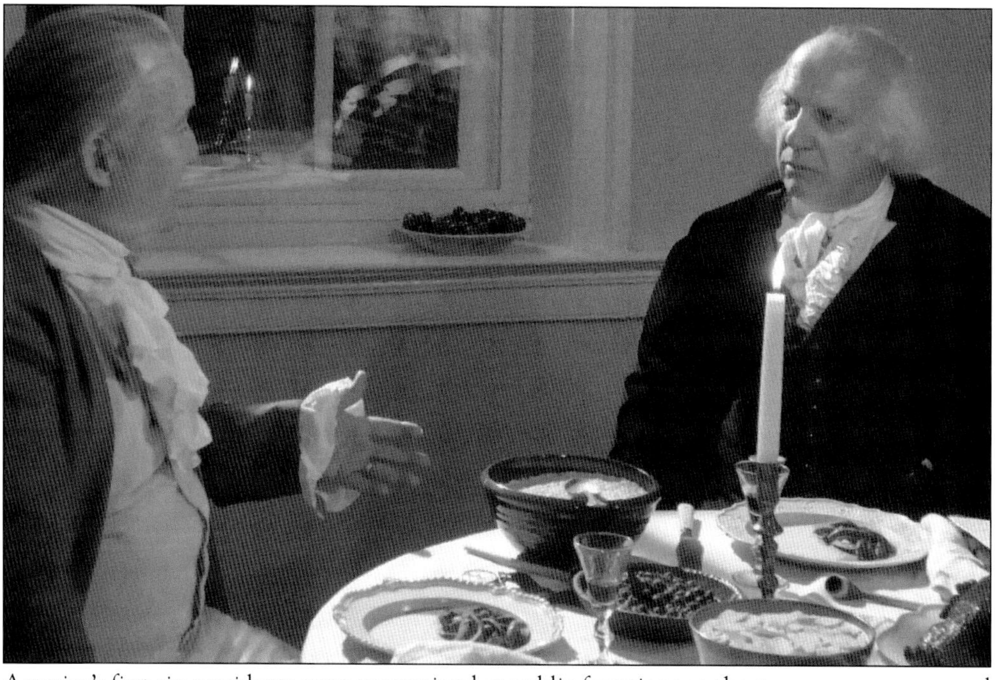

America's first six presidents were entertained at public functions at the tavern, as were several presidents and first ladies in the 20th century. James Madison dined at the City Hotel, which was then managed by William Caton, on May 9, 1809. Here, John Douglas Hall (right), portraying Madison, dines with reenactor Don McAndrews.

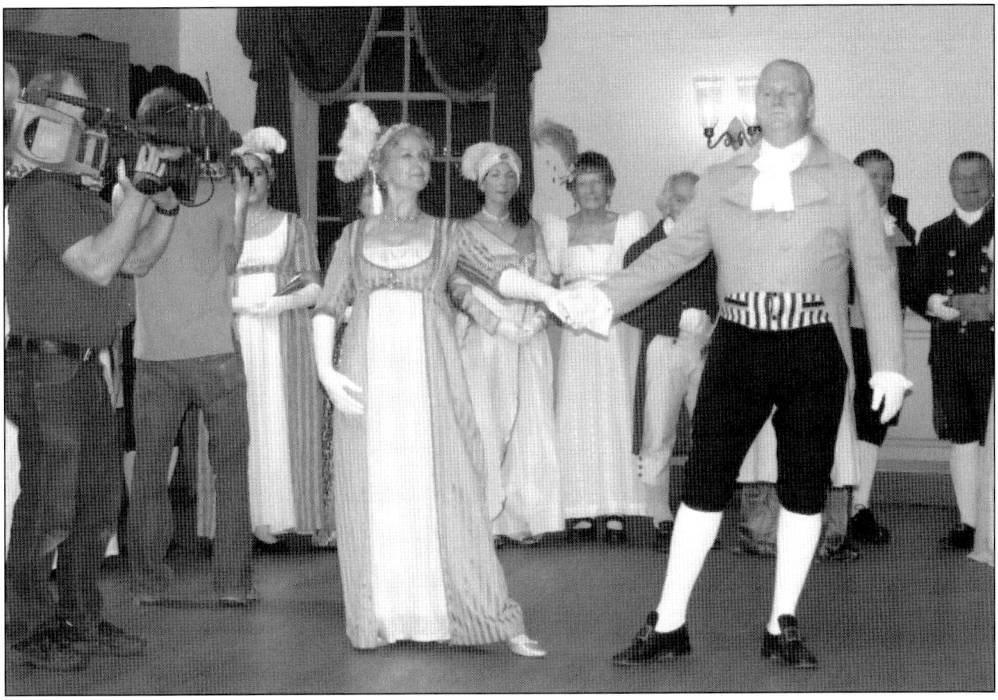

The museum's Ballroom, with its lovely woodwork, continues to be popular as a backdrop for interviews, documentaries, and a variety of other film projects. This production featured the museum's 18th-century dance program. Pictured here is the museum's dance master, Corky Palmer, along with his wife, Cindy.

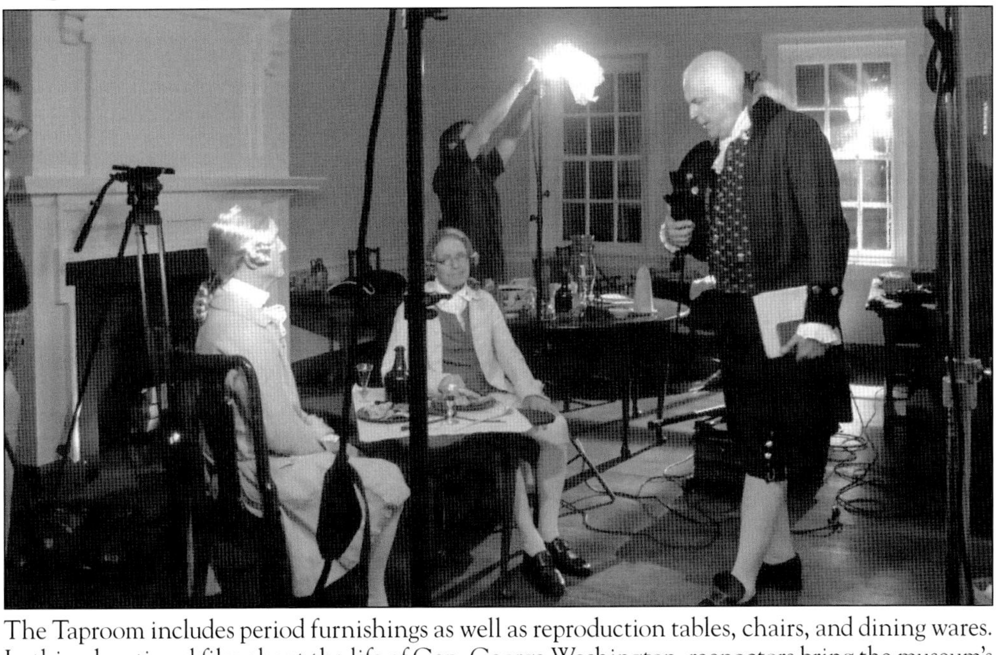

The Taproom includes period furnishings as well as reproduction tables, chairs, and dining wares. In this educational film about the life of Gen. George Washington, reenactors bring the museum's Taproom to life. Dean Malissa (right), as Washington, greets tavern patrons portrayed by Shane (left) and Larry Kippenhan (center).

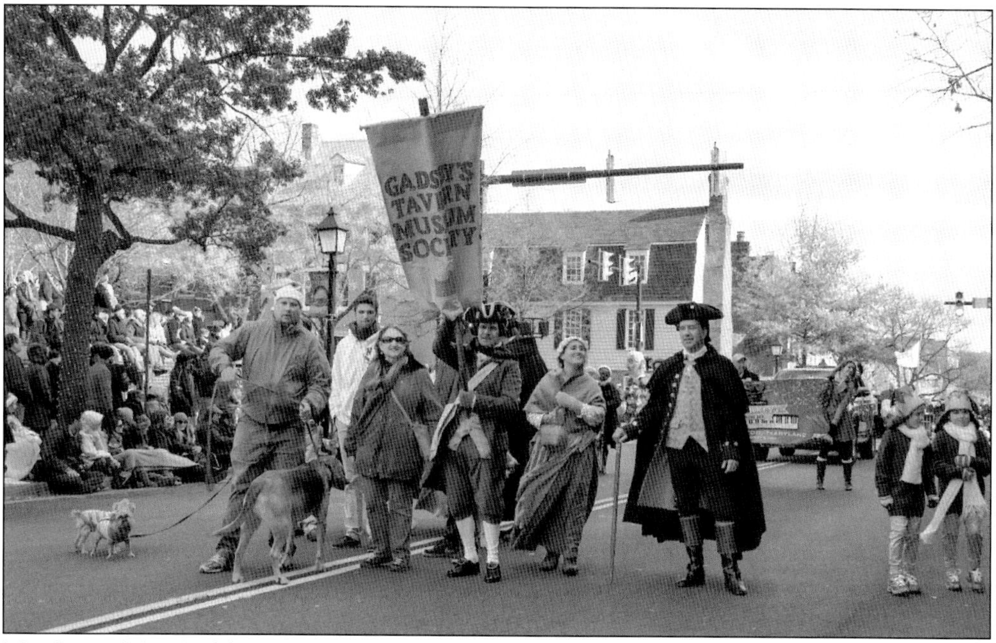

Members of the Gadsby's Tavern Museum Society support the museum through advocacy and financial assistance. The Society holds events throughout the year, including an annual fundraiser, a member appreciation evening, and a Tavern Dog Contest. In addition, members and their dogs march in each of the three annual Alexandria parades. (Joey Wang.)

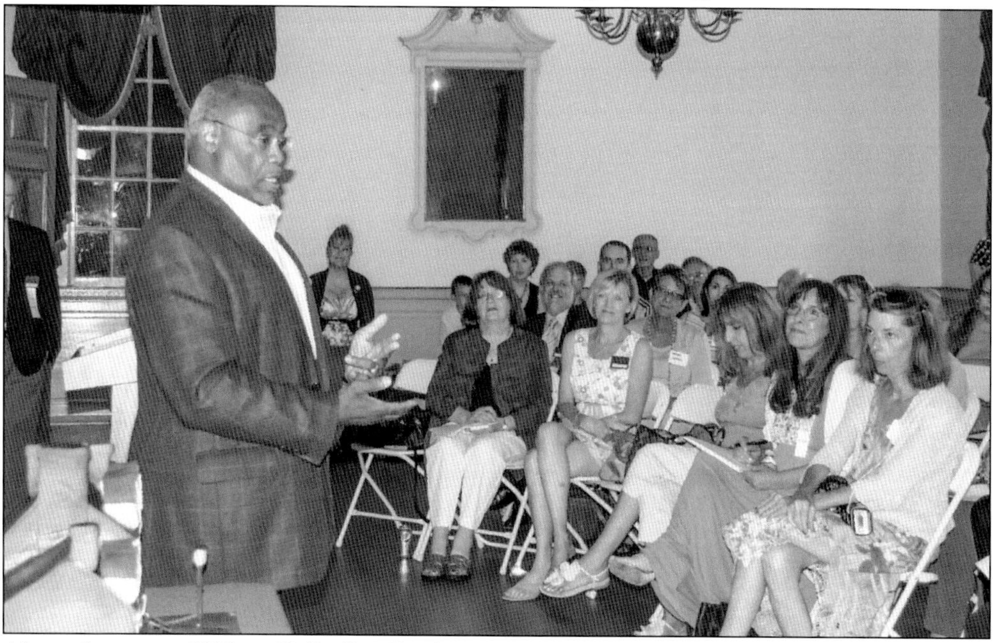

Alexandria mayor William D. Euille offers his appreciation for the support of the Gadsby's Tavern Museum Society at its 20th annual meeting. At each annual meeting, the Society presents a gift to the museum. Over the years, gifts have ranged from disaster preparedness supplies, to marketing funds, to a c. 1790 Alexandria-made chair. New members are always welcome. Information may be found on the museum's website.

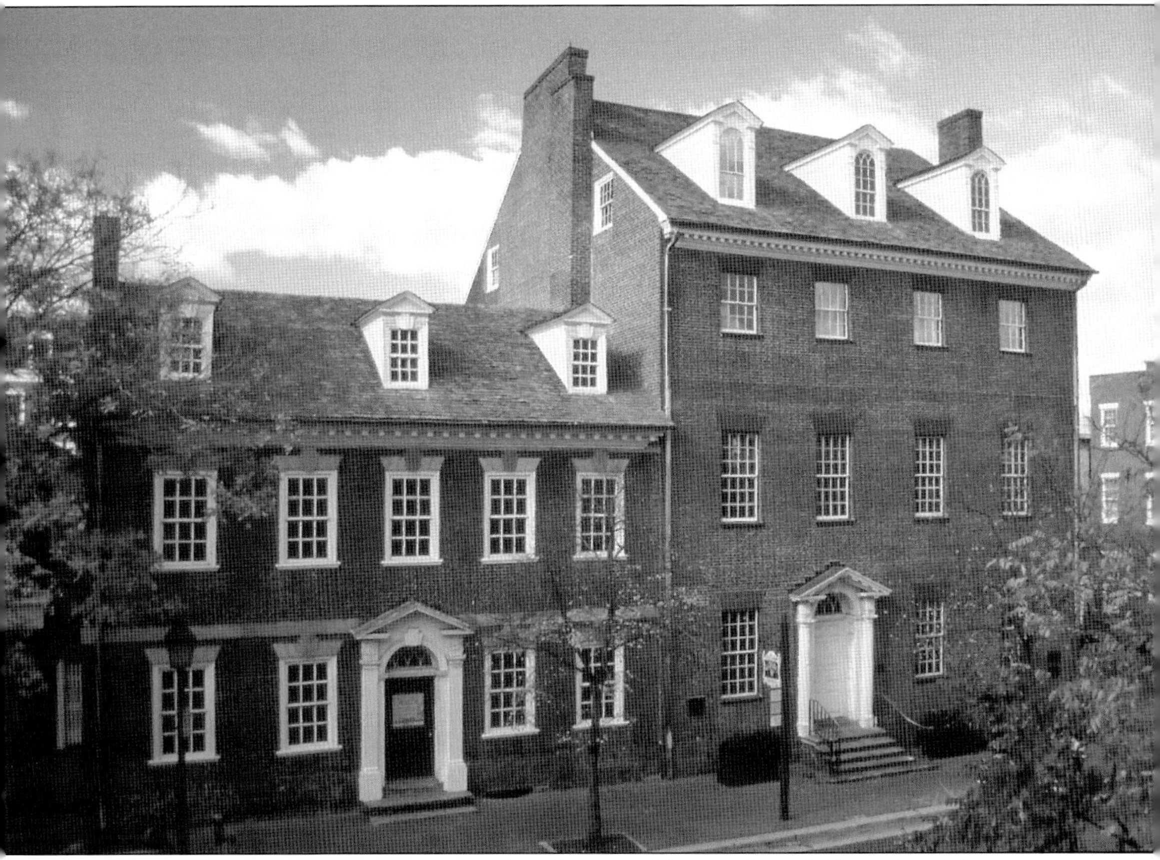

Today, Gadsby's Tavern Museum is owned and operated by the City of Alexandria. The vibrant historic house museum welcomes more than 25,000 visitors per year. The museum, open for tours year-round, offers a wide array of programs that invite the public to experience John Gadsby's Alexandria. The Federal-themed restaurant, Gadsby's Tavern, continues to operate on the first floor of the 1792 building, serving a period-inspired menu to be enjoyed by the modern palate. American Legion Post 24, still headquartered in the 1878 City Hotel Wing, actively supports the museum as well as numerous other community organizations. For more information about Gadsby's Tavern Museum, please visit www.gadsbystavern.org or stop by the museum at 134 North Royal Street, Alexandria, Virginia, 22314 for a tour.

Consistent with our mission to preserve history on a local level, this book was printed in South Carolina on American-made paper and manufactured entirely in the United States. Products carrying the accredited Forest Stewardship Council (FSC) label are printed on 100 percent FSC-certified paper.

MADE IN THE USA